THE CANONICAL TRADITION IN
ANCIENT EGYPTIAN ART

CAMBRIDGE NEW ART HISTORY AND CRITICISM

General Editor:
Norman Bryson, *University of Rochester*

Advisory Board:
Stephen Bann, *University of Kent*
Joseph Rykwert, *Cambridge University*
Henri Zerner, *Harvard University*

Also in the series:

Norman Bryson: *Calligram: Essays in New Art History from France*

Michael Camille: *The Gothic Idol: Ideology and Image-Making in Medieval Art*

Stephen Bann: *The True Vine: Essays on Visual Representation and the Western Tradition*

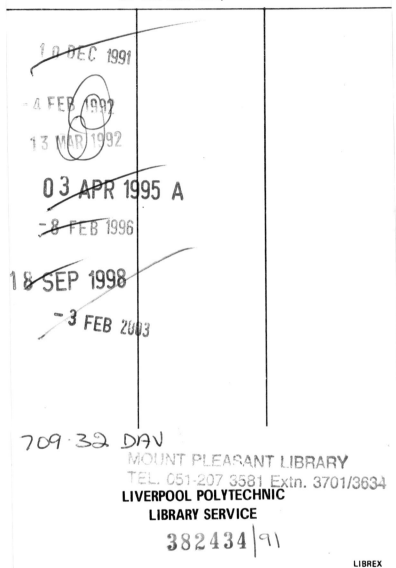

The Canonical
Tradition in
Ancient Egyptian Art

WHITNEY DAVIS
Northwestern University

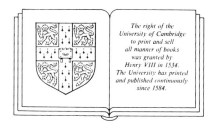

The right of the
University of Cambridge
to print and sell
all manner of books
was granted by
Henry VIII in 1534.
The University has printed
and published continuously
since 1584.

CAMBRIDGE UNIVERSITY PRESS

Cambridge
New York   Port Chester   Melbourne   Sydney

Published by the Press Syndicate of the University of Cambridge
The Pitt Building, Trumpington Street, Cambridge CB2 IRP
40 West 20th Street, New York, NY 10011, USA
10 Stamford Road, Oakleigh, Melbourne 3166, Australia

First published 1989

Printed in the United States of America

Library of Congress Cataloging-in-Publication Data
Davis, Whitney.
The canonical tradition in ancient Egyptian art / Whitney Davis.
    p.   cm. – (Cambridge new art history and criticism)
Bibliography: p.
ISBN 0–521–36590–2 hard covers
1. Art, Egyptian – Themes, motives.   2. Art, Ancient – Egypt
– Themes, motives.   3. Composition (Art) – Egypt.   I. Title.
II. Series.
N5350.D34   1989
709'.32–dc   89–679

British library cataloguing-in-publication applied for

To My Parents

CONTENTS

ILLUSTRATIONS

PREFACE

The present book is a shortened and extensively revised version of my Harvard doctoral dissertation of the same title (1985). After several years away from that project, working on other problems, I have now tried to correct my interpretations in the light of comments, more recent scholarship, and my own changed points of view on various issues.

Yet I have resisted writing an entirely new study. I am extremely conscious of the unsatisfactory nature of some formulations and, in particular, of the danger of reification running throughout my presentation; but I have stuck with my original aim to write a general, synthetic, and accessible treatment. In a "history of art" of the future – a logically possible if not a desirable history – we could translate my talk of historical actors like "style," "tradition," "canon," or "rules and system of production" into talk about real historical individuals and their actual cognitive activities. The best writing I know of in art history already tries to do this in various ways, even though it cannot avoid generalizing or moralizing from our present perspective and for our present concerns. Paradoxically, a total cognitive history would, if absolutely true to its subjects-in-history, be both overwhelming and unintelligible to us as readers, for it would merely reprint their cognition; at least, and so far, it cannot avoid being academically specialized to a daunting degree. These days many of the protocols of a cognitive history are put to use, casually or rigorously, and are better understood at a theoretical level than ever before, but even in 1989 there is still a need, I think, for what I offer here as a provisional, large-scale, grossly formulated historical sociology of representation.

In terms of the study of particular Egyptian works, probably the greatest recent advances have been made in the analysis of late prehistoric, protodynastic, and early dynastic art.

I have approached this phase of the history of canonical Egyptian art – the phase of the "canonical synthesis" (see Chapter 6) – from a particular point of view. In this book I am especially interested in the role of objects like the Oxford, Hunter's, or Narmer Palettes in the formation of the canonical tradition. My way of integrating these non- or precanonical works into an analysis of the canon risks a degree of either teleological or anachronistic reasoning. The late prehistoric and protodynastic materials certainly deserve a full and specific study in their own terms. Because I hope to preserve my general emphasis on the overall qualities and history of the canonical tradition here, no extra space could be found for such a detailed analysis. I attempt a full semiological treatment, as well as offer some iconological suggestions, in a separate monograph, *Masking the blow: the scene of representation in late prehistoric Egyptian art*. There I consider late prehistoric/early dynastic works like the Oxford, Hunter's, Battlefield, and Narmer Palettes as disjunctively related in their pictorial metaphorics and as exhibiting similar figurative preoccupations.

★ ★ ★

In the course of working on the subject of this book, I incurred many debts. An early draft of what has now become the analysis of canonical rules was written in 1977 but then put aside. At that point I had the benefit of comments from Edward Brovarski, Paul Frandsen, David Gordon Mitten, Karol Myśliwiec, William Kelly Simpson, and Claude Vandersleyen. Hans-Wolfgang Müller of the Egyptian Collection, Munich, particularly encouraged some writing on early dynastic art, supported in 1970–80 by the Joseph Pulitzer Fund of the Department of Fine Arts, Harvard University. In 1980–1, Harvard generously enabled me to travel for an extended time in Egypt and Greece as a Sheldon Traveling Fellow. In Egypt, the Department of Egyptian Art of the Boston Museum of Fine Arts contributed materially to my work, helped me secure access to sites, and invited me to take part in the work of the Giza Mastabas project under the direction of Professor William Kelly Simpson. I also thank the German Archaeological Institute and the American Research Center in Egypt, in Cairo, and the Epigraphic Survey of the Oriental Institute, University of Chicago, in Luxor, for the use of libraries and for other kindnesses. At the Cairo Museum I was able to make many notes and drawings, for which I thank the director and his staff. The help of Dr.

Mohsen has been critical in obtaining photographs for this final publication. When it became clear that some of my research would result in a dissertation, the Department of Fine Arts at Harvard supported further months of travel in Europe and America to study research collections of Egyptian antiquities; I especially thank Oleg Grabar and David Mitten for their support at this point. The basic draft was composed in 1983–4 in the idyllic quarters of the American School of Classical Studies at Athens. The Society of Fellows at Harvard provided the best possible atmosphere for the completion of the thesis, in 1985, and fostered links between this Egyptian work and other projects I was pursuing on prehistoric art and on theories of depiction and style in culture. My co-Junior Fellows will see legacies of our talks in this book.

Aspects of my research on the rules of production and on semiotic and anthropological interpretations of Egyptian art were presented in papers for the annual meetings of the American Research Center in Egypt (1979, 1983, 1984, 1988) and the International Congresses of Egyptology (1982, 1985); preliminary publication of the analysis of rules (in *Göttinger Miszellen*, nos. 47, 56, 64, and 75) elicited many valuable responses. Invitations to lecture on the canonical synthesis in the early dynastic period for Rice, UCLA, Johns Hopkins, Northwestern, and elsewhere provided strong incentives to organize my research.

In retrospect, a few experiences stand out as especially significant. Francesco Pellizzi offered a searching scrutiny of, and substantive suggestions for, an article on canonical representation for the journal *Res* (vol. 4, 1982); no one could ask for a better sounding board. Roderick and Susan McIntosh invited me to take part in a seminar on complex society in Africa (School of American Research, Santa Fe, 1984), at which Henry Wright and others commented on my view of the archaeology of early Egyptian art; although only some of my paper remains in what is now Chapter 7 (and I thank the McIntoshes for permission to use it), the seminar helped me understand my whole project better. T. J. Clark also commented at written length on that paper, raising proper doubts and calling for further thought; he will find echoes of many conversations on canons, Gombrich, reference, and other topics throughout this book. An invitation to lecture on Egyptian art at the Fourth International Congress of Egyptology (Munich, 1985), thanks to William Kelly Simpson, Dietrich Wildung, and others, forced me to consider the Egyptological paradigm from an art historian's perspective.

PREFACE Edward Brovarski, David Mitten, and Irene Winter, readers of the material that finally became the text of a dissertation, were patient, attentive to detail, and full of ideas; I thank them profoundly. Norman Bryson's encouragement and advice on rewriting for publication have made this book possible.

Curators around the world have been unfailingly helpful in providing information on photos and facilitating work in their collections (photo acknowledgments are provided in the captions). For their enormous help in reading and criticizing parts or the whole of various drafts and in providing information, advance reports, or publications, I thank Barbara Adams, Johan Ahr, Edward Brovarski, Norman Bryson, T. J. Clark, Paul Frandsen, Beate George, Oleg Grabar, Werner Kaiser, Alan B. Lloyd, Peter Manuelian, Pierre de Maret, David Mitten, Hans-Wolfgang Müller, Karol Myśliwiec, Winifred Needler, Francesco Pellizzi, Bengt Peterson, Gay Robins, William Kelly Simpson, Roland Tefnin, Claude Vandersleyen, Dietrich Wildung, Henry Wright, and Henri Zerner. All errors and unclarities remaining are my own responsibility.

CHAPTER I

INTRODUCTION

THIS study considers drawing, painting, relief, and sculpture produced in dynastic Egypt from the establishment of the dynastic state at the end of the fourth millennium B.C. until the middle of the fourth century B.C., the last point at which a native Egyptian ruled the country. For reasons which will become obvious, however, I emphasize Egyptian image making in the late predynastic and early dynastic periods and in the high Old Kingdom (c. 3000–2100 B.C.). Architecture and the "minor arts" will only be considered tangentially, although ceramics and stone vases enter the discussion because they had a role to play in the development of painting, relief, and sculpture. In addition to finished works, I will refer to unfinished, preparatory, and pedagogical works; the evidence of manufacture itself will be extremely useful.

THE ARGUMENT

Only one fundamental distinction between types of drawing, painting, relief, and sculpture will be elaborated here. Whether official or private, funerary or mundane, religious or secular, whether made for residence, temple, palace, or tomb, whether traded abroad or consumed at home, I am interested in Egyptian *canonical representation*, that is, the making of images regarded as well formed according to particular standards of correctness. In effect, this permits me to examine almost all works produced by the ancient Egyptians for any purpose. However, it does not imply that there are no further substantial differences between official and private production or between temple and tomb imagery. I simply will not consider such differences. The difference between two-dimensional and three-dimensional images and between drawing and painting will sometimes be relevant; but for the moment, these media can be considered simultaneously as canonical or not.

In theory, canonical work was and can now be distinguished from noncanonical work. Although little noncanonical work has survived, in principle canonical and noncanonical production must be considered in relation to one another for either to be fully intelligible.

A robust definition and grasp of canonical representation enables us to understand a wide range of formal and historical phenomena in Egyptian art – above all, its extraordinary coherence or invariance. The long-lived, comprehensive stability of Egyptian art was the largely successful achievement of an academic system for making such correct images. I will argue that canonical images were all governed by a unitary set of formal and iconographic principles. How these were embodied and enforced and what they were intended to achieve are questions requiring analysis. In approaching them, I suggest throughout that the principles were a specific *selection* from a range of conceivable, noncanonical alternatives. This selection was a *social decision*; the canon was a *social institution*. Although the real historical sociology of this institution is largely unknown, this book is a description of some of its elements: I focus on the character of the principles, the means by which they were produced and perceived, and the problems of defining the origins, development, and limits of the system.

SOME ASSUMPTIONS AND PROCEDURES

Some elements of this argument have by now become commonplace in other branches of the general history of art, yet as far as possible I will not assume them here as self-evident. Argument or example must show, for instance, that a single set of rules was used to produce images or that the canon was a social institution rather than the "natural" expression of the ancient Egyptian "mentality." Some elements of the argument have not received adequate formulation in art history: I hope to demonstrate their power and usefulness.

The argument assumes the form of evaluating a hypothesis. *If* we maintain an adequate notion of canonical representation, *then* we can make sense of many puzzling phenomena – leading us to the tentative conclusion that our notion has been confirmed in some respects. To my mind, it makes sense to see just how far the hypothesis can take us, at the risk of seeming to overreach our evidence.

I assume throughout that the invariance of Egyptian art cannot simply be taken for granted. There are good precedents here: Plato's remarks in the *Laws* (656–7) on the law-bound purity and "intrinsic rightness" of Egyptian forms have shaped the classical and postclassical Western understanding of Egyptian production.[1] In the literature of Western art history and criticism, Egyptian art has always stood for more than the historical art of ancient Egypt. Typically it has been seen as the paradigmatically "conceptual" art – "stylized," conventional, highly abstract.[2] The opinion of generations of casual viewers cannot be far off the mark: The most striking visual fact about Egyptian images is their *sameness* – one work is more or less like another.

For many connoisseurs, one response to Egyptian art has been to wish away the rule-governed, conventional, and highly repetitive features of Egyptian images and the standardized, mechanical conditions of their social production. In distinguishing one work from another (sometimes for historically important purposes but sometimes quite irrelevantly), connoisseurs need to assume the fact of style and stylistic variation; however, *the fact of style is a problem*. This problem appears throughout art history – it may even define the discipline – and it finds a perfect laboratory "test case" in ancient Egypt. The sheer volume, range, and chronological or geographic diversity of the remains hold incredible potential for systematic analysis.

Unfortunately, histories of Egyptian art tend to sketch a few quick points about the overall qualities of Egyptian style (Aldred, 1980: 11–30; Smith, 1981: 15–23) and turn in much greater detail to issues of historical "development," where stress is naturally placed on the unique features of each individual artifact. By contrast, I will say little about the features of individual objects, which are always necessarily different from one another; I offer descriptions of works not as complete assessments, in the way of catalogue entries, but only as brief reminders of the few features that concern my argument. The problem is to determine what might be an *interesting or significant* type of invariance or of variation: Our problem will be the *relation between* single works of art and the preexisting standards of design, the "canon" of Egyptian art.

Some critics have always insisted that it is in the relation between invariance and variability, between program and

3

production, between competence and performance, that we will understand the history of art. "Art products," Aristotle argued (*De part. anim.* I.1.640a), "require the preexistence of a homogeneous cause, such as the art of a statue which precedes the statue." More recently, Heinrich Schäfer (1974) saw behind the multitude of objects making up the history of Egyptian art the parallel history of a single principle. I will not follow Schäfer's interpretation of this principle, but his insight that an invariant method is the key to understanding relations of similarity in Egyptian art remains as valid now as it was in his original statement of the idea in 1919.

As we will see, the method consists in authorizing several means for the maximization of invariance or, conversely, the control of variation. Since no two objects can be identical – entropy would predict ever-diversifying variations – a noticeable degree of invariance among individual, separate works of art points to an intentional perpetuation of style: To do justice to the puzzle, I argue that *invariance is not just an inevitable but an intentional property of Egyptian art.* An adequate history of Egyptian art should take us back to, must give us some account of, sameness.

Three other assumptions are worth noting very briefly. First and broadly, I take representation to be the site of reflection upon and manipulation of the maker's and the viewer's knowledge of the world. In some situations representation becomes a means by which the world can be regularized and dominated. The success of this project of domination depends upon conditions not all arts or artists can or wish to meet. We measure the rationale, dynamic, and success of representation not transcendentally but historically, in relation to what we can reconstruct of the interests and intentions of human agents. Inevitably – and risking circularity – we are able to learn about these agents only by examining their fossilized remains in behavior, language, and the practices of production. However inadequate our archaeology, I assume the need to approach questions of interest, intention, and individual or social meaning. In fact, I will make the strong claim that representational practice simply *is* thought, *is* intention, *is* ideology: We do not look for ideology in a representation or explain production by its ideological function or meaning, for in considering the history and rules of representation we are necessarily already and always considering thought, intention, ideology.

Second, then, our object of study is *a practice of representation* – all of a piece, a style, an administration, an economy, a technology, an idea, a historical sociology of making and viewing, a *Lebensform* (Wittgenstein, 1921; Wollheim, 1980). Archaeology gives us access only to some elements of this practice but the practice is a whole: Indeed, it is the whole of history itself.

Third, implicitly and sometimes explicitly throughout this volume, I compare canonical representation in Egypt with *other practices* – other practices we know about in the general history of art. It is difficult, in this, to escape the charge that ancient Egyptian representation has been considered in terms devised for the study of some of these other practices. In fact, at the very least comparison of canonical art with possibly noncanonical art in Egypt itself is essential, and I make no claim that I have evolved a "neutral" language of description for *all* practices.

Since I attempt to explore an argument and certain assumptions, this book is not a work of reference nor a balanced survey of formal and historical information. Such projects require different formulation and are available (e.g., Smith, 1981). Occasionally I revise chronologies or attributions accepted in the literature; here the primary evidence is cited as far as feasible. In fact, no work of reference or survey of primary evidence could be produced without making interpretative assumptions about the nature, status, and significance of the object of study. Therefore we might just as well attempt, as systematically as possible, to articulate these assumptions – in opposition to constant efforts "to forestall that systematic articulation and totalization of interpretative results which can only lead to embarrassing questions about the relationship between them and in particular the place of history and the ultimate ground of narrative and textual production" (Jameson, 1981: 32).

Purely for convenience, I frequently use well known works like the Third-Dynasty wooden relief panels of the official Hesire (Quibell, 1913) or the Fifth-Dynasty funerary temple reliefs of Sahure (Borchardt, 1913). It is an important peculiarity of Egyptian art that *any* canonical work serves as an exemplification of general principles. No doubt this is a truism. However, I begin by supposing we should attend to it above others. For published reproductions of works discussed, citations have been offered, where possible, to volumes easily accessible to English-speaking readers (e.g., Smith, 1981). Comprehensive collections of excellent photographs may be found in Lange and Hirmer, 1967, Michalowski, 1969, and Vandersleyen, 1975b; to save space, these references have been omitted, as has reference to Porter, Moss, and Malek's *Topographical Bibliography*, which is inaccessible to uninitiated users who do not know the provenance of a particular work.

As all of my comments here imply, this book is designed for art historians, archaeologists, and anthropologists unfamiliar with specialized Egyptological evidence but interested in the status of Egyptian art in and for the general history of art or civilization. Egyptologists will already know the sources and their difficulties and will not require this book. Because the main drift of the text is interpretive and synthetic, references are highly selective, but readers should find enough for initial needs. I warn that the many complexities of and counterexamples to my general points are not exhaustively examined: I am writing for a nonspecialist who could use a map of the forest before analyzing each and every tree.

I have avoided explicitly "theoretical" discussion of the art-historical concepts of reference, style, canon, convention, tradition, or culture assumed and occasionally revised here. Theoretical topics such as the properties of variability in the replication of artifacts or the origins and social conventionalization of reference and style certainly require careful dissection, and I have offered some of my own views elsewhere (Davis, 1986, 1987, 1988a, 1989): Although a reader might wish to follow these up, I hope my arguments in this book will simply seem naturally appropriate to Egyptian art. I believe the central theoretical challenge for contemporary art history will be to underwrite all of its algorithmic descriptions of production ("formal," "structural," "social-historical") with a genuine archaeology of the actual cognitive representation *of* those algorithms *for* individuals in society (to be called, perhaps, a natural history or historical sociology of mind). My approach to this challenge is entirely provisional in this book, only one small step in the whole argument that should be made. In this book I probably do no better than foist a fairly elegant morphological grammar and quite straightforward social history off onto my objects of study; "confirmation" only obtains in the power my algorithms may have in accounting for variability in the record. But this is a necessary condition of writing history, if not a sufficient one.

CHAPTER 2

THE CANONICAL REPRESENTATION OF FIGURES AND GROUPS

I N this chapter I consider the principal canonical systems for the construction of individual figures in an image and of groups of figures in a "scene" or "composition." Consideration of these systems does not cover all aspects of canonical representation exhaustively; some examples of further, more specific conventions will be noted in the following chapter.

INITIAL SIMPLIFICATIONS

In order to conduct a sufficiently powerful analysis in a brief compass, I will make several analytic simplifications. First, in considering the two-dimensional rendition of the human figure, I focus specifically on figures of adult male officials and rulers. Details of anatomy, costume, scale, or pose were sometimes rendered quite differently for women, children, the lower classes, and foreigners (Schäfer, 1974: 17, 59–60). Canonical rules were applied more or less rigorously according to the social status of the subject, as well as other factors. My simplification is justified because canonical systems were first devised, it seems, for the representation of rulers (see Chapter 6).

Second, I generally consider figures facing right for simplicity in description, since if the figure was oriented in the other direction some details were necessarily different (Smith, 1949: 274–6; Russmann, 1980; von Recklinghausen, 1928, whose broad conclusions go too far). The simplification is also justified by the overall rightward orientation of most Egyptian two-dimensional representation (Fischer, 1977: sec. 4, 1986). Orientation, however, occasionally had symbolic significance; for instance, deceased individuals depicted in Old Kingdom tombs (like deceased parents of the patron) face left, that is, toward the realms of the living (Kanawati, 1981: 219–20).

Third, again for simplicity's sake, I do not rigorously observe the distinction between drawing/painting and relief, but

Figure 2.1. Wooden Relief of Hesire, from His Mastaba Tomb at Sakkara, Third Dynasty. Courtesy Cairo Museum.

consider these together as two-dimensional representation distinguished from freestanding sculpture. In principle, relief techniques permit the manufacture of very "sculptural" or three-dimensional forms. Some classes of Egyptian production, like funerary likenesses of individuals standing in deep niches, are best understood as kinds of architectural sculpture. Nevertheless, the technique of deep-relief modeling of partially engaged architectural sculpture was rarely exploited by Egyptian artists.

Fourth, I focus the range of our historical gaze. Observers have often attempted to identify the point at which the normative Egyptian representation found its most ideal manifestation. The classical formulations were certainly well established by the Fourth and Fifth Dynasties of the Old Kingdom, c. 2600 B.C. (Smith, 1963). My analysis throughout applies first and foremost to good-quality work of the classic Old Kingdom – not because it is the "best" or "most" canonical work but because it is the first canonical work (see Chapter 6) and therefore a less complex art-historical case instance (Figures 2.1, 2.2, 2.3).

This simplification must be handled cautiously. Needless to say, striking variations occurred after the Old Kingdom, modifying Old Kingdom preferences in some respects. For lack of space, I do not review First Intermediate Period, Middle Kingdom, early Eighteenth Dynasty, Amarna, Late Period, or Greco-Egyptian production from this perspective. Most variations in canonical procedures in these periods do not seriously affect our understanding of the principal systems

Figure 2.2. Painted Limestone Relief of Wepemnofret, from His Mastaba Tomb at Giza, Fourth Dynasty. Courtesy Lowie Museum of Anthropology, University of California, Berkeley.

and can be safely omitted from an outline morphological analysis. They could be accommodated easily in an expanded analysis, as forms of predictable or permissible variation. In Chapter 4, some rules for the transformation of style or motif will be noted and examples of sequences of variation from the Old through the New Kingdoms cited.

Nonetheless, although Old Kingdom art provides a yardstick for our purposes, the Egyptians themselves hardly saw matters in this light. In all probability Old Kingdom artists did not think of themselves as being "classical" or "conventional": They could only have regarded themselves as practicing a certain proper way of making images. In some cases later artists deliberately referred back to classic Old Kingdom formulations – the best-known case is the archaizing tendency of Twenty-sixth Dynasty (Saite) art – but these and other conventionalizations may not be merely or wholly a "quotation" from the past.[1]

A prime justification for these simplifications is the basic overriding fact that throughout Egyptian history the human figure was represented in two dimensions in the same way. The canonical formulas remained the standard from which variations could be understood has having a purpose or assuming a particular, pointed significance.

INTEGRATED CONSTRUCTION

The human figure posed a tripartite problem for the Egyptian artist. First, he faced the problem of components: A figure has various parts, not all of which are distinguished equally easily, and not all of which are necessarily seen at the same time. Second, he faced the problem of proportions: There are relations of size among the various parts of a figure, however these are identified and depicted, and the whole figure has a scale vis-à-vis others. Third, he faced the problem of aspect: A viewpoint from which to present the individual components in their proper proportions must be selected. These three problems do not spring, in any way, from visual or scientific appraisal of the figure as an organic unity and certainly involve some artificial distinctions (for instance, between parts and wholes, points of view and coordinates of projection). They only provide a preliminary way of describing "the Egyptian method" (Arnheim, 1954: 112–16; Hagen, 1986) as a unified – if not a unitary or wholly unambiguous – enterprise of representation.

Briefly, the method consisted of special solutions (1) to the
problem of components, by the selection of section contours
for parts of the body, (2) to the problem of proportions, by
the use of a canon of proportions, and (3) to the problem of
aspect, by the construction of the "frontal-profile view" (Figure 2.4). Each of these three features of the method does not
in and of itself fully constitute it. In combination, however,
they create that "stiff and formal" figure familiar to us from
textbook characterizations of Egyptian art. The method of
combination is itself deliberate, although not easily described
without reference to the material it works upon; it may be
the most distinctive quality of Egyptian art, for parallels to
the Egyptian treatments of components, proportions, and
aspect can be located in the arts of many other ancient and
modern cultures (see Hagen, 1986 for a helpful analysis from
the point of view of metric, affine, and projective geometry).

The canonical treatments of components, proportion, and
aspect are not exactly comparable. They are not equally re-
solved or, perhaps, equally conscious solutions to equally
clear-cut representational problems. Whereas the canon of
proportions had to be worked out mathematically and taught
verbally or by demonstration, the artist's treatment of components and aspect may have been less self-conscious. There-

Figure 2.3. Limestone Re-
lief of Nofer and Atten-
dants, from the Exterior
Facade of His Mastaba
Tomb at Giza, Fourth Dy-
nasty. Courtesy Boston
Museum of Fine Arts.

11

fore it makes sense to consider each solution separately, before tackling questions of their combination and of the resolution of the method as a whole.

My analysis of construction attempts to integrate a number of matters often considered separately (Schäfer, 1974: 277–309 and Smith, 1949: 273–332 are the indispensable sources). For example, we will see that the proportional system is in a sense dependent upon a prior conception of the aspect of the figure and that the choice of aspect involves demands about the preservation of information concerning components and proportions. Although these problems are often difficult to describe clearly, in general my aim is to stress the logical interdependencies and systematic, deliberate, calcu-

Figure 2.4. Canonical
Principles of Components,
Proportions, and Aspect.

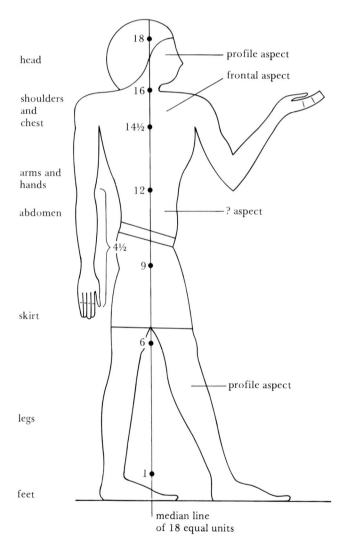

head

shoulders
and
chest

arms and
hands

abdomen

skirt

legs

feet

18

16

14½

12

4½

9

6

profile aspect

frontal aspect

? aspect

profile aspect

1

median line
of 18 equal units

lated nature of the relevant variables. This analysis under-writes a larger conclusion (see Chapter 3) that methodical invariance was not the result of "natural" tendencies of Egyptian thought, innate qualities of Egyptian psychology, or even the constraints of Egyptian perceptual and practical life.

COMPONENTS AND CONTOURS OF THE HUMAN FIGURE

It is visually obvious that in an Egyptian representation (Figures 2.1, 2.2, 2.3), the component parts of the human figure – hands, feet, legs, head, and so on – are not joined with one another in the rendition as they would be anatomically articulated in reality. Although true as far as it may go, this observation defines the method in terms of what it was not; moreover, it seems to assume some absolute (and fantastical) standard of lifelikeness to which Egyptian images could be compared. A description produced in this way is bound to be misleading. In other words it is necessary, although more difficult, to specify exactly what Egyptian artists represented.

The direction of an adequate positive description initially seems clear enough. The Egyptian artist apparently set out to isolate particular and single views of the component parts of the body (or object). For simple objects, the view was usually fully frontal (that is, with a "frontal" plane of an object, however that is in turn defined, parallel with the picture plane – see Hagen, 1986: 168–76), fully profile, or in "plan." The plane of the object is perpendicular to the line of sight and its contours are closed. Clearly this drawing is not necessarily of any world we "normally" perceive.[2] Furthermore, many objects and components of objects are much too complex to be reduced easily to simple bounded views. All of this amounts to saying that the canonical image must be a reductive analysis of complex objects. How, then, is the analysis carried out?

Perhaps the canonical method isolates characteristic views of objects. This hypothesis is often taken to be an explanation of Egyptian images. However, we clearly need further explanation: What is or should be the characteristic presentation of an object such that the characteristic plane will be parallel to the picture plane?[3]

It seems the artist chooses a view displaying as much of the particular part of the body as possible. Unless depicted holding an object, the hand presents all four fingers and the thumb. The torso presents both shoulders. In fact, the artist

13

draws the most substantial section of a component (Figure 2.5). More precisely, (1) the component is cut by an intersecting plane between the most distant opposite surfaces of the component, in real measure; (2) a view of this plane as perpendicular to the line of sight and at optical infinity is taken; (3) its outermost closed contours are drawn (see further Hagen, 1986: 182–4, 188).

This formulation differs significantly from many accounts of the Egyptian method, in which it is assumed that the frontal (profile, plan) drawing is of a particular chosen surface of an object "seen head-on and close up" (Schäfer, 1974: 96–7, although elsewhere Schäfer is forced to recognize interior sections for sculpture). By contrast, the artist sets out to draw the broadest section of the three-dimensional volume. Because he was drawing sections and not surfaces, the Egyptian artist obviously never needed to consider the facts of foreshortening and highlighting (or illumination): These are properties of the curving and differentially illuminated surfaces of things and not of sections taken perpendicular to the line of sight. Painterly elaboration of the section outline was rarely made and virtually never in order to suggest the play of shadow at the "edge" or to suggest a fictive depth of some measure separating figure and ground.

Surfaces are never actually represented in Egyptian drawing except in cases where the surface of the component is (it happens) coextensive with its thickest section. This may occur, although not invariably, in the representation of walls, boxes, flat pieces of ground or water, and so on, where the

Figure 2.5. Principles of the Section-Contour Drafting of Solids with Curved and with Flat Surfaces.

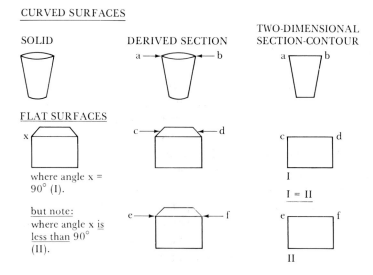

CURVED SURFACES

SOLID   DERIVED SECTION   TWO-DIMENSIONAL SECTION-CONTOUR

FLAT SURFACES

where angle x = 90° (I).

but note: where angle x is less than 90° (II).

eye is confronted with a perfectly flat surface coterminous with its section.

Details of objects lying on top of surfaces (handles on boxes, facial features) are merely applied to the section laying under them at an appropriately measured point. It is not always clear whether this point is a "real" measure across the section (say, equidistant from the two opposite surfaces) or a repositioning to conform to other standards (for instance, consider the position of nipples and navels on the body – although this construction is inherently ambiguous anyway). Insofar as details are separate components of a figure, they are themselves reduced to the relevant section contours. The composition or construction of a full figure is therefore in part the additive superimposition of section contours.

The degree to which effects of volume are as it were re-introduced into the figure (added to the section contours) varies greatly. In relief work, considerable modeling is some-times attempted. At other times, "surfaces" – that is, the areas between the outermost contours of the section – are far smoother and unrelieved. In painting, muscular and other details of anatomy are sometimes drawn in or even colored differently; at other times the component is simply blocked out and colored uniformly within the contours.

As many observers have noted, in general the contour of the body and the contours of its chief components (head, upper torso, arms, middle torso or abdomen, waist/thigh area or skirt, legs, feet) are significantly more important than any detailing, modeling, or internal relief.[4] In a sense, the history of Egyptian art is a history of the contour line.

THE CONTOUR IN SCULPTURE

Even freestanding monumental stone sculpture ultimately re-flects the control of the contour line. Sculpture based upon a fully three-dimensional core never took hold in Egypt. The useful dichotomy proposed by Richard Hamann (1908), fol-lowing Michelangelo, should be brought to mind here: Egypt does not sculpt *von innen heraus*, "out from within," but rather *von aussen heran*, "in from without." For reasons to be ex-plored, the Egyptians were not particularly interested in the potential tension of a block and the interior sculptural form, as worked out, for instance, in a Michelangelo *Captive*, or in projecting a form upward and outward into surrounding space, as developed, for example, in a work by Myron (although see the special block-statue type, Radwan, 1973).

Egyptian sculpture proceeds from a set of contour drawings on the block surface (Figure 2.6). Control over the block of stone was obtained by cutting in from these outlines, that is, by reproducing on the four vertical surfaces of the block the section contours of the two interior axial vertical planes of the figure, intersecting at right angles at the median vertical line of central gravity.[5] In this procedure, a "pure" side view of a figure had to be sketched on the two side surfaces of the

Figure 2.6. Principles of Contour Drawing on the Four Sides of the Sculptural Block.

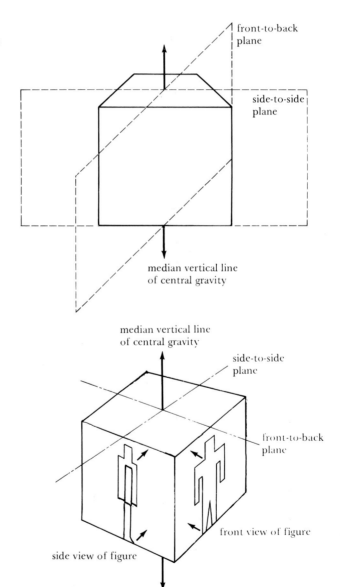

block, although canonical technique in two dimensions does not usually employ such pure views in the construction of the figure (Eaton-Krauss, 1984: 2–3; Edgar, 1905: 148; Schäfer, 1974: 305). Egypt's freestanding sculptural work can therefore be seen as a unique synthesis of drawing on the flat and downcutting, relief working, and modeling what is essentially always a planar section contour of a form.[6]

The sculptor's difficulty, of course, lay in juggling the requirements of drawing upon and modeling *four* planes. The drawings were dissolved as the sides of the original block were cut down and away. However, the structure had already been imposed on the new surfaces as they were arrived at in the progress of the work. Although no doubt not always easy to control, this arrangement proceeded successfully and mechanically for several reasons, including the simple fact that two of the four planes were usually mirror identical. Presumably a sculptor was most appropriately trained, in fact, by practicing the working of drawings into relief; heavy abrading and polishing could take care of any overly hard edges where two drawings cut down from the surfaces happened to meet at right angles. When stone was expensive and its transport difficult, a sculptor naturally favored methods conveniently discovering the form in the block and providing him with exact means of loosing it.[7] Moreover, in Egypt the generalization of canonical two-dimensional techniques to the three-dimensional media was apparently considered advantageous in itself; canonical sculpture derives directly from earlier canonical relief (see Chapter 6).

These points apply chiefly to the manufacture of stone sculpture. Eaton-Krauss suggests that in Egypt "the wooden statue was much more common than the number of surviving specimens suggests" (1984: 6, cf. 58). She disputes the common wisdom that Egyptian patrons preferred stone statuary to wood (see Drenkhahn, 1976: 59); ebony and cedar, for example, were luxuries "obtainable only through the royal monopoly on foreign trade" (Eaton-Krauss, 1984: 59) and therefore conceivably as valuable as quarried stone. Technical exigencies probably account for some of the more notable differences between stone and wood sculpture. For example, fear of breakage in Old Kingdom stone statuary explains why protruding accessories of costume are not shown or are abbreviated (Smith, 1949: 38). Wooden statues were often made in pieces, and there may be some essential conceptual difference between stone sculptures extracted from a quarried block and wooden statues built up from separately turned units.

Some evidence implies that sculptors in wood were associated with other carpenters while sculptors in stone were affiliated with the stone vase industry (Drenkhahn, 1976: 60).

BAS-RELIEF

Contour also overridingly directs the representation of individual parts of a figure in Egyptian bas-relief. Given the qualities of Egyptian relief (Figures 2.1, 2.3), it is worth recalling that relief potentially does permit the subtle grading of an outline contour back into the negative surface; potentially, there can be an almost imperceptible transition between figure and ground. Rather than suggesting depth or other phenomena (such as foreshortening) in this manner, the Egyptians used contour to effect a strong contrast between figure and field; bas-relief figures stand out from the ground, sharp clear contours overriding the modeling of edge. As I have already noted, modeling of an exquisite sophistication could certainly be carried out within the outermost contours: Examine the modeling of the leg muscles or torso of a figure in many reliefs. However, even internal modeling must "flatten" three-dimensional detail onto the flat "surface" – the two-dimensional shape – stretched between the section contours. Therefore it will always seem unnaturalistic to some degree, at least in the rendition of the palpable volume and texture of objects.[8]

THE RATIONALE OF SECTION CONTOURS

Although the visual and technical preeminence of the section contour and outermost contour line is easy to observe, it is not obvious why these contours were selected as most important in producing a correct representation. For the moment, I will not consider possible symbolic or metaphysical meanings of the canonical image (see Chapter 7) and simply evaluate elementary psychological and formal factors.

Presumably the use of the contour reflects the artist's mental procedure: He mentally isolates component parts of a figure before setting out to represent it, and contour is his graphic means of delimiting what has been delimited mentally. Yet the question is begged: Why should the artist graphically or mentally visualize certain contours rather than others, namely, section contours? In choosing certain contours, perhaps certain enclosed shapes are thought to reveal more than lines that do not describe an intelligible enclosure and are therefore more complex or less immediate. Again, however, what are the criteria by which intelligibility or clarity – two terms often applied to Egyptian art – is recognized? How does the artist know some lines to be principal and some to be secondary?

Rhys Carpenter's analysis of this problem in Greek art (1962: 93–5) applies equally to Egyptian art. Carpenter argues that "graphic outline" or "significant contour" defines a two-dimensional "areal shape" in relation to the whole range of more or less informative stereometric views an artist could obtain: An outline selects the most informative view. These "fully recognizable and completely intelligible silhouettes" are identical with the few unforeshortened views it is possible to obtain. They are the most informative because, not being foreshortened, they must reveal most surface area (compare Hagen, 1986: 174–5). Although this is a helpful formulation, it is not, I think, completely satisfying. Unforeshortened views are not necessarily more informative about other aspects of form than area, nor is it exactly true that unforeshortened views always reveal most area (one might look without foreshortening at the narrowest side of an object or directly at the apex of an angle of two sides). On Carpenter's principle alone we cannot establish that "it is these [unforeshortened views] which the archaic draftsman and sculptor will elect to reproduce" (1962: 95). Certainly the archaic artist does select certain kinds of unforeshortened views – but in Egyptian art, because they are section contours, descriptive of stereometric volume in a way other kinds of "unforeshortened views" cannot be. We might wish to say, in turn, that this is so as it were naturally – the Egyptian method does directly express a fundamental feature of visual perception. As the eye scrutinizes a shape it does tend to focus – both in the point location and frequency of individual saccadic registrations – upon what Gestalt psychologists call the simplest outline, generally the line joining the outermost points perceived to belong to a unitary field (Arnheim, 1954: 27–64; Kennedy, 1976).

This account is partially incomplete. Other variables being equal, the most encompassing and complete shape will be perceived "naturally"; the section contour draws this shape. Yet it is easy to construct an object that would distract the eye from its natural tendency to see the simplest outlines, and indeed what is natural loses any meaning once we begin to draw: We could thicken some lines or illuminate some parts of the surface such that the "unitary fields" of our perception were delivering very little information about the actual geometry of the planes of an object or about its volume. Despite this difficulty, it is possible to say that isolating the section contour – through tactile exploration of the object and by measurement – is one means of formulating at least one kind of objective, that is, geometrical, picture of the most encompassing and complete form of the object.

THE CANON OF PROPORTIONS

We have seen the components of the figure in Egyptian art to be isolated units bounded by contours, a planar analysis of the full mass existing in three dimensions. Canonical methods isolated and transcribed the most substantial section contours. Nevertheless, how and why these components have been composed in a particular way to create the figure cannot be fully understood without examining the Egyptian systems of proportion and aspect.

A system of proportional rationalization apparently was used by the sculptor of the Narmer Palette (see Figure 6.14), which is generally and probably correctly dated to the early First Dynasty. Proportional rationalization does not appear in all early dynastic art and never, as far as we know, before the First Dynasty. Moreover, it is not entirely clear whether the Narmer Palette makes use of the system that would later become the canonical system of proportions.[9]

Proportional studies have yet to be conducted on relief sculptures in the Upper Egyptian style of the late Second Dynasty – the Gebelein reliefs and monuments of Khasekhemuwy (see Chapter 6 for a review of this material) – but as these works are stylistically continuous with the Narmer Palette and other very early canonical works, they may bridge the gap between the possible early appearance of the proportional system and its fully evolved expression on the carved wooden panels of Hesire from the beginning of the Third Dynasty (Figure 2.1; see also Figure 3.3) (Iversen, 1975; Quibell, 1913).

The early history of the proportional system remains obscure at points, but its general course seems clear enough: The crystallization of the canonical conventions in the early dynastic period involved proportional rationalization and, finally, the selection of a particular canon of proportions (see

Chapter 6). However, we are still far from understanding precisely how the system functioned and what its significance or symbolic connotations might have been.

Several misconceptions have crept into much of the analysis of proportional systems in ancient art and in Egyptian production. Therefore it is worth recalling in general terms what proportional systems do and do not achieve and, in particular, what the Egyptian system does and does not achieve.

First, the Egyptian proportional system was not merely a "gridding" device by which a preparatory design could be transferred to the large surface of a wall or from a small model to a large unworked block. This interpretation of the lines and grids surviving on some Egyptian paintings and reliefs had been put forward by several scholars before the metrological basis of the proportional canon was identified.[10]

The proportional system did make use of the grid which, like any system of coordinates, could be used as a copying aid. As samples from the Old Kingdom indicate, however, the system of proportions could be used without the full coordinate grid. Determining the length of a given unit of a figure according to a proportional canon can be carried out whether the artist uses a grid, or simply a single vertical line intersected by horizontals (C. R. Williams, 1932: 8–13), or even only an optical (nontechnical) judgment.

An intersected vertical could fix the ratio of the length of one part of the figure to the length of another part. A grid system could take into account ratios of breadth as well. These ratios were apparently always rather more variable than ratios of length, which perhaps implies that the initial scheme of proportions did not calculate them explicitly. (For example, it may be that the underlying ambition of the system was to enforce certain ratios between different units of height in the human figure.) Taste initially preferred a "slender" figure, but in the Fourth Dynasty the heavy-shouldered statuary of Mycerinus and Rahotep (Reisner, 1930: 118; Smith, 1949: 107) perhaps reflects a change in standards of breath proportion.[11]

Any grid drawn over a figure can serve as a copying device; the proportion grid was not, however, any variable grid. In surviving specimens individual coordinates of the grid bear invariable relationships with individual points of reference on the figure, with modifications only appearing when the number of grid squares was modified. In the "canonical" system of proportions analyzed by Erik Iversen (1975), the figure to its hairline is eighteen units high (the grid is eighteen grid squares high), and each unit is equivalent to one "fist" (Figure 2.7). Although this system was not the only proportional system used in Egyptian art, it is best understood at the moment. The figure "fits into" the grid; that is, it has been proportioned so that points on the figure are regularly keyed to the proportionalities obtainable between multiples of the fist (up to eighteen): The foot is three squares long, the knee-cap falls on line 6 of the grid ($= \frac{1}{3}$ of the total height of the figure to its hairline), the front of the belt in line 11, the nipple at line 14, and the top of the shoulders at line 16. The length of the forearm from the elbow bone or crease to the tip of the thumb (or fingers) is $4\frac{1}{2}$ (or 5) grid squares in the eighteen-square system and is therefore equivalent to $\frac{1}{4}$ (or $\frac{5}{8}$) of the total height of the figure to its hairline.[12]

Figure 2.7. The Eighteen-Square Grid Canonical Proportional System. After Iversen, 1975: Pl. 3.

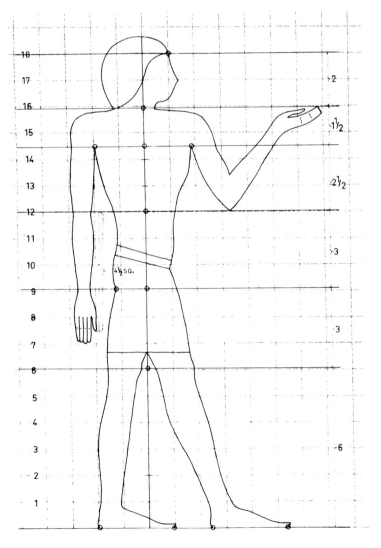

To a great extent, the proper proportional relations of the parts of the figure were the proportions of the human body as assessed in Egyptian metrological research. As Iversen says (1971a: 58), "As a standardization of the natural proportions of the body these ratios constitute in themselves a system of human proportions, an elementary canon, which was fully established at the beginning of dynastic times when the artistic traditions of Egypt were inaugurated."

Detailed analysis of the canonical proportional system(s) has been carried out by other writers and still requires much further work. In a series of fundamental studies, Gay Robins (e.g., 1983a, 1983b, 1983c) has shown that in the New Kingdom some artists used a twenty-square system (as in the tombs of Tuthmosis IV, Haremhab, and Ramesses I), adding, for example, an extra square between the knee and the navel and in the thorax to achieve "more natural proportions" for the leg (1983b, 1983c). At Amarna, artists added two extra squares above the waist to arrive at a second kind of twenty-square system (Figure 2.8) (Robins, 1983a, although see Gilderdale, 1984 for complexities). In the tomb of Ramesses I, the twenty-square grid was used at the same time as the eighteen-square system. Conceivably at other points in Egyptian history other such modifications were introduced. They should all, of course, be distinguished clearly from noncanonical deviations, such as those in the First Intermediate Period, where ratios of length and breadth were not system-

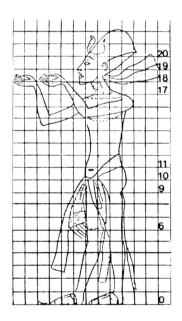
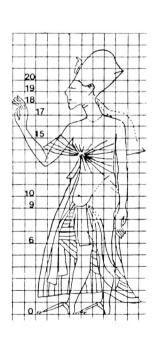

Figure 2.8. Examples of Canonical Construction Using a Twenty-Square Grid, from Tomb Reliefs in Private Tombs at Amarna, Eighteenth Dynasty. *Left*: Tomb of Apy; *Right*: Tomb of Mahu. After Robins, 1983a: Fig. 3.

atically calculated or controlled, that is, where a proportional system was not used or was only partly used.

For my purposes here, it is crucial to see that the Egyptian canon achieves only one or a closely related set of the many possible effects a proportional system might have in a representational art. In the Egyptian system problems of volume, the degree of foreshortening, or the special ratio of the distance of a figure from the eye to its perceived height and breadth – matters other proportional canons have taken up as crucial to the final effect – were passed over. This was so because the proportional system worked with or upon a figure constructed in a certain way (see above) from a certain aspect (see below). The proportional system simply instructed an artist at what scale he was to draw individual component section contours for inclusion in a figure constructed according to the frontal-profile aspect.

Second, it is necessary to distinguish the proportional canon from both the method of extracting section contours and the method of coordinating aspect. A misconception about the proportional canon has held it to be responsible for the frontal-profile stance itself: For example, Panofsky (1955: 59–60, but cf. 57) took the system to be both an anthropometry, an analysis of body sizes and proportions, and a theory of construction that "precedes the design and predetermines the final product." Although an artist could certainly determine the dimensions and relative proportions of parts of an object, this in no way determines that initially the object should be viewed frontally or in profile – or in any particular aspect at all. Whether head-on (frontal) or perspective (incorporating foreshortening), the view comes first; only after it has been conceived does the artist refine the relative proportions of the parts made visible in the drawing from that point of view. In practice the artist actually draws the figure with advance knowledge of the proportions he wishes to obtain, but the use of a proportional system does not in itself determine the view.

In the second edition of his pioneering analysis of proportions in Egyptian art, Iversen (1975: 33–7, and cf. 1971a: 58–61) introduces a novel discussion of the median line in figure drawing (see Figure 2.7). He claims to derive a law that "in their two-dimensional projection, parts protruding from the three-dimensional plane must be seen in profile, [and] parts extending on the plane [at right angles to the line of sight] en face." This description of the Egyptian method of projection – of the way in which a view of a three-

24

dimensional object is transferred to a two-dimensional surface – similarly misconceives it as an explanation for the canonical system of proportions, in an exact reversal of Panofsky's error. Proportional systems are not necessarily determined by projective systems. Consider grids superimposed upon a "perspective" drawing of a cube and a "flat" drawing of a square in an "Egyptian view" (section-contour view, Figure 2.5). The coordinates of the grids over cube and square correspond with points of reference on both figures, such as the seven corners of the cube in the perspective drawing and the four corners of the square in the Egyptian drawing. We can reproduce exactly the proportions of the first drawing in other drawings simply by knowing in advance what equivalences will map each figure into a proportional coordinate system. The fact that we are using perspective projection in the one case and Egyptian "metric projection" in the other (Hagen, 1986) does not necessarily explain the character of the proportional systems in either example.

These considerations only prove that the proportional canon in Egyptian art was exactly that: First and foremost, it provided exact understanding of ratios of length and breadth among different component parts of the body.

It seems the ratios were themselves determined by measurement and careful observation, although a balance between "naturalistic," empirical observation and a calculation of simple, regular ratios was always held. Schäfer (1974: 333) argued that the Egyptians would not have studied living bodies to work out the basis of the system. In a sense, an artist need never have measured a body in order to have been able to draw it so that the width of the fist was equivalent to one-eighteenth of the total height of the standing figure to its hairline. Where then did the ratio derive its authority or legitimacy? Schäfer suggests that proportions were derived from "exemplary" works of art which struck viewers as especially well formed. Surely exemplary works simply exhibited faithful attention to the canon of proportions – which must therefore have been operating already and have been known to the maker of exemplary works. Schäfer did not realize that in fact the proportions partly conform to the Egyptian measurement of the "natural" body ratios. Because the overall aspect of the figure initially establishes certain ratios or measurements as relevant in figure drawing, only a fraction of empirical observation could have been put to actual use in the proportional system. In order to explain the good fit between proportional canon and Egyptian metrology itself based on an organic standard, we must assume that the Egyptians conducted a certain amount of research on human body proportions (for instance, Robins, 1983d shows that the canon "follows the natural proportions for the upper limb," but not for the lower limbs "where instead there is an elegant elongation of the lower leg").

The proportional canon offered a scientific, calculated basis for an idealizing naturalism, regularizing, standardizing, or normalizing the obvious diversity in actual human proportions. In fact, it was perhaps through the study of regularities that the Egyptians hoped to uncover characteristics of the human figure not necessarily evident in a view of any particular body. Although he mistakenly regards the Egyptian proportional system as a "theory of construction," Panofsky rightly argues (1955: 56) that "proportions could be investigated with reference to the object of the representation as well as with reference to the representation of the object."

The study of proportional systems in ancient art has long been tempted to propose an equation between proportion and ancient ideals of beauty, harmony, or perfection: Proportional observations are often taken to deliver the facts of beauty. As we have seen, however, one needs to know already what kind of form one prefers before proportions are useful for the discrimination of more beautiful or more perfect examples of its representation (see Bernheimer, 1961: 9; Choisy, 1899: I, 56). This is not to say that the adoption of a proportional system was insignificant, but if there are determinable historical reasons for the Egyptian preferences in proportioning the human figure according to a particular set of ratios, current scholarship has not yet been able to find a plausible account of them. Here I can only go so far as to suggest that proportional systems were part of the overall effort to regularize graphic activity, but any proportional system has this effect, and the specific symbolic meaning of equations like 1 fist = $\frac{1}{18}$th of the total height of the figure, if any, remains obscure.

So far, it has only been possible to reconstruct the proportional system applied to standing figures of socially significant adults (but see Iversen, 1960). Other figures in common poses were likely accorded a proportional formulation which was a straightforward variation on the main canon (Robins, 1985). The degree to which proportional formulas were applied to all figure drawings is as yet an open question. It seems that the systems were so well known that the full grid and even the single intersected vertical were not always plotted out (C. R. Williams, 1932: 61). The evidence of *ostraca figurés* suggests that proportional regularization was not universal; most figure drawings on ostraca, a mixed bag of preparatory, copy, humorous, and other drawings, exhibit typical canonical treatments of components and aspect, with deviations from canonical "perfection" mostly in matters of proportion. Furthermore, in periods of high variability in Egyptian art, associated with decay in the productive sector of the economy, the first and most dramatic deviations from canonical standards again involve matters of proportion (Smith, 1949: 217–34).

The proportional system was apparently crucial to the final overall effect of a drawing – to its finish, elegance, and precision. It was apparently for this reason that Greek sculptors adopted the Egyptian canon in the late seventh or sixth century B.C. (Davis, 1981a; Guralnick, 1978). Despite the fact that the proportional canon is logically and historically a final refinement in Egyptian drawing, the use of a highly regularized system of proportions is compelling evidence for the existence of a systematic canon of practice. We must be able to account for the desire to push regularization to such comprehensive and subtle degrees.

THE COORDINATION OF ASPECT

Perhaps the most striking formal element of the Egyptian canon, the frontal-profile aspect (*Abstand*) invariably appears and is the "coordination toward unity," in Riegl's words (1927: 98) – the coordination of the basic rules for body components and proportions.[13] The matter has been well served by Schäfer's description of the human figure in Egyptian art as *geradansichtig-vorstellig* or *geradvorstellig*, "based on frontal images," but it is best to retain the English term frontal-profile for the aspect of figures.[14]

As we have seen, parts of the body are drawn from one position, head-on to a particular section contour, preferably (but not in the event invariably) the most "substantial" section contour. The resulting figure is partially viewed frontally (eyes, shoulders, parts of the chest and abdomen) and partially viewed in profile (head, arms, one of the breasts, and legs).

It is important to note that the coordination is a conventional compromise, a further canonical rule; it is not uniquely determined by the other rules for component contours or proportions. In the drawing of cylindrical volumes like arms and legs, the artist obviously has a choice between several roughly equal but somewhat differently shaped two-dimensional section contours, depending on whether the cylinder is viewed from "front," "back," or "side." The arms appear as we would see the section contours of a standing figure presenting its profile to us – that is, for the nearer arm we appear to see the side of the arm outermost from the body, and for the farther arm we appear to see the side innermost to the body. The aspect of the hands is treated specially according to circumstance. The legs are handled differently; although also presented in profile, in the classic canon they appear as if with two right feet or two left feet. Furthermore, the "aspect" of other parts of the body in the areas of the upper torso, lower abdomen, and upper hips and thighs is somewhat ambiguous.

The standing figure can be regarded as bisected by a vertical median axis, which is often drawn in preparatory work on the image, around which one might "rotate" the various body parts – with proportions fixed by horizontal or grid indicators – to reconstruct the "correct" foreshortened view (Figure 2.7).[15] The correct foreshortened view – what the artist is analyzing in the frontal-profile aspect – turns out to be of a man with one arm at his side, the other arm free (often grasping a staff or rod), with one leg freely advanced or advancing, the other leg at rest. The overall frontal-profile view is perhaps somewhat ambiguous from an observer's point of view. For example, from narrative contexts we know certain figures are supposed to be moving while others are quite still, in a "presentation" or "receiving" pose, but these possibilities cannot be differentiated visually in the canon:[16] At least two and possibly several interpretations could be attached to the single picture offered by the canonical image.

With the frontal-profile aspect, the Egyptians solve the problem of transferring a complex three-dimensional sighting (that is, a view of an object in depth) to a two-dimensional surface. Many earlier commentators wondered how such a peculiar, nonnaturalistic drawing could have persisted and sought an explanation in the allegedly childish, illogical, or unscientific approach of pre-Greek cultures to representation. Yet the canonical aspect is a sophisticated and logical convention. The canon demanded the most substantial depictions of individual components of a figure. Neither a completely frontal nor a completely profile coordination would sufficiently fulfill this demand. A fully frontal view would expose the whole torso and certain facial features (eyes and mouth), but the character-istic shape – that is, the largest possible area bounded by a sec-tion contour – of the legs, feet, and other facial features (nose and chin) would be lost. A profile view would expose certain facial features very well (nose and chin), as well as the legs and feet, but the eyes, shoulders, and breast would seem to disap-pear altogether. To obtain the most complete coordination of all features, some blending of the strictly profile and strictly frontal is required. Now certainly one kind of blended (oblique) view is available if the artist is willing to foreshorten forms. However, foreshortening obscures the facts of propor-tion; for instance, the lengths of the two arms are equal, but in a foreshortened figure one arm might have to be shown as shorter than the other. Overlapping of forms (one arm behind the body) further obscures the articulation of distinct parts.

In sum, for the artist to control and realize his knowledge of the invariable distinctness and proportions of component parts, he requires a coordinated aspect that allows him to combine as many substantial section contours as possible. A short experiment at the drafting board will show that the Egyptian frontal-profile construction of the human figure, although ambiguous in some passages, is nevertheless the only available construction that satisfies this rule and simul-taneously minimizes the necessity of ambiguous section con-tours (for cylindrical volumes or other difficult components).

THE CANONICAL THEORY OF COMPOSITION

An understanding of canonical composition is essential to a clear appreciation of canonical intentions. The subject poses a number of possibly intractable problems (Schäfer, 1974; Smith, 1949: 333–50, 1965: 137–47, 168–79; Groenewegen-Frankfort, 1951: 78–141; Hanke, 1961; Meyer, 1975a, b); study of individual figures has certainly outstripped our knowledge of their arrangement on a surface. Although it was at this level that canonical formulas were often adjusted to accommodate narrative requirements, architectural con-text, and so forth, to survey the gamut of arrangements re-quires a superhuman familiarity with the whole vast range of Egyptian reliefs and paintings. Nevertheless, canonical compositional principles are organically related to or even derived from principles we have already seen at work in figure construction. Building from our knowledge of construction already sketched in this chapter, it should be possible to isolate briefly the routine aspects of compositional practice.

We must be cautious with descriptive definitions, for the Egyptians arranged figures on the two-dimensional plane surface of the ground (Figure 2.9) – a wall, a roll of papyrus – with intentions entirely different from those of Western illusionists. Illusionists accepted the representational value of the ground as a field or "space" not merely empty of figures but signifying "air," "atmosphere," measurable spatial "distance" between objects, a stretch of earth, floor, or ceiling, and so forth, in turn allowing the construction of compositional relations in which the edges or "frames" of the image become a "window" through which the viewer looks back into coherent space (see White, 1957 for the Western tradition of illusion). By contrast, the Egyptians probably did not conceive of the ground or background of the image as a "field" or "space" (see further Hagen, 1986: 211–13).

The tendency of modern historians to publish Egyptian art as individual vignettes in separate photographs or line drawings tends to promote the idea that framing of the modern kind appeared also in Egypt. It is therefore worth stressing that even bordering effects that served representational functions – like the register lines to be considered momentarily – were conceptualized very differently in Egypt than were visually similar effects in our tradition.

Egyptians did produce some objects that look somewhat like the framed "window" of the canvas in Western painting.

Figure 2.9. The Principles of Compositional Organization (Examples of Traces of Artists' Guiding Lines at the Tomb of Perneb). After C.R. Williams, 1932: Pl. 10.

For instance, for the artist's convenience they apparently
sometimes painted on small panels set up on "easels." In the
mastaba of Mereruka, the owner is shown painting on such
a panel (Figure 2.10); there are a few similar instances.[17] If
we look closely at this panel, however, it is obvious that it
was not conceived as a substitute window.

It is also tempting to interpret various procedures as efforts
to animate the plane surface of the ground or to assign to it
a representational value. Groenewegen-Frankfort (1951: 78–
141) has presented a brilliant analysis of topographical
groundlines in Egyptian art, lines added above the register
line do occasionally turn the plane surface into a "world,"
and indeed it appears that some effects of recession were
occasionally attempted. I consider these innovations noncanonical (see Chapter 4). Canonically, even a topographical
groundline is actually just one more individual, separate figure – that is, a shape, a block of ground, drawn like any other
figure by drawing its section contour. The artist is free to
dispose his block of topography, his landscape figure, however he will – that is, according to criteria which may have
nothing to do with a conception of the totality of the plane
surface as coterminous with a coherent "space." In most
cases, of course, the groundline is not topographical anyway
and is identical with the bottom edge of the image or register
within the image.

Western composition tends to use not only a representa-

Figure 2.10. Limestone
Relief of Mereruka Painting the Seasons, from His
Mastaba Tomb at Sakkara,
Fourth Dynasty. After
Duell, 1938: Pl. 7.

tionally significant ground but also a closed, nonfigurative formal armature, "invisible" in the image, for the arrangement of figures on the surface. The typical cone composition of Italian High Renaissance painting underlines the emotional or psychological unity of the various figures. Compositional unity of this kind, based on geometric or abstract plans where figures were fitted into the frame by formally associating them with one another, was generally avoided in Egyptian art. The most important exceptions were a few compositions produced in the late Eighteenth Dynasty at Tell el-Amarna (see generally Davis, 1978; Frankfort, 1929; Nims, 1973; C. R. Williams, 1929–30); some of these depend upon a circular armature which emphasizes the familial bonds of the domestic group of the king, Akhenaten, and his family (Figure 2.11). However, the exception simply dramatizes the canonical preference for an open, indefinitely additive format.

Although the plane surface of the compositional field is not conceived either as a space or as a finite and indivisible unity, none of this tells against the fact that canonical artists used several regularized procedures for arranging figures. Unfortunately these have not been well studied in positive and particular terms.

Some Egyptian compositional preferences can be attributed to a sense of decorative order (Gombrich, 1984), such as a wish to maintain uniform distances between figures on a plane surface. The repetition of forms establishes a rhythmic continuity which can convince the eye that separate figures belong together; some types of repetition, like the *rhythmes ondulatoires* identified by Badawy (1959), can be quite sophisticated. Other techniques also suggest that figures must

Figure 2.11. Principles of "Concentric" Composition for the Relief Stela of Akhenaten, Nefertiti, and Their Daughters, from Tell el-Amarna, Relief and Line Drawing Eighteenth Dynasty. Courtesy Egyptian Museum, West Berlin, and after Davis, 1978: Illus.

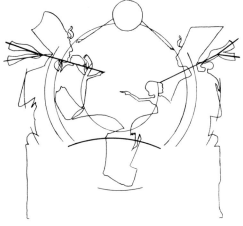

be associated. The visual axis of a group of figures tends to fall in any empty center rather than run through any form (Balcz, 1930). This approach to symmetry seems to have been chosen over the other option of bisecting a form. Since two figures are mutually related to a central axis, the eye infers that they are grouped. In none of these instances does the empty ground have a representational value.

What then does the ground do? I will begin by defining the ground in canonical representation as that which holds figures apart. This function is critical to the general canonical aim of picturing a world which has not been collapsed into a momentary image but rather is "unpacked" or "unfolded" in order to display certain constant qualities (see Chapter 7).

In avoiding compositional integration in the Western sense, the Egyptians used several devices to separate distinct entities from one another visually and to hold them apart. The most important of these was the register line or, more generally, register composition. Leaving aside special contexts, variations in register size throughout a large monument, or other exceptions, in general register composition divides the whole two-dimensional drawing surface into horizontal bands of equal height. The bottom of each band is drawn as a register line, usually unadorned. The drawing surface was not necessarily coextensive with the total surface area of a wall but with the surface area of a wall above and/or below a certain height. It is probable that drawing surfaces were themselves deliberately and carefully defined, although little systematic study of the question has been undertaken. Selection may have had something to do with visibility, perhaps using a viewer's eye level from the floor as the bench mark, and proportionality, for instance, maintaining sets of registers of given heights in proportional relation to heights or lengths of architectural units (in some Old Kingdom tombs, the height of an individual register was always $\frac{1}{20}$th the length of the longest wall of the chapel [Badawy, 1981]).

In Egyptian canonical representation, several other ordering preferences tend to be invariably associated with register composition. They are not logically or formally dependent upon register composition and can be independently varied. The four most important of these conventions were the equidistance, isocephaly, fixity, and coterminousness of figures.

First, a series of figures is placed in a register band according to simple spacing rules, most often a rule specifying equal distance between all figures in the band. Variations from this rule are generally simple fractions or multiples of the constant (for instance, half or twice the general distance between figures).

Second, isocephaly literally refers to the fact that the heads of all figures in a register are placed at the same level. Therefore all figures in a register are of equal height. In combination with the rule of fixity, this specification eliminates the possibility of scale variations being introduced into figure construction through the demands of compositional foreshortening (taller figures closer to the viewer and so on). Isocephaly is best understood as the rule of compositional proportion.

Third, the rule of fixity specifies that all figures in a register are firmly rooted to the register line at all possible natural points. The overwhelming majority of human figures have both feet, toes and heel, placed on the register line, all four feet of a hooved animal are placed on the line, and so forth. Variations from this rule are certainly permitted, but always have a determinate representational significance as a departure from the norm – for instance, as representing a special action or activity like jumping or prancing.

Fourth, in some ways the rule of coterminousness was the most powerful and profound of the compositional conventions. Speaking rigorously, it specifies that if mapped on to each other, all figures in a register band would be (more or less) geometrically identical. Informally speaking, it specifies that all figures in a register band should possess the same (or nearly the same) constructed aspect. In combination with the rule of isocephaly, it means that all figures in a register band look more or less alike. The rule seems particularly potent when operating within individual registers, but it seems to have significant power for entire compositions and indeed for the entire repertory of drawings in canonical art. Again, variations from this rule are certainly permitted, but always have determinate significance as variations – for instance, as representing a figure different from others in some significant physical respect or state (corpulence, weariness, old age, and so forth). Although the rule of coterminousness can be described as a compositional rule – it refers to a kind of pattern or regularity enforced on the drawing surface and involving many separate figures – essentially it is best regarded simply as the invariant use of the single canonical construction of the figure. In the broadest possible phrasing of the matter and speaking for the ideal case, the rule specifies that compositional placement in itself does not affect the construction of the figure. In this respect, Egyptian art is fundamentally different from an art which uses non-object-centered coordinate projection systems (like perspective projection) (Marr, 1982: 300).

We are now ready to ask what registers are intended to represent. I will assume throughout that in considering registers we are also including the four associated conventions of equidistance, isocephaly, fixity, and coterminousness, despite their logical independence from the register division of the drawing surface. Consider the way in which a register composition (Figure 2.10) represents an ordinary view into real space. To describe the register as "compositional" at all has led some commentators to take it to be a way of transferring the whole of a single view of a three-dimensional "world" of real space to a two-dimensional surface. In fact, the device is really a means of transferring only some elements of more than one three-dimensional view.

An actual three-dimensional view of space includes a plane extending back into far space from the viewing eye. Objects, figures, and groups are seen to rest or to move upon this ground plane. In order to transfer this view to the two-dimensional surface, it is argued, the Egyptian artist takes it and tips it up, forward and "flat" against the surface (Carpenter, 1962: 177). Each register would therefore represent the piece of ground upon which a figure or group rested or moved. However, this account implies that any figures in the topmost register are farthest from the viewer; the bottommost register is closer. This pattern does not seem to occur regularly in canonical composition. In many cases the position of a figure in the register is unrelated to its absolute distance from the viewer. Furthermore, topmost figures are not necessarily smaller than bottommost figures: Scale relationships depend upon the relative importance of figures rather than their absolute distance from the viewer (for *Bedeutungsmassstab* or "hierarchic scale," see Frankfort, 1948: 7; Schäfer, 1974: 230–4).[18] It appears that quite separate, stacked registers can represent parts of a single procession or action, appearing optically to a viewer of real space as a single upright long plane intersecting the perspective horizontal plane of the ground and at right angles to the line of sight, that is, as "moving past" the eye. The stacking of registers fractures this single plane.

All of these considerations suggest that registers conduct the viewer through a first view of a three-dimensional world in a particular way. Registers represent the pieces of the ground plane we would see – whether we actually see them or not from any single, fixed viewing position – if or when we see all figures as completely separate from one another, not touching or overlapping. If we want to see figures as separate, separated by a patch of ground, then we have to move in and through a space, stopping to take a series of clear views whenever figures are seen no longer to be touching or overlapping from our point of view. All of these many, separate sightings can be organized if we connect all the separate patches of ground plane lying under each individual figure, whether or not they are actually seen to be continuous patches from any single, fixed viewing position. This, then, is what registers represent: The artist draws all the patches of ground that we would see when we see all separate figures as discontinuous from each other, and he draws them as if they were continuous. In other words, register composition (like the rule of coterminousness) makes it possible to draw individual figures in a certain way.

Not surprisingly, as I have argued elsewhere (Davis, 1976), the groundline of register composition originated in the predynastic period in decorative scenes of figures in files or rows and in a technique of separating figures in a complex group by orienting their baselines in a consistent fashion. Once discovered, the groundline suited narrative and other purposes so well that it was maintained with "extraordinary tenacity" at all times in Egyptian history.[19]

Whereas in the Western tradition, then, composition is most often a means of formal integration, in Egypt composition was principally a means of dis-integration or, speaking positively, of maintaining clarity and distinctions. Artists individually investigated and constructed and then separately "slotted in" each element and action taken in by a single view into real space from a single, fixed position. The artist obtains these views by bringing objects to a position (in his "mind's eye"?) where the appropriate section contours can be isolated and by moving figures to positions where they are not seen to touch. Canonical composition as it were draws lines under the results of this research.

In general, the viewer of an Egyptian image could not have acquired a view like that of the image from any single point of view he might adopt, could never see that view which the image finally composes.[20] Canonical representation both incorporates and supersedes what the individual observer experiences as his view of the world or, more generally, as viewing the world. This direction of interest must be at the heart of the historical and theoretical meaning of canonical representation. The coherence of the world, it proposes, consists of structures and relations that the eye has not originally registered or (a metaphysical point) that the individual has not himself initially constituted or obtained as viewer placed somewhere in his world: And this is the world of which the canonical image is a representation (see Chapter 7).

CHAPTER 3

VARIABILITY, CONVENTION, AND LAWS

I N the preceding chapter I asked what rules the canonical Egyptian artist followed in order to produce the images that he did and, more precisely, all and only the images that he did. Since the formulation of an algorithm in answer to this question is not as simple as it looks and many existing formulations do not quite capture the visual facts, my analysis was inevitably tendentious in a number of respects.

I claimed that the artist isolates and draws the section contours of the components of an object or figure. He constructs the whole figure so that he may include as many section contours as possible, although this will involve him in a few ambiguous passages of anatomical description (for example, in the rendition of the abdominal area). Construction must also respect a complex, finely tuned proportional canon – which actually has the simple duty of telling the artist at what scale a component section contour should be drawn. In putting together a group of figures drawn to these specifications, the artist combines several views of the group, namely, a series of same-scale nonoverlapping presentations of identically constructed figures which can only be obtained by fragmenting a unitary view into space. He uses the plane surface of the drawing surface to hold figures apart, but connects them with "continuous" register lines – representing the separate discontinuous patches of ground upon which figures individually stand – and follows simple spacing rules. In approaching a complex group in this way, the artist is assured of obtaining the individual views of separate figures, which in turn allows him to isolate section contours and arrive at correct construction. Construction, proportion, and composition are interdependent: To present proportional data correctly, the artist must use a certain kind of construction of aspect; to obtain a view of an object that permits the most substantial section contour, figure grouping must be approached in a certain way; and so on. If he follows all and only these invariant specifications and respects the limits of conventional standards for more variable details, the artist will obtain a canonical image.

VARIABILITY

Before considering in more detail what the status of this algorithm might be, it is important to stress that the vast proportion of what appears to be variable, idiosyncratic detail in Egyptian representation is fully canonical. In my limited space, it is simply impossible to produce a complete list of all the individual conventions developed for the rendition of particular objects, actions, and so forth; I have focused only on the most general principles regulating drawing as such – the drawing of any object or action. Despite the Egyptians' extraordinary interest in the properties of the natural world, specifically different one moment from the next and potentially demanding a mode of representation infinitely capacious, flexible, and attentive to diversifying difference, a highly formulaic quality can be isolated in any Egyptian representation conforming to the general algorithm. This obvious point is worth making because many commentators have taken the "naturalism" of Egyptian art to lie outside the domain of canonical control. The "naturalistic" interests of Egyptian artists are often brought forward as evidence that the Egyptian artist was doing something more (that is, more creative, more "artistic") than abiding by regularized mechanical prescriptions for production. (As we will see, there is indeed a limit to prescription or a moment in drawing when the artist has no rule, but the account of this limit in crude Romantic aesthetics that attempt to liberate the Egyptian "artist" from the Egypt whose languages he used fails to understand it correctly.) Note, then, that a detailed history of increasing naturalism in Old Kingdom art (Spiegel, 1957) is simultaneously a history of an increasingly formalized style: Conventionalization of canon is simply a different category of analysis than the lifelikeness of the image, and one cannot be used to show that the other lacks force. Our real task is to understand the nature of the established conventions – "naturalistic" or not – at any given time in Egyptian history.

The conventions themselves, of course, vary from one subject to another. Drawing an animal was not regulated by precisely the same standards used for the representation of

VARIABILITY,
CONVENTION, AND LAWS

the human figure. For example, sketches of flying birds typically combine the form of the bird seen at rest with a concern for its movement in flight. Especially in *ostraca figurés* monkeys are gymnastic and playful (Figure 3.1*a*), qualities not normally ascribed to human figures in Egyptian art. In New Kingdom monumental reliefs horses are elegantly proportioned; care lavished on basic outline form does not preclude secondary attention to movement, for the horses strain forward, leap, or prance skittishly ahead of the monarch's chariot. Although one could multiply these cases (see the handbooks of Klebs, 1915, 1922, 1934; Vandier, 1964), they should not be seen as naturalistic noncanonical variations; they are examples of canonical conventions of naturalism.

The many surviving *ostraca figurés* document the great range of Egyptian visual interests and graphic abilities.[1] Dating primarily from the New Kingdom, these trial studies and informal sketches include formal presentations of the canonical human figure, conforming to preferences discussed already, and comparatively naturalistic but fully conventional studies of animals in motion. Composition ranges from the register band to registerless arrangements most closely re-

Figure 3.1. Three Painted Limestone Ostraca. *a.* With Climbing Monkey, Human Keeper (?), and Birds in Tree, from Deir el-Medineh, Probably Eighteenth or Nineteenth Dynasty. *b.* With Three Wild (?) or Hunting Dogs Attacking a Hyena or Boar (?). *c.* With Horse Resting (?) or Gnawing Its Hoof. After Vandier-d'Abbadie, 1936–59: II, Nos. 2004, 2211, 2157.

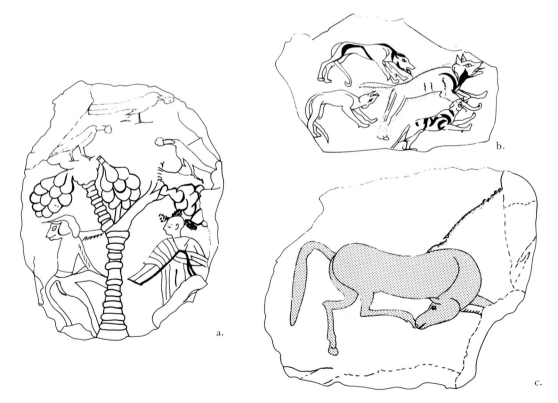

a.

b.

c.

sembling the "bird's eye" planning used in some predynastic representations (Davis, 1976); in some thematic contexts, the spread-out arrangements were not uncanonical (see Chapter 4). Portraiture may be extremely lifelike in some respects or strictly idealizing. Line may be "painterly" or controlled as if by careful ruling. In all of this diversity, techniques of rendition and expression from the naturalistic to the diagrammatic ends of the conventional continuum have been mastered.

Occasionally drawings on the ostraca break from Schäfer's frontal *geradvorstellig* rule or, in our terms, from the conventional canonical algorithm for components, proportions, aspect, and composition (Figures 3.1*b*, *c*). No doubt there are a number of ambiguous drawings throughout the corpus of Egyptian representations, and in the ostraca they may simply be students' unsuccessful efforts to learn or copy or a master's attempt to work out a canonically acceptable presentation. Whatever the reason for the noncanonical result, in general the difference between a canonical and noncanonical convention, realistic or idealizing, is easy to see – for the general algorithm does establish a strict criterion of correctness for the construction and composition of figures and groups.

"PORTRAITURE"

The addition of variable, often lifelike detail to the general format for a well-formed canonical image is nowhere so much in evidence as in Egyptian "portraiture."[2] On the one hand, in some contexts the canonical drawing of a human face and body idealized and beautified the subject (see Figures 2.1, 2.2, 2.3). The purpose was both propagandistic and religious. An image presented a man as strong and successful. Conventions of presentation varied from case to case and from epoch to epoch; in some instances corpulence was an attribute of the powerful courtier, but in others it may be a grotesque attribute. From the idealizing point of view, the personality or physiognomic peculiarities of an individual were secondary matters. Indeed it is commonly said that Egyptian tomb sculpture explicitly avoids specificity at the level of physiognomic detail, for the tomb statue served only as a receptacle, "waiting for animation" (Panofsky, 1956: 15) by the soul of the deceased (see the classic treatment of Steindorff, 1910).

On the other hand, inspired by other religious and various secular imperatives, the image of a man should also be recognizable as his image. As the sculpted image may be occupied by the soul or be his only monumental memory on earth, we can understand a patron's desire to live on in some familiar form – this "anxiety to produce statues that the *Ka* could not fail to recognize as himself" (Berenson, 1953: 19).

For a variety of reasons, at some points Egyptian officials and monarchs rich enough to commission "portrait" images were seemingly interested in individualized likeness (Figure 3.2). As the functional contexts of image making permitted both individualizing and generalizing likeness, there is no particular reason why individualizing likeness could not have been as conventional as we can imagine. Of course, it may be asked how we know that a "likeness" depicted actual details of a real individual's physiognomy; but just because we could in principle identify such "realism" does not, by my earlier arguments, show them to be nonconventional or noncanonical. It is often and in some cases probably correctly assumed that features of images like wrinkles, folds of fat, fleshy noses or lips, and so forth were efforts to depict the actual characteristics of individual patrons. It is also conceivable that a symbolic point was being made: For example, is corpulence an attribute of an individual or a general attribute symbolizing contentedness or social success? Needless to say, in all of this the selection of realisms was a conventionalized undertaking: Late Period "portraits" depict sitters as author-

Figure 3.2. Granite Sculpted Portrait of Amenemhet III, Twelfth Dynasty. Courtesy Ny Carlsberg Glyptothek, Copenhagen.

itative, world-wise, fatherly statesmen and priests, as had the great royal portraits of the high Middle Kingdom (Figure 3.2). These works are stylistically and psychologically coherent, implying that they were fully canonical. More problematic are the somewhat awkward works that include one single idiosyncratic "signature element," an individual realistic detail in an otherwise generalized likeness. Perhaps these were intended to depict striking features of individuals (like Nofer's nose, see Figure 2.3) (Smith, 1949: 304) or hereditary characters; it seems likely that these efforts were not intended to break the bounds of the canon but rather to "fix" the image precisely, for the viewer, within the range of canonically acceptable presentations of the patron's self.

As a measure of these relations, let us briefly consider two "portraits" of one man, presumably manufactured at the same time, for the same tomb, serving the same memorializing function. The tomb panels of the high official Hesire from Sakkara in the Third Dynasty (Figure 3.3; see also Figure 2.1) are excellent illustrations, not only for their great technical accomplishment – the image is no more than eighteen inches high – but also because they seem to be the earliest surviving examples of the fully evolved Egyptian canon in its "basic form" (Schäfer, 1974: 283). As Iversen (1955) showed, the figures on the panels conform to the eighteen-unit system of proportions. In the treatment of the outline components, hands, feet, torso, and so on, and in the selection of aspect all of the panels are almost absolutely canonical.

On one panel (Figure 3.3), Hesire is seated before his offering table on a low backless seat. The details of the chair legs, in the shape of bulls' feet, and the thongs attaching legs to seat, crisscross braided, are carefully incised, almost sculpturally modeled. Hesire wears a long robe (although the hem at the neck has not been shown), grasps his staff and wand to his chest with his left hand, and extends his right, palm up, to the table. His scribal pot, palette, and brush – not so much items of his occupation as symbols of his high rank – are slung over his right shoulder. This overall formula for official majesty has been slightly modified by the inclusion of individualizing features. Ostensibly Hesire is a young and potent man; his short, well-trimmed mustache formulaically establishes him as a handsome courtier. His expression, however, is weary, middle-aged, deeply experienced: His collarbones, as well as the prominent descending muscles of his neck, have been strongly modeled to make the entire upper body seem tense. More lightly, the sculptor adds the tendons and bones of elbows and ankles, although as his feet rest gently on the low base of the offering table Hesire could not really be in a state of muscular tension. The physique is powerful, but the proportions of the figure exhibit the peculiar thinness of breadth characteristic of perfect full grid presentations of the proportional canon. Hesire's face unequivocally reflects the burdens and responsibilities of titled office.

We have enough comparable examples from the Old and Middle Kingdoms to be able to read these signs fairly reliably. The strong jaw is clenched, the jawline tough and precise from the lower, dented chin to the base of the ear behind the

Figure 3.3. Detail of the Wooden Relief of Hesire, from His Mastaba Tomb at Sakkara, Third Dynasty. Courtesy Cairo Museum.

wig. The mouth, curving down beneath the clipped mustache, small and thin-lipped, is a highly individual feature: The usual convention for human lips calls for more fleshiness. The lower face has been deeply marked by a middle-aged cleft from the side of the nostrils to below the corners of the mouth, although as Smith (1949: 18, 22) observes, this furrow can also be seen, less dramatically, on other portraits of the period and is probably quite conventionalized in itself. Between a high, prominently modeled cheekbone and a protruding browridge, the eye appears slightly sunken, dropping perceptibly in the front corner. It is revealing that the cosmetic line of the eyebrow is not included. Subtly, we are given to know that we are seeing Hesire in a private moment of naturalness or perhaps – given the context – in thoughtful contemplation of his mortality. His braided wig overhangs his brow somewhat, again a briefly poignant departure from public propriety.

The significance of all of these details can only be appreciated in relation to a range of typicalities and, specifically, in relation to a second panel on which Hesire stands officially and in public, apparently receiving (or making) offerings (see Figure 2.1). Wearing an ornamental short kilt, outdoor and public dress, and a long uncurled wig, slightly dandified with its four waves at the top, he carries his short staff in his right hand, his rod and scribal implements in his left. On this relief much more attention has been paid to details of Hesire's anatomy. The collarbones are again prominent; the navel depression is carefully modeled, with the forward thigh muscle large and developed; the kneecap is markedly raised and set off by two diagonal ripples of muscle above; the shin bone is deeply modeled with a lighter long muscle in the calf behind; here the ankle is only slightly indicated, a foot bone rather unscientifically stretched along the upper length of the foot. Most of these details are or will become conventional signs of athletic physique. As usual for this period, in neither panel do we find much suggestion of musculature in the torso. Each fingernail has been depicted, as well as two tiny wrinkles above the right thumbnail. Compared with the seated figure, Hesire's face in this image is much smoother and untroubled. As on the first panel, his most distinctive characteristics appear – hook nose, high cheekbones, long high forehead, and a depression around the base of the nose – but the modeling is more restrained. Is this a composed, "official" expression?

Both panels (Figure 3.3; see also Figure 2.1) exemplify full canonical conventionalization of the human figure. Variation is restricted to play within these limits. In this canonical language, Hesire makes at least two statements about himself – about his personal and his public identity. A third well-preserved panel depicts a second official Hesire, but unfortunately the other panels are too seriously damaged for conclusions to be drawn about their place in the tomb's program.[3] With a language of dress, facial expression, anatomical detailing, and so on fully established, the significance of variable details would have been instantly appreciated – in this case, for example, as making a personal, private statement or as depicting the official identity of the sitter.

In canonical representation variable details do not have any sort of independent life of their own. They derive the resonance they possess from their specific place in a field of possibilities established by canonical preferences. Insofar as variable details belong to this domain at all (and in some images, some may not), they can only be regarded as fully canonical in themselves. The problem is often simply that our documentation in many cases is not adequate to discovering all of the individual canonical significations of the more variable ranges of the continuum.

In his important essay on the Egyptian capacity for and powers of "abstraction" (*Abstraktionsvermögung*), Otto (1972) interprets Egyptian art as balanced between two "poles," the abstract principle and the principle of *konkrete Naturfülle* (from Wolf, 1957). The latter, the representation of specific concrete things, individually different and distinguished, comprehends most of what we can take as variable detail in completely canonical art. The greater part of the representation of the concrete takes place within the canonical context, appearing selectively in authorized circumstances and using conventionalized formulations for realism or lifelikeness.

Nevertheless, Egyptian art is balanced between two poles, the canonical and the noncanonical. The canonical includes both variable and invariant elements, whereas the noncanonical is seldom allowed to be made manifest and to survive in the tradition although it may (for instance, in preparatory studies [Figures 3.1*b*, *c*]) be one of the grounds of the tradition as such. The real tension in Egyptian art, then, is not between two articulated principles, but between method and chaos, the spoken and the unspoken, articulated principle and merely potential practice, existing always outside the limits of recognized representations.

46

In addition to conventions of realism and of "portrait" likeness, a full catalogue of canonical conventions of representation in Egyptian art would have to include other matters
that my outline analysis (see Chapter 2) passed over silently.
These conventions are now only partly understood; for example, understanding color conventions – or the symbolic
meaning of different color schemes for the human figure –
will depend upon better knowledge of the Egyptian seg-
mentation of the color spectrum and other factors still being
studied.[4] Our full catalogue, in principle, would have to be
sensitive to assorted subtle differences between various artistic media. For example, my outline (see Chapter 2) applies
most readily to drawing and painting and to some types of
relief sculpture, and although quite canonical, some relief
work ought to be described in slightly different formal terms.
In relief there can be no such thing as pure profile (Krahmer,
1931: 62–3, and cf. Eaton-Krauss, 1984: 2–3; Schäfer, 1974:
74–9, 305), although the concept of profile logically enters
in to canonical constructions (it is identical with one kind of
section contour). Artists and patrons apparently sometimes
felt that the typical sculpted relief profile of the human face
failed to be completely intelligible. In some reliefs, sculptors
added both sides of the philtrum from the nose to the upper
lips (for instance, Simpson, 1977: No. 36), though in "pure"
profile theoretically only one side of the philtrum should
appear. We could make an intriguing survey of these efforts
to adjust canonical requirements and resolve ambiguities in
procedures. One striking case of adjustment was the mod-
ernization of the proportional canon in the Twenty-sixth Dynasty, accommodating formulas to new metrological
standards (Iversen, 1975: 75–88).

All of these problems, however, are too specialized or too
uncertain for detailed comment here. It is fair to say that the
principal conventionalities of a typical image have been described; at least, I have stressed the intelligibility of variations
as being dependent upon a canonical frame of reference. It is
therefore important to note that the study of Egyptian art
has traditionally been characterized by an ambition to reduce
formal description even further than the algorithmic/gram-
matical model I have been developing here must require.
Many observers have believed that the canonical images of
Egypt could be generated logically from a single overarching

rule, "principle," or "attitude." In one way or another, they have attempted to identify the single fundamental law of procedure. These efforts require our attention as we evaluate the status of my own morphological description.

Many Egyptologists are suspicious of claims that some mathematical absolute might animate Egyptian art and architecture, for such claims often proceed from wrongheaded estimations of the capabilities and intentions of Egyptian technicians, artists, and patrons. Nevertheless, there is no a priori reason to rule out analysis of this kind: There is no sense in which the Egyptian intellect was incapable of having known and articulated mathematical absolutes; some analyses are implausible, but others may point to important characteristics of Egyptian image making.

Some commentators have vigorously argued that the Egyptians used the derivation and ratio of the "golden section" (the $\emptyset$ ratio of 5:8). Badawy (1965) showed that this ratio can be detected in a few engineering efforts and in the preliminary ground-plan design of some buildings (see also Varille, 1947: 15). The architectural historian Moessel (1926: 32–3) recognized the presence of 5:8 constructions in the compositional design of Egyptian sculpted stelae. The arc of the top of the stela is thought to represent the sky; one wonders if the perfect geometry suggested a cosmographical or mystical meaning or if the meaning required a perfection of construction (Schäfer, 1974: 235; Westendorf, 1966: Figs. 14–15). In a neglected volume by the Norwegian artist Else Christie Kielland, *Geometry in Egyptian Art* (1955), a number of tomb- and wall-relief figures and compositions are analyzed as products of careful geometric constructions based upon simple ratios like the golden section (Iversen, 1975: 25–6; Roeder, 1956; Senk, 1956; Wolf, 1957–8).

If we accept the measurements of buildings, stelae, or figures and compositions proposed by Badawy, Moessel, and Kielland – there is room for doubt about the accuracy of some measurements – it is true that 5:8 and other similar simple ratios between parts of the whole can be detected. The question, of course, is to know how to interpret these observations, for some kind of proportional relation can always be formulated between any parts of a whole. Does this imply that the $\emptyset$ analysis is fanciful or that the repeated use of particular $\emptyset$ ratios must have been meaningful?

Carpenter's remarks on the system of "dynamic symmetry" as a rule for the proportioning of Greek vases make instructive reading as a parallel problem in the history of art

(1921, 1962: 81–90, on Caskey, 1922, Hambidge, 1920). Carpenter concludes that no invisible, axiomatically geometrical system is at work in the design of Greek vases; rather, non-geometrical preferences based on the visible qualities of forms and the routine metrology were responsible for the shaping and perfection of those forms – in some cases approaching geometrical or harmonic purity according to some rigorous definition.

Although Kielland is able to analyze one or two Egyptian reliefs as a detailed embodiment of an intricate system, the measurement of other reliefs does not yield any regular result at all. Does this imply that some artists were producing images according to rigorous preplanned specifications of relationship and others were simply striving for a more generalized optical perfection? Perhaps some artists were better technicians, performing their work more exactly according to a precise system: This would explain why some Egyptian compositions are quite regular but others deviate from the supposed standards. Carpenter notes that in Greece, however, objects quite clearly produced by the same artist vary widely in their alleged exactitude. Furthermore, the tolerance of metrological and proportional errors in construction is relatively wide, that is, it is apparently based on simple visual preferences not fine enough to distinguish small errors, not narrow enough, that is, to be based on a geometrical system calculated to a fine degree.

Yet peculiar features of Egyptian construction may indeed result from employing ratio systems of relationship. We have seen that the superimposition of a proportional canon, whatever ratios of relationship it happens to use (for example, one fist = $1/18$th of the height of the figure to its hairline), follows upon the visualization of the whole figure viewed from a particular aspect. Nevertheless, the Egyptians did choose to use a particular proportional system which, by the very logic of proportional mathematics, must inevitably embody particular kinds of ratio relationships (for instance, ratio of a figure's fist to its height to hairline = 1:18). An understanding of more simple and elegant ratios and a preference for their use might have entered into the selection of the particular proportional system applied in Egyptian canonical representation; given canonical interests in clarity and intelligibility, there is no particular a priori reason why this could not be so. It turns out, in the event, that the ratio of the total height of the figure (18 units) to the height of the figure as high as the navel (11 units) happens to be more or less the golden

49

section ($\emptyset$) constant (here 1.6363 for the value of $\emptyset$ as 1.618), as does the ratio of the height of the figure from the junction of the legs (9 units) to its height from the junction to the armpit (5½ units) (and therefore further, 18:11 = 9:5.5) (Badawy, 1965: 62–4; Kielland, 1946, 1955). In the Late Period, by coincidence (?), the adjustment of the proportional system to the new metrology brings the ratio results to 1.615, a much closer approximation of the $\emptyset$ constant at 1.618 than that achieved in the "classical" proportional canon.

With the information available to us at the moment, it is not easy to settle between two alternative interpretations of these observations: The proportional canon was (1) deliberately devised to embody the $\emptyset$ constant relationship between total figure and height of figure to the navel (and so forth); (2) constructed for other reasons (which, as we have seen, are not known but would have to do, perhaps, with the metaphysical or other "meaning" of the fist as a relevant module for figure drawing, and so forth). Or was it the case that, simply to satisfy visual preferences for a certain "naturally agreeable" optical harmony, the proportional canon coincidentally happens to embody the $\emptyset$ constant relationships? Interpretation (1) is certainly the most economical but also makes the strongest claim. Despite the several incompletenesses of interpretation (2), it is probably the one art historians and Egyptologists would accept at the moment. Interpretation (2) covers all the facts of interpretation (1) and accounts for the many deviations or unregularities to be observed in the record, for we simply assert that visual preferences are rather loose, tolerating considerable margins of error or difference.

THE REDUCTION OF CONVENTIONS TO AN UNDERLYING
PSYCHOLOGICAL PRINCIPLE OR ATTITUDE

Although some single, simple mathematical or geometrical absolute, like the 5:8 ratio of the golden section, may have been at work in the selection of some rather than other proportions in the overall construction of figures and compositions, as my analysis of the general algorithm implies (see Chapter 2), many other conceptual operations are going on simultaneously in the drawing of the figure. Some are not mathematical or harmonic at all and are geometric only in the broadest sense that, for example, section contours must ultimately enclose some kind of geometry – rather complex polygons or other shapes of the component parts of the figure. It seems highly unlikely that these conceptually diverse operations could be reduced to a single simple harmony.

The quest for fundamental canonical "laws" has led in another direction as well. At the root of these inquiries is the general belief, best expressed by Schäfer (1974), that it makes sense to derive the principles of Egyptian art – whether described as a collection of conventions and practical procedures or as algorithmic laws for drawing – from an underlying "perceptual attitude," specified by Schäfer and his followers (Brunner-Traut, 1973, 1974a) as *geradvorstellig* or "aspective." Aspective is the "framework" (*Gerüstsschicht*) for a superimposed "level of expression" (*Ausdrucksschicht*) (Schäfer, 1974: 90–2, 265–7; translations by Baines, 1974a: xvii, and see his 1985b). Since it is remarkably similar to Panofsky's iconological category of the "intrinsic meaning" or "content" of an image (1939: 3–5), Panofsky's clear words can be used: Unlike the "factual meaning," "expressional meaning," or "conventional meaning" of the image, the *Gerüstsschicht* ("framework," "intrinsic meaning") underlies and explains "both the visible event [that is, a particular work of art] and its intelligible significance [that is, the expressional and conventional meanings a viewer in a culture automatically assigns to it]" and "determines even the form in which the visible event takes shape"; it is "those underlying principles which reveal the basic attitude of a nation, a period, a class, a religious or philosophical persuasion – unconsciously qualified by one personality and condensed into one work" and "discernible in all other specific qualities of [a particular] style" (Panofsky, 1939: 5, 7–8). Like Panofsky's iconology and by virtue of its similar assumptions, Schäfer's work leads ultimately to a form of psychological idealism or idealistic *Kulturmorphologie*, that is, to claims about the essential nature of the Egyptian mentality.

According to Schäfer, in *geradvorstellig* representation – "not artistic form but the logical basis of that form" (Brunner-Traut, 1974a: 423) – the artist isolates "single frontal mental images" of aspects or views of complex whole objects, visualized in an unforeshortened format, with the "mind's eye" placed "close up to" it, uninfluenced by the relations of the view to the surrounding near and far spatial environment or by the environment's particular impingements on the object (differential illumination, occlusion, and so forth). The results of this "unrestricted viewing" are placed

51

"paratactically side by side" to create a depiction of the whole object combining several points of view (to use Brunner-Traut's 1974a summary of Schäfer's ideas). As it is the "framework" for individual acts of rendition, Schäfer (1974: 267) insists that "Egyptian artists were not even aware" of using *geradvorstellig* technique; it was supposedly arrived at "purely by instinct" (Brunner-Traut, 1974a: 424). Indeed, Schäfer and Brunner-Traut regard *geradvorstellig* or aspective representation as the basis of all pre-Greek representation (as well as of the drawing of young children) and as an innate or natural "perceptual attitude" shared by all Egyptians. This idealist, essentialist claim is highly undesirable (and in its homogenizing of pre-Greek representational practices quite inaccurate).[5] Yet as a description Schäfer's analysis of *geradvorstellig* is helpful, and I will take it that the "perceptual attitude" of the artist-viewer, supposedly "instinctual," could have actually been no more and no less than a practical decision about the viewing position of the draftsman and about the appropriate means of drawing the object from this position. In other words, the viewer decides to adopt the *geradvorstellig* representation – which I have analyzed in somewhat different terms (see Chapter 2) – as the most suitable means of making sense of perception and knowledge of the world, according to criteria we still know little about.

On the whole, Schäfer's own detailed analysis of the conventions of Egyptian representation does not require any more; *geradvorstellig* is not so much a way of seeing or thinking as a way of drawing. To be precise, a way of drawing is a way of seeing and thinking, and there is no use or power in explaining the qualities of the one by appealing to the other. In creating a pre-Greek perceptual attitude to account for pre-Greek drawing, Schäfer goes much too far.

It is important to recognize, however, that in another significant sense Schäfer actually does not go far enough. *Geradvorstellig* technique does not in itself uniquely determine what sort of drawing an artist should produce; it will not deliver all and only the images of canonical Egyptian art. The technical reason for this lack of fit between Schäfer's analysis of the "logical basis" of representation in Egypt and Egyptian representational practices as they can actually be observed is easy enough to identify. Consider that there are many possible *geradvorstellig* or aspective representations of a complex object. Suppose an artist must draw a box resting on the ground (Figure 3.4). If he chooses to depict only two sides of this box, there are still four separate aspective drawings available to him. If he chooses to depict more than two sides – for instance, if he wants to show different decorations on the various sides or the top as well as the sides – there are many more drawings available, all satisfying *geradvorstellig* principles and paratactic combination. Furthermore, at least from one common vantage point, the artist must solve an ambiguity in depicting his box: He has to decide between those aspective renditions that assume that the sides of the box are rectangular and those that assume irregular or sloping sides. Of these numerous aspective drawings, some are quite similar to each other and it hardly makes a difference which rendition is selected; but others are quite distinct.

Egyptian draftsmen experimented with different possible aspective representations of the same object. For instance, the paintings in the tomb of Hesire (Figure 3.5) contain several interesting examples of this experimentation, such as a series of drawings of beds in which two and possibly more solutions to the same problem have been adopted, either by different draftsmen or by the same draftsman exploring alternatives. But experimentation always had its limits. In fact, the catalogue of acceptable aspective solutions in Egyptian drawing is quite restricted. For one of the most complex objects of all, the human figure, artists at the beginning of the dynastic period accepted only one of the many possible aspective representations and maintained it consistently. We have already seen (see Chapter 2) that their choice involved the complex interpenetration of several specific rules. These conventions were not the same thing as aspective drawing itself; they were

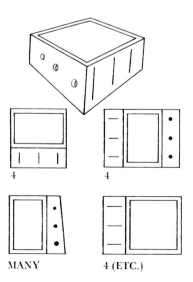

Figure 3.4. Model Box (*top*) with Different Possible Aspective Representations.

certainly more narrow and precise, presenting further constraints, beyond aspective, for a well formed construction.

Schäfer was undoubtedly quite aware of the need to describe and explain particular conventional choices. The *Ausdrucksschicht*, the "level of expression," presumably contains the various "expressions," styles, or conventions adopted in practice and in particular circumstances. As convention specified which aspective view was acceptable, it would have made sense to begin with the *Ausdrucksschicht* (indeed, there is nothing more to consider than representational practice itself), but Schäfer was interested in what he believed to be bigger game, the elucidation of aspective itself.

By contrast, I have attempted to isolate all and only the standards relevant to the particular "aspective" renditions that actually appear consistently in Egyptian canonical image making (see Chapter 2). Anything more general to be said about aspective representation may help us with certain problems in the psychology of representation or the general qualities of nonillusionistic drawing, but does not help with the specific formal and historical qualities of Egyptian art as such. Egyptian artists and viewers adopted the most suitable as-

Figure 3.5. Experiments in Aspective Representation of Beds, Paintings from the Mastaba Tomb of Hesire at Sakkara, Four Views, Third Dynasty. After Quibell, 1913: Pl. 14.

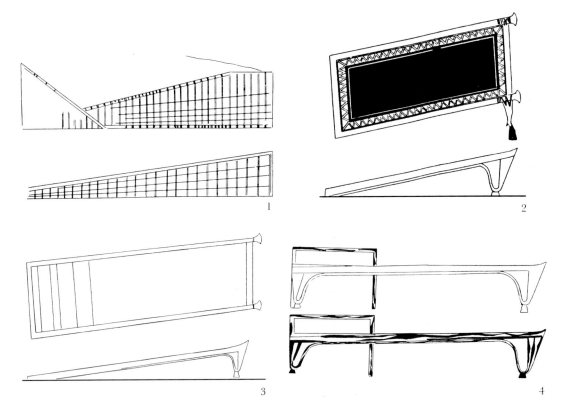

pective way of producing a drawing of what they intended to draw. Therefore we need to know what particular rules, assumptions, and purposes or, at the least, what history of selection (see Chapter 6) might have been responsible for the selection of this mode rather than other perceptually, conceptually, and technically possible modes.

Despite the possibility of a materialist critique along these lines (thought is representation), idealist commitments have continued to grip art-historical writing on Egyptian art. A culture's "mode of consciousness" is held to be responsible for the "basic form" of its cultural practice. For instance, in her remarkable book Groenewegen-Frankfort (1951) argued that cultural conceptions of temporal progression or the nature of the spatial continuum structured the way in which time and space were presented in Egyptian art.[6] Needless to say, Egyptian artists must depend upon Egyptian theories about the spatiotemporal continuum. This is not to say that these theories are an explanation for artistic practice; they are simply one of its conditions. Although Groenewegen-Frankfort herself is not guilty of the conflation, in general the traditional claims of *Kulturpsychologie* cannot be justified by arguing that art expresses or reflects deeper, wider cultural constants and concerns. Claims of this kind inevitably lead us away from a particular historical account of conventional choices (see Chapter 6). Just as I concluded that aspective is simply a way of drawing, we may ask where these "modes of consciousness" or "theories of the world" are if not actually in the practice of representation itself. An account of a society's distinctive cultural practices does not need to assume that knowledge or beliefs about the world are simply there waiting to be expressed or reflected in representation, just as it does not need to assume preferences or attitudes are simply there waiting to guide practical decisions. Representational practice is nothing more or less than knowledge itself: And the question should be about what the artist knows, that is, what he represents.

As a final difficulty, Schäfer's insistence on the "principle" of Egyptian art as *geradvorstellig* fails adequately to recognize that the history of the formation of the canon is the history of experiments, accretion, and adjustment (see Chapter 6) and that even the most precisely defined procedures within the overall system can remain visually and logically quite ambiguous as aspective in the first place. Aspective ambiguity is especially characteristic of the resolution of spatial relationships between forms (for example, lying in overlapping, intersecting, or vertically adjacent planes) and of the depiction of parts of the figure lying between converging but seemingly contradictory outlines. The three-quarters (non-*geradvorstellig*) view of the abdomen between chest, stomach, and back is one instructive example (see Figures 2.1, 2.7). The line from the left armpit to the navel at the front side of the body outlines the shape of the chest and belly in profile. The shoulders are viewed frontally. The line from the shoulder to the buttocks at the back side of the body, the side from which the face looks away, seems to be constructed in order to unite the frontal broadness of the shoulders with the more or less profile slenderness of the waist. The actual aspect of the abdomen is therefore not at all clear, for the anatomy lying between all of these outlines is undetermined as a specific section contour. The only details to aid us are the nipples and the navel, but they are merely applied to the plane area lying between the outlines, not inserted in a position that establishes foreshortening (see Mohr, 1943: 5; Schäfer, 1974: 282–5, who does concur that the torso has not been constructed in the same way or with the same definition as usual but gets around the difficulty for his larger argument by emphasizing mysterious "unconscious processes" in this part of the artist's effort at drawing). The area of contact between frontal lower belly and profile forward leg above the hip is another puzzling anatomical passage. Panofsky (1955: 58, n. 2) describes this as a passage of "graphic transition," for neither foreshortening nor other torsional constructions are applied; certainly the upper hips are not constructed from a head-on, "frontal" vantage.[7] However, if we drop an insistence on *geradvorstellig* or aspective as the basic rule of drawing, such passages are not at all mysterious; we would fully expect to find them. According to our analysis (see Chapter 2), they are section contours, the plane being taken through the part of the anatomy in question (such as the abdomen) between the two most distant opposite surfaces (such as those between the left front flank and right back rump). There is nothing in the algorithm requiring all section contours be frontal or profile (the abdominal section contour subtends at an approximately 45° angle from either an absolutely frontal or absolutely profile plane through the figure); and the artist is simultaneously obeying a complementary rule that he include as many substantial section contours as possible, which demands a few lines of "graphic transition" in the paratactic combination of those contours.

The existence of these "ambiguities" in construction (if we

wrongly enforce *geradvorstellig* as the final measure of clarity or success in drawing) hardly contradicts the central claim put forward here that the canon is a methodical, deliberated effort to map certain properties of the world, which is fully regularized, consistent, intelligible, and unambiguous given the requirements of all and only its several interpenetrating conventional rules. Although it is impossible to axiomatize Egyptian art, derive it from a single harmony, or reduce it to a unitary psychological "principle" or "attitude," typicalities can be identified; the limits of practice can be isolated; a rationale for most individual formal decisions regularly repeated in most practice can be produced. In all of this, canonical method is defined as a way of drawing and not a (natural, innate, instinctive) way of seeing. The canonical method has the psychological status of a choice, a selection, a convention – a purposeful commitment to what is conceived to be the most appropriate way of making images according to a representational ambition still to concern us in detail (see Chapter 7).

Nevertheless, there is a sense in which the strong definition of the "principles" of image making at work in Schäfer's analysis seems to be the most acceptable characterization of a central feature of Egyptian art. Any Egyptian artist represents his subjects canonically; he produces canonically correct images within a specific tolerance of variation. Despite the logical possibility of representing in some other way, in Egypt there was a fundamental asymmetry between the alternative possibilities open to an artist. Canonical methods were overwhelmingly successful. Except in rare circumstances, the "choices" for representation were not socially available choices at all. Therefore, in the end we might have to say that the Egyptian artist – whatever his way of seeing or knowing the world – knew no other way of drawing the world.

Our argument has not just come full circle to a Schäferian conclusion. Two critical points have been established by implication in our consideration of variability, convention, and law in Egyptian art. First, Egyptian society did select between alternatives, a selection we can invest with historical significance. Early Egyptian artists (see Chapter 6) selected to make these representations, the canonical images, instead of making something else, everything possible, or nothing at all. Although at any given point in Egyptian history, this was not a selection on the part of a particular artist, at some point in its history the society did in fact settle upon its procedures.

We must, then, consider the activity of some specifiable group of artists and patrons at some specifiable point in history as having nominated canonical images for continued regard and reproduction.

Second, that the artist knows no other way of making an image is purely a social fact. By the logic of the case, there are no a priori reasons to believe that the artist would, left utterly to his own devices, draw according to the canonical rules – which, after all, have shown themselves in my analysis to be sophisticated, precise, and particular. Most important, in Egypt there was no likelihood that the artist would ever be left to his own devices anyway, such that we could ever see what, "naturally," he would have done. The social fact, then, becomes a psychological fact: That the artist knows no other way of drawing is a way of saying that he had no opportunity, means, incentive, education, and so on for making any other kind of drawing. It was not essential mentality, natural disposition, or even the practical limits of ordinary skill which limited the artist to one way of making an image, but rather the fact that he belonged to and could not escape from a social institution.

CHAPTER 4

THE ORDER OF ICONOGRAPHY

SUBJECT MATTERS AND ICONOGRAPHY

IN an art as alien to us as that of ancient Egypt, it is not always clear what object a particular aggregation of lines, shapes, and fields of color denotes. From our point of view, ancient Egyptian art is filled with unidentified objects, items of costume, and so on. Strictly speaking, this is not in itself an art-historical problem. For the art historian the simple identification of a subject matter as such, as an object denoted, must be conducted in the context of an analysis of iconography. Among other things, iconographic analysis broadly identifies the image as such, as well as objects denoted in images; it attempts to specify that set of figurative forms taken by original makers and viewers as a symbolic whole, as representing. It determines whether and how individual images were associated in larger signifying organizations or representations. Finally, it may suggest what connotations the image possessed for original makers and viewers. Although we can usually identify subject matters – we can see that figurative forms depict human beings, animals, and objects – we may not understand iconography in the art historian's strong sense, that is, in terms of what the picture represented. This book will end (see Chapter 7) with a general specification of what a canonical image represented, but this is not a conclusion arrived at easily: We cannot simply see the representation in the same way that we can see that a set of lines in the representation denotes a human being, a chair, or a box.[1]

The bewildering variety of subject matters in Egyptian art has periodically been catalogued, on the largest scale chiefly by Klebs (1915, 1922, 1934) and Vandier (1952–69).[2] More circumscribed projects list, describe, and compare every example of the depiction of specific subject matters, such as human activities, kinds of architecture, or man-made objects.

The evidence is generally arranged chronologically in order to reveal "stylistic developments" in the depictions. Although these compendia are useful, they do not take us far in understanding iconography. For one thing, the coherence of a system of representation may be obscured if it is broken down into what we see as the minimally identifiable subject matters. Conversely, the significance of a motif for the representation (for example, as allegorical) might not be appreciated if it is wrenched from its total semiotic context. Furthermore, the atomization of the iconography into motifs and conventions, individually and lovingly traced by the connoisseur, may seem to be an orderly method of analysis, but potentially it is logically disorganized. Histories of motifs are extremely redundant and in the abundance of descriptions significant invariant patterns are lost to view. To follow the evolution of a single motif prevents us from appreciating how and why two, several, or many motifs might invariably accompany one another, might accompany one another only in certain contexts, or might mutually exclude one another.

ASSUMPTIONS AND PROBLEMS OF ICONOGRAPHIC ANALYSIS

Unfortunately, iconographic analysis must solve several problems of its own. A picture can be "of" or "about" its subject in complex and oblique ways. For example, a painter may produce a picture of Winston Churchill as a child; unless instructed or otherwise informed – say, by good knowledge of Churchill's characteristics – we may never see this aspect of the subject: We may only see a picture of a child. Similarly, a picture of thirteen men seated at a table without further explanation may not be seen as a representation of the Last Supper. Although the subject matter may seem transparently identifiable – an interpretation like "man leading oxen" or "slave slaughtering a calf" is probably correct – it may simply be too minimal, telling us what a form denotes but not necessarily what it is about or is to be seen as. We need to do justice to the most interesting elements of image making – to metaphor, quotation, and so on – and the apparently calculated ambiguity of Egyptian denotational techniques. (For the distinctions in this paragraph, see further Goodman, 1971; Panofsky, 1939; Wollheim, 1980.)

In producing a complete interpretation, an appeal is often made to the common visual culture of artists and viewers in a unified community (viewers somehow "knew" to expect a Winston-Churchill-as-a-child picture in some contexts), but the community may be unified only by the very common skills we have posited (Davis, 1989). In the case of ancient Egypt, we must reconstitute the visual culture using the apparent signification of images and not the other way around.

We cannot assume a priori that our identification of the image – as a basic unit of the perception and reception of acts of visual communication or of an iconography – is what ancient viewers themselves perceived as semiotically coherent. For instance, because in our culture, a picture frame usually establishes the outer limit of a single internally coherent image, we may be tempted to believe the same of various bordering effects in Egyptian art. However, in Egyptian composition register lines, lines of inscription, and so on, may instead mark off internal subunits of a larger association of figures meant to be viewed cumulatively. The boundary of the wall or drawing surface itself may not even be the frame; coherent compositions in Egyptian art sometimes cross from wall to wall or involve surfaces in several rooms of a building (see further Tefnin, 1983). Moreover, presuming we can identify the image itself, we cannot assume a priori that we understand the association between its separate figures in a scene or "narrative." We need to explore what reasons might justify the interpretations we believe to be successful.

Sometimes an interpretation of a group of figures must be proposed only on the basis of our perception of internal formal patterns, such as repetitions or rhythmic configurations. How do we know that what we perceive as association, action, or narration was originally seen this way? Since an ingenious formal analysis will always be capable of identifying some patterning in an image, how do we determine what patterning was relevant to original makers and viewers? Writing on this problem of the "coherence of significant scenes" in archaic arts, Groenewegen-Frankfort (1951: 10) insisted that we should never trust visual "self-evidence" to determine "whether a conglomeration of figures is intended to represent coherent action." As she argues, to describe a canonical composition as a "scene" at all probably does assume a "connotation of dramatic actuality" not present in canonical art. Although it is extremely tempting to use our own sensitivity to pattern to specify the meaning of an image, henceforth it will be accepted here that this method cannot be used without reinforcement.

There are, of course, a few external guides to interpretation. For one, Egyptologists often rely heavily on associated inscriptions in interpreting Egyptian images. This modern procedure may have little to do with what Egyptian viewers experienced. We do not really know whether original viewers found images interpretable by reference to inscriptions or that inscriptions functioned as "labels," "names," or expositions. Not many viewers of a public image could even read the hieroglyphs accompanying it. Perhaps, a cycle of pictures – like a sequence of Ramesside war or hunt reliefs – explained a text for those who did not understand the script. In one famous Ramesside war relief the major texts about the conflict, the so-called Poem and the Bulletin, are certainly architecturally and perhaps conceptually relatively self-contained in relation to the complex reliefs with their short inscriptional "labels" (overview in Kuentz, 1928); it seems unlikely that these long texts were meant to decode the images (but see Tefnin, 1981).

Unfortunately, even from our point of view, inscriptions do not do any more than identify primary subject matter with some particularity. For instance, although the proper name and titles of a figure may be provided by the inscription – the denotation is precisely established – many specifically iconographic problems of connotation remain unresolved. Occasionally inscriptions served as interjections, the equivalent of the speech or thought "bubble" in a modern comic strip. Yet such interjections do not decode the image; they are part of the image itself and require explanation. Finally, some inscriptions probably can be regarded as independent explanations of the image, like a label or caption. Here, however, it would be misleading to believe that the ambiguous qualities of an image have been anchored or fixed by the precise, definite specifications of written language. Language itself is made up of levels of connotation or metaphor beyond its minimal denotative functions. What assures us, then, that the "label" is really speaking straightforwardly about the image? The linguistic operation requires explicit analysis on our part and therefore the presence of inscriptions of this kind actually compounds interpretive difficulties.

In addition to script, the presence of other highly coded elements may assist in interpretation. Figures in a scene often gesture conventionally in exclamation, command, or other individual action (Groenewegen-Frankfort, 1951: 42; H. Müller, 1937). Since canonical aspect is often ambiguous about the possible rest, action, attention, and so forth of the figure, the gestures may be useful in specifying the nature of actions. Nonetheless, the gestures themselves were subject to canonical formalizations and may be little more than a "pictorial conceit" with little value as a guide to complex orders of connotation (Groenewegen-Frankfort, 1951: 33–34).

In the full interpretation of an image, what Gombrich (1960) calls the "beholder's share" includes the viewer's more or less successful reconstitution of meaning – based not only on explicit aids, like captions or gestures, but also on his knowledge of a tradition of signs with established referents, his perception of coherence on the basis of trial-and-error experiments in interpretation, and so on. Artists and viewers share information of a routine, unaesthetic kind; once in possession of it, interpretation is easy and automatic for an ordinary viewer in ordinary cases. Egyptology may be able to retrieve a proportion of this background to the Egyptian image. However, other interpretative skills must have been far more complex; explaining an image required more than simply knowing the world of Egypt as it were before that world included images. It utilized specialized aesthetic preferences or semiotic skills, some of which could not have been articulated clearly at the time and for which we have no independent evidence.[3]

A first step – and it is only a first, simplifying step – recognizes that an individual image made sense to an original viewer in terms of some overall understanding already in his possession, a wealth of possible iconographic distinctions, associations, and transformations. In the circumstances, iconographic analysis depends upon four rough-and-ready methods. First, stylistic analysis of iconographies suggests that procedures developed early on for the distinctive presentation of separate themes survived in the tradition, remaining especially characteristic of the units for which they were first evolved. Stylistic differences can be used to infer symbolic distinctions. Second, historical analysis may identify the primitive and perhaps simple character of several themes. *Urgeschichte* has its uses in arriving at the *Urgestalt* of an iconographic category that we believe may have existed. Third, syntactic analysis, as it might be called, attends to the internally marked, coded, or differentiated aspects of the total output of messages. We might be able to determine the "syntax" of a representational "language." Fourth, and most problematic, semantic analysis suggests that representation

articulated a definition, classification, and valuation of experience. Internal clues and external evidence may help us to
reconstitute these original categories.

In this chapter I employ all of these methods in a tentative
sketch of some of the principles of organization and variation
animating Egyptian iconography. Limitations of space preclude a thorough theoretical assessment of each method, but
it makes sense at least to attempt some initial outlines.

The image can be regarded as a particular variation within
a field of invariant, canonical iconographic possibilities, governed by rules of interpretation. Knowledge of this repertory
and of the rules for putting it to use constituted the primary
condition of an original viewer's understanding. As we will
see, not all modes of iconographic transformation necessarily
establish a single, easily intelligible, invariant iconography,
but Egyptian artists and patrons chose to depend upon such
rules.

VARIATION BY EXPANSION AND CONTRACTION AROUND AN INVARIANT CORE

Egyptian canonical iconographic programs seem to expand
and contract. However, each program maintained a "core"
motif, often historically the most archaic element, which invariably appears in every context of use in a highly invariant
form. Expansion and contraction occurs through the manipulation of a cluster of available details modifying this core.
Additive modification of a core element is the most common
source of iconographic variability and flexibility in Egyptian
art and was probably the most stable of the canonical iconographic principles. It could nevertheless be supplemented
by other principles of establishing and transforming meaning,
which were often used simultaneously by an artist in a single
work.

One core motif, the king of Egypt striking down an enemy, apparently first appeared in the time of Narmer; its
most explicit presentation is on the Narmer Palette (see Figure
6.14), which apparently depicts Narmer's victory over a
Lower Egyptian people. A similar grouping appears in the
painting in Tomb 100 at Hierakonpolis, of Nagada II date
(Asselberghs, 1961: Figs. 33–4; Case and Payne, 1962; Williams and Logan, 1987: 253–5), and presumably represents
the formal origins of the motif; the figure of the chieftain in
this painting may not, in context, have been seen to possess

the attributes of the later pharaoh.[4] Other documents from the time of Narmer or of unnamed kings of the early First Dynasty (Horizon A) present versions of the smiting motif in which a royal emblem, such as a *serekh* of the king, confronts a defeated enemy (Arkell, 1950; Williams and Logan, 1987: 263–4, 282–5, for the relief at Gebel Sheikh Suleiman). On the Narmer Palette the image of Narmer has been given most compositional attention, space, and scale. As we have seen, the system of components, proportions, and aspect, later fully canonical, has been used to carve the figure of the king in the slender style preferred by the sculptors of early dynastic Abydos and Hierakonpolis. This motif is clearly the dominant subject of the palette or, as Schäfer (1974: 154–9) puts it, the central "symbolic image." However, other details are included. Some of them become quite standard components of the motif, like the presence of the king's attendants or servants standing behind him or the "hieroglyphic" rebus to the upper right of the main image on the reverse (S. Schott, 1950: 22–3) giving the number of defeated enemies brought down by (or led to?) the pharaoh.

Narmer's artist also employs two rather different modes of iconographic organization. Divided off from the main scene by a register line, we are shown in dramatic detail – a sort of "blow up" – the contorted bodies of two naked, fleeing or slaughtered enemies. On the lowermost space on the obverse, a royal bull, metaphorically representing the king, is shown breaking down the walls of a fortress with its horns and trampling yet another naked enemy. Iconographic development through such divisions and metaphorical substitutions can be considered separately as distinctive principles.

The core motif of the lone king striking down his enemy continued to be used throughout the early dynastic period, establishing it firmly in the canonical repertory. There were probably material reasons for the initial emphasis on this motif. Both Narmer and Djet commemorated (military?) expeditions in the eastern desert near Edfu (Edwards, 1971: 22–5). In the reign of Den in the middle First Dynasty, an ivory carver produced a fine incised drawing of the motif, recording the "first occasion of 'Smiting the East' " (Figure 4.1).[5] Named with the royal *serekh*, Den grasps a kneeling captive by the hair before striking, a graphic detail that gained great popularity in the Old Kingdom. The standard of Wepwawet is thrust into the ground before the king, an early statement of a close relationship between this god in jackal form and the monarch of Egypt. The locale, it seems, is the desert, for the groundline moves upward on the right and encloses various dots as if to show high rocky ground. This topographic specification also becomes canonical. In Vandier's words (1952: 859), the style is "already quite animated, but conventional at the same time": For this motif canonical artists circumvented the convention for a resting stance – here the

Figure 4.1. Carved Ivory Label of King Den "Smiting the East," from Abydos, First Dynasty. After Spencer, 1980: No. 460.

Figure 4.2. *a.* Cliff Relief of King Sekhemkhet Smiting an Enemy and Standing in Majesty, Wadi Maghara (Sinai), Third Dynasty. After Petrie, 1906: Fig. 47; Smith, 1949: Fig. 32. *b.* Cliff Relief of King Sanakht Smiting an Enemy, Wadi Maghara (Sinai), Third Dynasty. After Gardiner and Černý, 1952–5: Pl. 1, no. 4.

feet are placed far apart, the arm raised – but in so doing created a distinctive convention.

Owing to the destruction of monuments, the Third and Fourth Dynasties present a slight gap in our documentation of the variability of this convention. In the early Third Dynasty the reliefs of Sekhemkhet at Wadi Maghara (Figure 4.2*a*), once attributed to the First Dynasty, present a fine and fully canonical scene of the king, with pear-headed mace held over his head in a straight line parallel with the groundline, grasping a kneeling enemy by the topknot (Gardiner and Černý, 1952–5: I, Pl. 1; Petrie, 1906: Pls. 45–7; Schäfer, 1974: 282–3). Like Narmer, Sekhemkhet wears the White Crown of Upper Egypt, a tunic is drawn up over the left shoulder with the right bare, and from his belt a long "tail" hangs down his right and rear leg. He carries a dagger in a belt and, in the hand grasping the captive, a large wand. This paraphernalia has become more or less standard regalia for this scene. His wide-legged stance duplicates that of Den on the ivory tag (Figure 4.1). This group of king and enemy is placed on the same groundline behind two striding figures of the king, one wearing the Red Crown and other the White, both likewise facing to the right. Similarly, a fragmentary limestone relief from Wadi Maghara shows Sanakht of the Third Dynasty, wearing the Red Crown, about to strike a kneeling enemy (Figure 4.2*b*) (Gardiner and Černý, 1952–5: I, Pl. 1, no. 4, and see Smith, 1949: Pl. 30c; Spencer, 1980: No. 18). The fragment includes the *serekh*, standard of Wepwawet, and the word for turquoise, possibly the resource for which Sanakht's expedition set out.

Royal artists in the Fifth and Sixth Dynasties added a good deal to the core motif. In the Fifth Dynasty, instead of a single captive grasped by the hair, artists present a whole cluster of captives drawn overlapping one another. The king grasps the topknot of the chief enemy in scenes at the temples of Neuserre, Sahure, and Pepi (Leclant, 1980; Smith, 1949: 176–85) and possibly also at the temple of Unas (Labrousse, Lauer, and Leclant, 1977: doc. 39). The groups are taken to represent a foreign army or its leaders. In the Sixth Dynasty, Pepi II seems to refer to several different enemy races, that is, one image records a multitude of victories (Jéquier, 1938: II, Pls. 36–40). Elsewhere in the temple, he singles out a captured Libyan grasped by the hair for particular attention in the more ancient mode (Figure 4.3), but the scene goes on to show, behind the captive, the Libyan's wife, two sons, and followers (Jéquier, 1938: II, Pls. 8–11), almost exactly copied from Sahure (Borchardt, 1913: Pl. 1) and recopied seventeen centuries later by Taharqa at his southern temple in Kawa (O'Connor, 1983: Fig. 3.17; Smith, 1965: 22, Fig. 80). Less material along these lines survives from the Sixth Dynasty pyramid temple of Teti, although Smith (1949: 202) noted a fragmentary block with the word for bedouin, which may have belonged to a series of smiting the Asiatic or receiving booty (apparently Lauer and Leclant, 1973: Pl. 33e).

Inspecting prisoners, receiving booty, and showing off the spoils of war was a common addition to the victory motif. (Sometimes, in the iconographic "division" and "substitution" to be considered momentarily, such scenes could actually stand in for and evoke the core motif of the smiting pharaoh, not itself included in the composition.) On the Narmer Palette (see Figure 6.14) the king and his attendants inspect two rows of decapitated enemies. A fragment of a relief from the pyramid temple of Weserkaf apparently belonged to a scene of inspecting prisoners, although it is unclear whether the king was figured here (Smith, 1949: 181–2). The inspection scene is well preserved at the temple of Sahure, where the goddess Seshat is shown recording the booty of a Libyan campaign (Borchardt, 1913: Pls. 1, 3; Capart, 1927: Pl. 27; Groenewegen-Frankfort, 1951: Fig. 3), and resembles similar fragments from the Unas temple (Labrousse, Lauer, and Leclant, 1977: docs. 40, 41). Sahure also displays bears and other spoil captured in a Syrian campaign.

Additive manipulation of a core element can also be observed in canonical hunting iconography. The core motif

Figure 4.3. Heavily Damaged Limestone Relief of King Pepi II Grasping and Smiting an Enemy, from His Mortuary Complex at Sakkara, Sixth Dynasty. Reconstructed after Jéquier, 1938: Pl. 8.

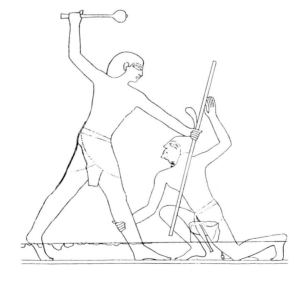

usually included four elements. First, the wild animals, the victims of the hunt, flee before wild carnivores or the hunters and their dogs, away from the chariot or the hunters' arrows. Second, a particularly fleet, tough carnivore or hunting hound brings down a panic-stricken creature in flight, pouncing or diving for the throat: This was probably the most ancient as well as the most powerfully evocative image, as artists' experiments in depicting it suggest (e.g., see Figure 3.1*b*). Third, the owner of the dogs or the human hunter observes the chase and often actively engages in it. Finally, the chase takes place in a special locale, namely, the rocky desert lands, flinty dunes, or mountainous wadis. As with representations of royal victory in battle, representation of the hunt oscillates from explicit to emblematic presentation of these standard features.

Predynastic and early dynastic artists had produced many images of animal chase and battle, such as an enigmatic scene of several carnivores and a fantastical creature with griffinlike wings preying on desert game on the Oxford Palette (see Figure 6.9) (Asselberghs, 1961: Fig. 128). Canonical artists in the early dynastic period selected from these ranges of possibility – the iconographic valence of the Oxford Palette was probably quite disjunct from that of later dynastic images[6] – the single motif of a lone hound pursuing a fleeing antelope or gazelle and grasping its throat, presumably, in these contexts, standing for the master's success (or for Egypt's mastery over nature itself). This image formed the core of elaborated Egyptian hunting iconography. On the canonical sculpted steatite disc of Prince Hemaka (Figure 4.4), deposited in his tomb in the reign of Den in the First Dynasty (Smith, 1981: Fig. 24), the scene of the animal figures in this deadly contest above all stresses the instant of physical contact. The legs of the animals are relatively widely separated, their necks and heads stretch forward, and their bodies are elongated. Since canonical representation generally avoids showing a brief moment of this kind, with this core image such representation comes as close as it ever would to spatiotemporal specificity.

Animals rearing up in the action of the hunt appear in the reliefs on protodynastic carved palettes, and for later scenes of the hunt, artists always remained uneasy about the ordinary canonical rule that figures be rooted, four-footed, to some register or groundline. For instance, at the end of the Third Dynasty at Medum, the draftsman of Rahotep's corridor pictures a gazelle kicking its front hooves in the air, rearing up to dash off in the chase (Figure 4.5a); perhaps to soften the implausible line of the register and to indicate the special location of events, he adds small hillocklike humps near the running creatures as suggestions for desert ground (Petrie, 1892: Pl. 9; Smith, 1949: 241 and Pl. 33, 1965: 64). Dating also to the transition from the Third to the Fourth Dynasty, a fragment of a painting on the south wall of the outer brick corridor of the mastaba of Atet at Medum represents the hunting dog seizing the raised back leg of a gazelle (Kantor, 1947: Pl. 16b; Petrie, 1892: Pl. 27).

In a more consistently canonical manner, other scenes placed the figures with all four feet attached to the groundline, as in the beautiful but technically idiosyncratic reliefs on the facade of the mastaba of Nefermaat at Medum (Kantor, 1947: Pl. 16a; Petrie, 1892: Pl. 17). The well-preserved hunt scene on the west and south walls of the chapel of the Chief Master of the Hunt Methen at Sakkara (Figure 4.5b) (Fechheimer, 1923: Pls. 116–7; Lepsius, *Denkm.*: II, Pls. 3–7; Smith, 1949: Fig. 60), shows animals making contact with one another in only three of the ten registers. The register line is used canonically to identify and separate the elements of a confusing view (see Chapter 2). As usual, Methen includes the observing figure of the hunter/owner himself.

By the Fifth Dynasty, modifying elements like the rearing ruminant or leashed dog were evidently standard features of hunting scenes. Sahure's pyramid temple preserves a hunt scene in its "most complete and monumental form" (Smith, 1949: 179, on Borchardt, 1913: II, Pl. 17; Groenewegen-Frankfort, 1951: Fig. 4). In addition to the observing owner,

Figure 4.4. Steatite Disc with Relief Carving and Insets of Wild Animals, from the Tomb of Prince Hemaka at Sakkara, First Dynasty. Courtesy Cairo Museum.

pursuing dogs, and moment of the kill (e.g., Figure 4.6*a*), the artist includes other seemingly novel details, such as a scene of a wounded hyena pawing at an arrow in its muzzle (Figure 4.6*b*). To the wavy groundline of the desert, he adds a number of desert plants, each individually different (Figure 4.6*a*). In the cycle of the seasons reliefs of Neuserre and Unas, the desert animals give birth to their offspring in a naturalistic setting – almost "pure landscape" (Groenewegen-Frankfort, 1951: 54–5) – of flinty desert scattered here and there with low shrubs. At Neuserre a nearby huntsman with impatient dogs and game bag reminds us that the young animals were sweet to the taste and would soon find their way to the royal tables. Further fragments of relief scenes of the hunt from the causeway of Unas, a reconstructed scene from the complex of Pepi II (Groenewegen-Frankfort, 1951: 54; Jéquier,

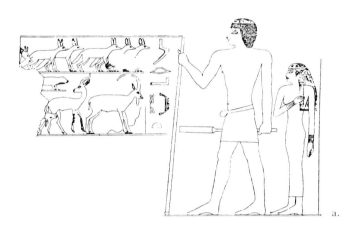

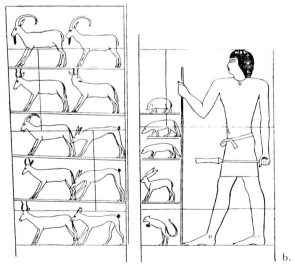

Figure 4.5. *a*. Wild Animals and Desert Ground, Painted Tomb Relief from the Tomb of Rahotep at Medum, Fourth Dynasty. After Petrie, 1892: Pl. 9. *b*. Hunt Scene, Painted Tomb Relief from the Tomb of Methen at Sakkara, Fourth Dynasty. Reconstructed after Smith, 1949: Fig. 60.

1938: Pl. 41), and other Old Kingdom materials suggest that Old Kingdom royal sculptors on the whole preferred what might be called a classicizing manner for the hunt scene, that is, figure constructions and compositions close to the other canonical iconographies (compare Figures 4.5a, b, 4.6a, with Figure 2.9). Movement is reduced, the groundline strictly organizes the scene, rules of fixity and coterminousness are generally respected; moreover, emphasis is placed on the owner's triumph as much as on observation of the animals.

It appears that over a span of several generations the overall direction of iconographic transformation was toward constant addition to established formats. The trend may have been due to pressure on patrons and artists to differentiate their deeds and their monuments from those of their predecessors, at least at a symbolic level (absolute expenditures on building programs or decoration apparently did not significantly increase); another iconographic transformation, the "expressive magnification" to be considered momentarily, probably had this cause too.

Figure 4.6. a. Detail of a Hunt Scene, from a Relief in the Funerary Complex of Sahure at Abusir, Fifth Dynasty. After Borchardt, 1913: Pl. 17. b. Detail of a Hunt Scene (Hyena with an Arrow in Its Muzzle), from a Relief in the Funerary Complex of Sahure at Abusir, Fifth Dynasty. After Smith, 1949: Fig. 70 (1).

It is more difficult to evaluate similar trends over centuries or whole millennia. For instance, compared with the victory motif and its accretions in the Old Kingdom, some New Kingdom presentations of the theme are extremely elaborate. On an outer wall of the Hypostyle Hall at Karnak, Seti I is depicted returning to Egypt after a great victory, with captives trotting beside him tied to great ropes (Groenewegen-Frankfort, 1951: Figs. 25–6). The greater variety of works surviving from the New Kingdom complicates the story. On

a.

b.

72

a chariot ornamented with stucco reliefs, Tuthmosis IV shows himself disposing of Syrians in one of the most aggressively vigorous compositions in New Kingdom art (Figure 4.7), an achievement of compression or "contraction" and in effect quite expressionistic (Groenewegen-Frankfort, 1951: 116–7, Fig. 24; Smith, 1965: Fig. 211). In addition, then, to certain internal and somewhat autonomous pressures to elaborate the program, in assessing its additive transformation we must also consider the context and medium of the image and the expressive purposes of different users.

VARIATION BY EXPRESSIVE MAGNIFICATION

The hunt was evidently dear to an Egyptian courtier, presumably as a gentlemen's activity in which he could prove his skill and courage or display his dogs and equipment. Not surprisingly, a courtier's desire to distinguish himself in the hunt was matched by his wish to commission a lively, individual, and personalized representation of it. Pressure of

Figure 4.7. King Tuthmosis IV Smiting His Enemies, Painted Stucco Relief from His Chariot, Eighteenth Dynasty. After Smith, 1965: Fig. 211.

73

this sort leads to what I will call the expressive magnification of elements of an iconographic field.

Just as the hunt was finally regulated by strict codes of etiquette, expressive differentiation, despite its often dramatic results, did not really involve breaking significant canonical rules. Rather the patron sought to have standard elements used in novel and distinctive ways, just as he would attempt to handle his bow with special flair.

Since the record of surviving scenes is probably unrepresentative in some respects, it is often difficult in practice to be sure that an individual scene counts as expressive differentiation. If we have only one case of distinctive variation, perhaps we are forced to consider it as an instance of true innovation, to be considered below. However, a priori it is likely that the conventional was always more common than the truly novel. Unusually prominent or especially detailed scenes in a composition are probably clear-cut instances of expressive differentiation: The patron and artist extracted an element from the standard repertory and made it the centerpiece of an individual variation. By and large, a standard element was magnified.

For instance, in the Old Kingdom, Nebemakhet's artist devoted special attention to a mother gazelle suckling her young in an extensive swamp scene (Figure 4.8a), a motif that may appear variously in hunt scenes, scenes of the master's domains and the bringing of offerings, or scenes of the cycle of the seasons (Figure 4.8b). Perhaps to underline his special fondness for the activity, near the end of the Fifth Dynasty Prince Raemka unconventionally placed two registers of a hunt scene directly under his offering list, a central element in the whole tomb program; his hounds pounce on a hyena and a gazelle and his huntsmen lasso antelopes (Smith, 1949: 195). Some private patrons paid special tribute to the desert lion (the tradition goes back to the Hunter's Palette of Nagada III, see Figure 6.10, although the iconographic value of this early representation may be disjunct from its canonical

Figure 4.8. Two Details of Swamp Scenes. *a*. With a Suckling Gazelle, Painted Tomb Relief in the Tomb of Nebemakhet at Giza, Fourth Dynasty. *b*. From the Tomb of Ptahhotep at Sakkara, Fourth Dynasty. After Smith, 1949: Fig. 237.

a.

b.

value). At the end of the Fifth Dynasty, the official Ti depicted a lion shaking a gazelle by the throat (Smith, 1949: 192). Unfortunately, several similar scenes from other contexts are extremely fragmentary and it is impossible to tell what this vignette signifies. Artists working on private commissions probably felt relatively uninhibited about the register line. Raemka's sculptor roots some animals to a wavy desert groundline placed considerably above the actual register line. Ti's gazelle is shown hanging from the lion's mouth rather than as collapsed on the groundline. The core image of the hound pulling down a lone animal turns up frequently somewhere in these scenes: A painted panel from the late Fifth Dynasty tomb of Akhetmerynesuwt presents two hounds bringing down and slaughtering an oryx (Smith, 1949: 198–9).

The Sixth Dynasty hunt scenes of Mereruka and Ptahhotep are the most developed, distinctive, and differentiated to survive from the Old Kingdom. (Other very fragmentary material might alter our picture of achievements if it survived better: See the remarkable fragment from the mastaba of Fetekta, Smith, 1949: 205, Fig. 216c.) In Mereruka's tomb (Figure 4.9a) (Duell, 1938: Pl. 25; Smith, 1949: Fig. 92a), between fences set up to trap the animals, slender hunting dogs tear apart an antelope, unconventionally drawn as stretched between two registers from which the dogs reach up and down, that is, as lying on the earth surrounded on all sides by snarling dogs. To the right of this group, a man pulls back with all of his weight on a rope binding three

VARIATION BY EXPRESSIVE MAGNIFICATION

Figure 4.9. *a.* Hunt Scene, Painted Tomb Relief from the Tomb of Mereruka at Sakkara, Sixth Dynasty. After Smith, 1949: Fig. 92a. *b.* Hunt Scene, Painted Tomb Relief from the Tomb of Ptahhotep at Sakkara, Sixth Dynasty. After Schäfer, 1974: Fig. 151.

a.

b.

75

antelopes, straining away from him up a hillock. Immediately below, on a narrow strip with its own minute register line, rabbits, hedgehogs (?), and a young gazelle crouch in terror behind plants and rocks. In the center of the lowest register, a desert lion clamps its jaws over the muzzle of a wild bull, swatting the bull's head with its left raised paw. To the left, another hunting dog leaps on the back of a fleeing antelope while a second antelope, glancing back, makes its escape; the scene is apparently repeated for a slightly later moment in time on the right of the register, where the dog now brings the antelope to the ground and tears its throat, the second antelope escaping to one side. In the magnificent reliefs in the mastaba of Ptahhotep (Figure 4.9*b*) (Schäfer, 1974: Fig. 151; Smith, 1949: Pl. 55b), many of these evidently standard elements as well as two groups of copulating lions and jackals and a plenitude of topographic indications also appear.

VARIATION BY DIVISION

Occasionally one feels that an Egyptian artist was more interested in an individual small detail than in the rest of a composition. This possibility may have naturally given rise to the phenomenon of iconographic variation through the division of a coherent theme into two or more subelements, henceforth manipulated quite independently and often marked off from one another by standard bordering effects.

The iconography of victory presents an early, clear, and dramatic instance of variation by division. The capture and binding of prisoners had been depicted in protodynastic compositions as one of the activities of the king, like smiting, or as a metaphorical substitute for the king, like a royal *serekh* or standard (examples in Williams and Logan, 1987: 247, 256, 268, 271, etc.). On the Narmer Palette (see Figure 6.14), in addition to the kneeling enemy confronted by the king himself, the artist depicts two contorted bodies of what are apparently fleeing enemies at the very bottom of the composition, divided off from the core motif by the register line. The defeated, captured, and bound prisoner or his contorted corpse itself immediately become a favorite independent subtheme – as it were a separate icon for the original core theme of "king victorious over his enemy." In the first two dynasties, kneeling and standing bound prisoners were carved on ivory plaques, seals, and other objects (Figure 4.10) (e.g., Petrie, 1900–1: II, Pl. 4; Quibell and Green, 1900–1: I, Pls. 12, 15; Vandier, 1952: Fig. 561). More rarely running or fallen figures, perhaps derived from a more extensive battle scene like that on the Battlefield Palette (see Figure 6.11) (Asselberghs, 1961: Fig. 151), appear on early dynastic ivory plaques and labels (Quibell and Green, 1900–1: II, Pl. 16). At the end of the Second Dynasty, the sculptors of Khasekhemuwy incised the contorted bodies of corpses around the base of his graywacke portrait statues (see Figure 6.19) (Quibell and Green, 1900–1: I, 11, II, Pls. 39–41; Smith, 1949: 13). As Frankfort noted (1925: 124), the door socket from Hierakonpolis (see Figure 6.26) should probably be included in the theme of the crushed enemy. In the Third Dynasty the sculptors of Djoser produced several remarkable heads in the round, apparently of the foreign enemies or prisoners of the king, probably to decorate a throne base; the several examples of the format suggest how popular the motif had become (Borchardt, 1901: Nos. 296, 1165; Bothmer, 1982; Smith, 1949: 15).[7] In these examples the two-dimensional composition of the Narmer Palette, with victorious king above fallen enemy, is repeated in three dimensions.

VARIATION BY EQUIVALENT AND NONEQUIVALENT SUBSTITUTION

In a typical variety of iconographic transformation, one element of the core motif was replaced by another. Frequently

Figure 4.10. Ivory Furniture Leg in the Form of a Bound Prisoner, Early Dynastic Period. Courtesy Fitzwilliam Museum, Cambridge University.

the substituted element possessed an equivalent symbolic value in relation to the original element – not so much metaphor or metonymy as "isomeme." The overall value of the motif therefore remained relatively stable. For example, in canonical scenes of victory the king was not always depicted by his human person; he was often symbolized by a lion, bull, griffin, or sphinx. The substitution required some corresponding modifications in the way other elements were depicted, but it is striking in Egyptian art that little of this actually occurred: Other elements often preserved their ordinary literal format, and full-scale allegorization virtually never took place.

Major substitutabilities were coeval with the emergence of the canonical system itself. For example, on the Bull Palette fragment (Figure 4.11), more or less contemporary with the Narmer Palette (see Fig. 6.14), a great wide-eyed bull, probably symbolizing the king, straddles a hapless curly-haired and bearded enemy, crushes his right leg, and thrusts one huge horn through his left shoulder. The victim flings his arm back in horror as the bull's shoulders tense in preparation for the final gory toss. The royal bull appears on the Narmer

Figure 4.11. The Palette. Relief-Carved Slate Palette with Royal Bull Trampling Crushed Enemies and Standards Capturing an Enemy, Probably Nagada III/Early First Dynasty. Courtesy the Louvre, Paris.

78

Palette battering down an enemy fortress. On the roughly contemporary Battlefield Palette (see Figure 6.11), fat scavenger birds with huge wicked claws descend on the field of battle and gouge out the eyes of curly-haired enemy corpses, while prisoners are led away by the victorious standards, personifications of the royal army, and an official in a long robe. In the center of the field a lion, probably symbolizing the monarch, tears open the belly of a fallen chieftain as a scavenger bird makes ready to scoop up the entrails.[8]

It would be impossible here to cite the wealth of transformations throughout the dynastic period using this level of equivalence between the king and a great animal. The substitution was apparently well known in the Old Kingdom. A block from the causeway corridor of the Chephren complex at Giza preserves a fragment of what seems to be the king-as-griffin trampling his enemies (Smith, 1949: 182), replicated in important reliefs at the temples of Sahure (Borchardt, 1913: Pl. 8) and Pepi II (Jéquier, 1938: III, Pls. 15–16).

Substitution by equivalence can be multiplied indefinitely, not only for a single but also for several elements of the core, and a motif may ultimately come to appear very different from its core. For instance, a Middle Kingdom pectoral of Amenemhet from Dahshur, now in Cairo (Figure 4.12), shows the king as a falcon-headed lion trampling one enemy beneath powerful legs and grasping a second enemy by the topknot.

Now at some limit, substitution will open up a new ter-

Figure 4.12. Pectoral (Gold and Semiprecious Gems) of Amenemhet with the King-as-Griffin Trampling His Enemies, from Dahshur, Reign of King Sesostris III, Twelfth Dynasty. After J. de Morgan, 1895: Pls. 19, 21.

ritory of meaning. Rather than substituting an equivalent, a different element with a different meaning is inserted (or at least so interpreted), leading to a transformation in the overall role of the motif. In terms I have considered elsewhere (Davis, 1987), the image modulates or montages into another image. For instance, one transformation in canonical art substitutes the "plants of Egypt" for the figure(s) of the captive enemy, with the king striking them; the motif means that the king rules the Two Lands of Egypt, not that he has conquered enemies (Habachi, 1963: 22, Fig. 6).

To take a clearer example, in scenes of victory some early dynastic artists substituted a long harpoon or spear for the king's fighting mace (Kaplony, 1958; Williams and Logan, 1987: 259–61). Evidently this substitution in turn suggested that the canonical pose of the striding, victorious king could be used in representations of hunting as well as of battle (in a more general way, the predynastic hunter's attributes had been made over to the dynastic pharaoh already). For example, on one tablet of Den, the king, in canonical pose, apparently spears a large animal victim, perhaps a hippopotamus (Figure 4.13*a*) (Petrie, 1900–1: I, Pl. 14 [8]). On one seal, the creature may be a crouching lion, lanced by the king, although the scene is rather difficult to understand (Petrie, 1900–1: I, Pl. 32; Smith, 1949: 122, Fig. 39; and cf. Eaton-Krauss, 1984: 89). On a fragmentary ivory tablet, Den thrusts his harpoon into a pool of water; this scene is perhaps a representation of fishing (?) (Petrie, 1902–3: I, Pl. 11; Smith, 1949: Fig. 37). A scene from the pyramid temple of Pepi II

Figure 4.13. *a*. Incised Ivory Label with the King Harpooning, from Abydos, Reign of King Den, First Dynasty. After Petrie, 1900–1: I, Pl. 14 (8). *b*. Relief of King Pepi II Smiting an Ibex, from His Mortuary Complex at Sakkara, Sixth Dynasty. Reconstructed after Jéquier, 1938: Pl. 47.

a.

b.

in the Sixth Dynasty has been thought to represent the king hunting hippopotamus in this manner (Smith, 1949: 203). In a slightly different version of a similar substitution, a relief in the inner room of Pepi II's temple apparently shows the king grasping an ibex by the horns with his other arm raised to strike (Figure 4.13*b*) (Jéquier, 1938: II, Pl. 41). The scene has replaced the king's enemy with an animal rather than the king's mace with a hunting weapon. Old Kingdom private funerary scenes of men hunting animals with long double-ended spears, as in the tombs of Iasen and Nebemakhet (Smith, 1949: 169–71, 245–48), show the hunter standing in the typical smiting pose with legs widespread. Scenes of men lassoing wild game or throwing down a bull for butchery also make use of this pose as well (for example, the tomb reliefs of Akhetmerynesuwt and Seshemnofer, Smith, 1949: 198–200). All of these "hunt" or related scenes created by substitutive transformation of the victory motif should be kept quite distinct from hunting scenes derived from another core motif, the dog bringing down a fleeing animal.

Substitution may sometimes be complete – creating a new iconographic category – but usually it is probably incomplete or metaphoric: The old category has a shadowy existence in the new, or the new is meant to evoke the old and depends upon the viewer's knowledge of the old for part of its point. In my example, draftsmen of the variant spearing and lassoing scenes apparently drew upon the core motif of the king in victory in order metaphorically to associate the king with successful hunters and farmers or, conversely, to associate farmhands with activities which, at the apex of the state, were expressed in the king's exemplification of victory over natural and enemy forces.

Probably the most complex and potentially fertile of these principles of iconographic transformation, the metaphoric operations of nonequivalent substitution are not well understood. Art historians have been preoccupied with tracing the formal sources of motifs without interpreting iconographic disjunctions and their signification. Moreover, it is often difficult to know whether the Egyptians themselves would have interpreted a transformation as disjunctive – that is, as substantially preserving or substantially changing the underlying connotation of a motif.

In many versions of some motifs, for example, the figure of an official, the patron of the work, can substitute for the figure of the king, although the scenes are otherwise very similar to royal scenes. Should this substitution affect our understanding of the work? For instance, should we really treat "private" imagery separately from "royal"? Presumably the Egyptians understood very well the difference between the divine king himself and any merely mortal official; nonetheless the scenes may still be largely equivalent – for the king's acts were properly emulated throughout the land of Egypt by all who behaved in accord with divine laws.

To take another instance, the Egyptians differentiated between the theme of a master receiving the fruit of his land and the theme of a master hunting various animals on his estates, although both themes in a larger sense have to do with the master's control of a domain of the natural world. The two themes were generally presented separately in a program of decoration, using distinctive canonical conventions developed for the relevant core motif. What orders of nonequivalence could possibly account for this distinction – domestic animals ≠ wild animals, farmland ≠ desert steppe, receiving food ≠ procuring food, funerary sustenance ≠ daily sustenance, animals for use ≠ animals for sport, or others? We do not always have independent access to Egyptian systems of conceptual equivalence and nonequivalence. My examples have been drawn from a few relatively clear-cut categories, such as king = lion = bull, battle ≠ hunt ≠ farming. It is both one of the ironies and one of the challenges of iconographic analysis that it must reconstruct a conceptual system using representations and their transformations and not vice versa.

TRUE INNOVATION AND THE LIMITS OF VARIABILITY

Variation by addition to an invariant core, expressive magnification, division, and substitution were fertile, flexible, and comprehensive means of regulating iconographic transformations and especially of preserving stable meanings. The overwhelming majority of canonical representations were generated by these principles and therefore intelligibly related to one another as products of the same network of conceptual categories. A viewer who understood the principles, basic core motifs, and conceptual equivalents upon which they operated would have had an excellent chance of understanding any particular iconographic program he might have encountered. Knowledge of the canonical formal and iconographic principles, core motifs, and system of equivalences was the fundamental condition of the viewer's understanding of the image.

Precisely because it depended upon a limited set of principles, motifs, and equivalences, however, a sequence of transformations could potentially edge close to this limit. At a certain point, a further transformation could be produced as an organic development of an established chain but only as a contradiction of some other established canonical principle. If this transformation was accepted, repeated, and incorporated in the canonical repertory, we may think of it as canonical innovation. It involved rethinking priorities in the repertory, holding certain powerful demands in abeyance, and recognizing the appeal of others, however untested.

As an example, I will consider transformations in hunting iconography in the Middle and New Kingdoms. We have already seen that in the Old Kingdom this program was especially open to expressive differentiation and magnification. In later periods continuing transformations ultimately came into conflict with established preferences for the generalized depiction of topography, register-line organization of composition, and resting frontal-profile aspect of figures, and, as we will see at the extreme limit, with canonical representation of the hunt as a representation of human mastery or victory of any kind. Although often resisted, true innovation was often accepted in this context of conflict.

Middle and New Kingdom artists intensified the movement of animal figures and increased topographical depiction. To some degree, the temporary weakening of canonical controls in the First Intermediate Period may have encouraged these changes: For instance, the tomb chapel of Sobekhotep at Mialla had depicted animals in the "flying gallop" – with back arched, all legs extended, neck elongated, and body lifted, in some cases, off the groundline (Figure 4.14a) (see Smith, 1952). Although the effect is not at all primitive, the tomb is considered to "fall somewhat outside the main stream of Egyptian development" (Smith, 1949: 233). The tomb of Ukhhotep at Meir omits groundlines altogether and combines a hunt scene with an animal landscape (Figure 4.14b) (Blackman, 1915: Pl. 7, and see Groenewegen-Frankfort, 1951: 73). Elsewhere in the early Middle Kingdom, we are probably looking at the uncertainties of draftsmen who did not fully understand Old Kingdom conventions.

Royal work of the high Middle Kingdom tends to resurrect canonical prototypes. As Smith has shown (1949: 235), the hunt scene of Mentuhotep II at Deir el-Bahari follows Old

Kingdom models. (By contrast, Mentuhotep's battle scenes are thought to be "wild and quite unorthodox" [Groenewegen-Frankfort, 1951: 50, on Naville, 1898: Pls. 56–64].) Compared even with superior private relief sculpture and painting of the Old Kingdom, some Middle Kingdom private compositions also resist any tendency for the hunt scene to use noncanonical conventions. For instance, the hunt scenes of Intefiker and Djehutyhotep at Beni Hasan and Bersheh are described as "stiffly composed" (Groenewegen-Frankfort, 1951: 75; Smith, 1949: 239–41); they use a fully canonical register-line organization.

Some Middle Kingdom artists working for private patrons, nevertheless, performed a series of formal transformations on the representation of animated movement that initially appeared in the First Intermediate Period. Animals were drawn with feet widely separated; figures were allowed to overlap much more frequently than in other iconographic programs. For example, a strikingly elongated "leaping"

Figure 4.14. *a.* Hunt Scene, Tomb Painting in the Tomb of Sobekhotep at Mialla, First Intermediate Period. After Smith, 1965: Fig. 190b. *b.* Hunt Scene, Tomb Painting in the Tomb of Ukhhotep at Meir, Twelfth Dynasty. After Blackman, 1915: Pl. 7.

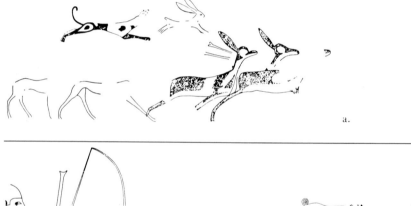

a.

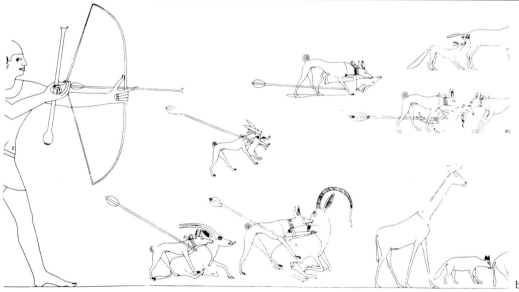

b.

hound is preserved on a small relief fragment from the now lost hunt scene of Akhtoy (Kheti) of the Eleventh Dynasty (Hayes, 1953: 164, Fig. 100). These experiments apparently swiftly resulted in the appearance of some novel, although not necessarily noncanonical, motifs. In the Twelfth Dynasty chapel of Senbi at Meir, dated to the reign of Amenemhet I (Figure 4.15a), established motifs like the pouncing dog, rearing hyena with an arrow through its muzzle, and wounded oryx kicking with hind legs were all used; essentially similar motifs had been used as early as the reign of Sahure in the Fifth Dynasty (Blackman, 1914: I, Pls. 6–8; Groenewegen-Frankfort, 1951: 70–73; Smith, 1949: Fig. 94, 1965: Fig. 191). Kantor (1947) has assembled a valuable list of several such "conventional groupings" in the hunt cycle, like the "seizure of the hind quarters," "meeting face to face," and "seizure

Figure 4.15. *a*. Hunt Scene, Tomb Painting in the Tomb of Senbi at Meir, Twelfth Dynasty. After Smith, 1965: Fig. 191. *b*. Hunt Scene, Tomb Painting in the Tomb of Antefoker at Thebes, Twelfth Dynasty. After Schäfer, 1974: Fig. 192.

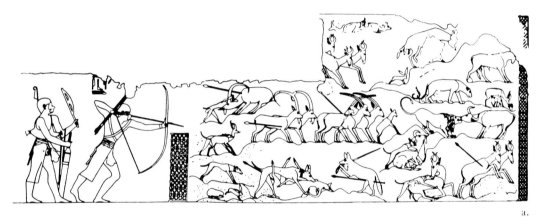

a.

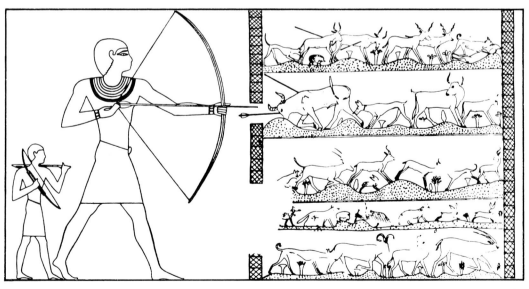

b.

of the prostrate animal." In most of them, care was taken to keep the figures as distinguishable as possible. However, Senbi's artist also draws a dog grasping the head of an oryx with the dog's head behind the oryx. Although an overlap of this kind may have normally been regarded as too ambiguous, for this representation of the instant of the kill it was highly convincing. Extensive overlapping was also permitted elsewhere in the composition. One of Senbi's rabbits appears to descend to the ground from a flying leap. Although most of the undulating desert groundlines follow the horizontal of the base register line, one winds sinuously up to the upper right corner of the composition. (Groenewegen-Frankfort [1951: 70–73] suggests that the higher contours were meant to be understood as more distant, although Evers's [1929] description of this effect as "Middle Kingdom perspective" surely goes too far [Schäfer, 1974: 268–9].) Under Sesostris I, the artist of Antefoker's tomb at Thebes (Figure 4.15b) (Davies, 1920: Pl. 7; Schäfer, 1974: Fig. 192) preferred a more conventional register arrangement, but also used the leaping rabbit and, at least in the uppermost register, allowed an extensive overlapping of figures.

By the New Kingdom, many of these lively, detailed, and "naturalistic" formulations were fully accepted in the canonical iconography of the hunt. In all surviving early New Kingdom hunt scenes, figures overlap and crowd, stumbling and falling in various contorted postures, amid a "landscape" of wavy desert groundlines. The hunt cycle seems to have been especially popular with private patrons in the reigns of Tuthmosis III, Amenhotep II, and Amenhotep III. Perhaps an increasingly wealthy, leisured, and well-traveled aristocracy engaged more frequently in the hunt itself. Evidently stimulated by contemporary explorations of the medium of painting and even by Aegean prototypes, artists became particularly fond of using the flying gallop for the representation of vigorous motion.

In the tomb of Amenemhet under Tuthmosis III (Figure 4.16) (Smith, 1981: Figs. 244–5; Wreszinski, 1923: I, Pl. 53), for instance, the tomb owner with bow and arrow faces four registers of dashing dogs and antelopes, stumbling bulls, and squawking ostriches. At the far right end of each register frieze, the artist inserts a large hillock as the termination of the wavy desert groundline. Standing just below Amenemhet, his son holds back the master's favorite hound, straining forward with his forefeet lifted high off the groundline. The directions of running figures are varied. In the uppermost register of fleeing animals, the excited creatures run together, toward, and past one another. Also under Tuthmosis III, a painter working for the official Inena (Smith, 1981: Fig. 247) dispenses with the vertical line conventionally used to divide the figure of the master from the desert "landscape" with running animals. Here the master lifts his bow and practically beneath his feet a hyena rears up, pierced in the face, and the hound strains to leap after a desert hare and wounded oryxes escaping across the field; the painting is a compressed amalgamation of motifs used since the reign of Sahure. Although Inena's painter uses a register line to define the horizontal direction of figures and their angles of placement he liberally stacks at least four tiers of running figures in one register frieze.

In the next generation, under Amenhotep II, a painter working for the official Rekhmire (Figure 4.17a) (Norman de Garis Davies, 1943: II, Pl. 43; Groenewegen-Frankfort, 1951: Fig. 14), using motifs from the standard repertory, abandons the base horizontal register lines and uses only the

Figure 4.16. Hunt Scene, Painted Tomb Relief in the Tomb of Amenemhet at Thebes, Eighteenth Dynasty. Photograph by Harry Burton, Courtesy Metropolitan Museum of Art.

Figure 4.17. a. Hunt
Scene, Tomb Painting in
the Tomb of Rekhmire at
Thebes, Eighteenth Dy-
nasty. Restored after
Smith, 1965: Fig. 192.

b. Hunt Scene, Tomb Painting in the Tomb of Puimre
at Thebes, Eighteenth Dy-
nasty. Restored after
Smith, 1965: Fig. 99.

undulating lines that stand for desert topography and normally float somewhere above the straight register line. Hope-
lessly confined between fence nets (painted vertically at either
side), the animals mill and dash, targets for the master's arrows. Three undulating lines of desert ground attach to either
end of the scene and isolate four registers or blocks of action.
Within these friezes, some animals are oriented diagonally
rather than horizontally. The painter was evidently concerned
about the implications of his innovations: Was the scene readable or too confusing? Underneath diagonally oriented figures, he places a short wavy line to show that the animals
are not falling or flying through the air but running across
the ground in various different directions. Furthermore, the
loosening of the strict register format opened up little patches
of empty space. Would these look blank or would areas of
the wall actually look unfinished? Not accepting an uneven
distribution of figures and empty space, blanks have been
filled with generalized sketches of desert plants.

Other patrons or painters were not as cautious and classicizing. One group of tomb decorators accepted a further
transformation: They abandoned any register or topographical groundlines whatsoever. Their works are not really an
evolutionary consequence of the painting for Amenemhet,
Inena, or Rekhmire; the two sets of paintings were produced
at the same time and therefore represent contemporary sectors
of taste. In the tomb of User, prepared between the reigns
of Tuthmosis I and III, groundlines were passed over entirely
at a time when the painters for Amenemhet and Inena were
still inserting some anchors. The same can be said for the
tomb of Mentiwy in the second generation, under Amenhotep II, and the extraordinary but badly damaged hunt scene
of Userhet in the third generation, under Amenhotep III (see
Mekhitarian, 1954: 58).

Although no doubt unconsciously, Puimre's tomb painter
(Figure 4.17b) (Norman de Garis Davis, 1922: Pl. 7; Smith,
1965: Fig. 99) returned to precanonical principles of composition. Although he used register lines, his conception of
compositional grouping actually took little account of them.
The painting is radical in its overpowering interest in swift
motion. No animals remain at rest; their bodies stretch and
gallop or change direction in what Kantor (1947) calls a "torsional" way. The creatures are not intended to be flying
through space or descending from the air, but running in and
among one another in different directions. A dog may run
at an antelope from the side or even from the front rather

89

than pursue, as register composition instructs, directly from behind along the same straight line of ground. Although Puimre's painter used canonical register lines to set up the major separations in his overall field, he hoped the eye could read off a far more precise description of what is occurring from the relative orientation of individual baselines.

One tomb painting produced by a member of this "school" or sector of taste can be regarded as truly innovative and, at the same time, as defining the limits of possible variation for a certain set of formal and iconographic principles. The innovations in the hunt scene painted for the official Kenamun under Amenhotep II (Figure 4.18) were never repeated. Only thin patches of this radically new and coherent vision by a brilliant and idiosyncratic painter survive (Norman de Garis Davies, 1930: I, Pl. 48, II, Pl. 48a; Nina de Garis Davies, 1936: Pls. 30–1, for excellent drawings; Smith, 1981: 248, for partial photo; see also Groenewegen-Frankfort, 1951: Pl. 37; Smith, 1965: Fig. 193). With bow and arrow, the tomb owner is shown preparing to shoot. The animals have not yet taken

Figure 4.18. Hunt Scene, Tomb Painting in the Tomb of Kenamun at Thebes, Eighteenth Dynasty. After Norman de Garis Davies, 1930: Pl. 48.

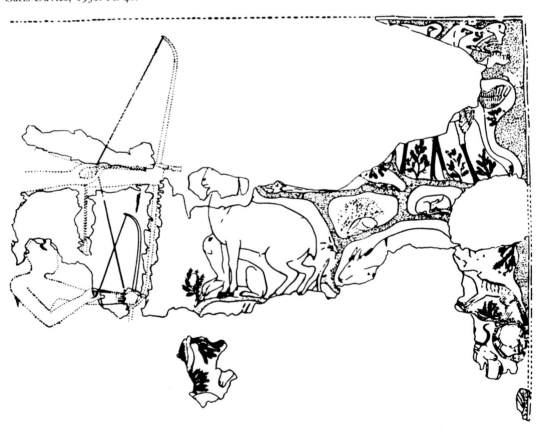

flight, however, and remain peacefully grazing. The "movement" in this scene, then, is as much an implied movement still to come – or perhaps not to come at all? – as the literal marking of real action, carried, this artist may have felt, to its extreme in a painting like that for the tomb of Puimre. Formal and iconographic transformations on the theme of movement simply come to a stop here; another conception of what occurs in the hunt is put in its place. Groenewegen-Frankfort (1951: 86, 95–6) has done most justice to this unsettling fragment:

[Kenamun's artist] solved the problem of depicting the animals in this setting by surrounding each creature – resting on, in some cases slightly overlapping, the wide pebbly strips – by a plain colored surface, which needless to say acts in contrast as *space*. It is true that the weird uneven network which results does not clearly suggest receding soil and that the plants and trees adhering to the strips in a variety of orientation are equally confusing. But it cannot be denied that this unique experiment in going beyond the mere abstraction of a skyline is the nearest approach to topographical coherence in pre-Amarna Egypt – it is, in fact, a typical true painter's experiment – and that it has the remarkable effect of both binding and isolating the animals in space. . . . Such dignity in the face of inevitable disaster could only be expressed in animal form and in the relation of hunter and prey. The very immobility of the ibex facing his murderer has the tension of a tragic situation realized and accepted. It is enhanced with great subtlety by the unusual posture which suggests imminent collapse yet emphasizes the proud bearing of the head and shoulders and also by the unexpected behavior of the hound who, lying down with forepaws crossed, looks up as if in awe and wonder.

In this painting each figure group has been set off from the others by dotted dark strips of desert ground completely surrounding it in a remarkable "projection" of desert "space." This innovative device may actually derive from formal division of another iconographic cycle, scenes of agricultural activity in which men and animals are depicted squatting beside or moving along such strips, standing for banks of earth or, striped with waterlines, for ponds and canals. Although it somewhat oversimplifies his complex relation to possible formal and iconographic sources in the canonical tradition itself, it would be fair to say that the transformational principles in Kenamun's painting amount to reversal and negation. The representation of movement was not simply differentiated and magnified; it was reversed, and the painter makes a moment of absolute rest the focus of the image. Similarly, rather than playing with the direction and number of baselines and groundlines, continually expanding and differentiating, the painter negates them altogether, although the exact nature of his alternative – a "projection" of receding space? – is hard to make out from the damaged fragment.

Compared with transformation by addition, magnification, division, and substitution, amounting to a cumulative conservation of a consistent thematic, transformations through reversal or negation are very strong modes. Typical of what are often called avant-garde experiments, they constitute a direct threat to the established iconography as it attempts to preserve and even to aggrandize a set of invariances through a sequence of transformations. Therefore they were resisted by an essentially classicizing, academic institution. Since they were not repeated, the innovations of Kenamun's painter were apparently noncanonical and were never to be assimilated in the repertory.

ICONOGRAPHIC INVARIANCE

In general, in canonical iconography as I have described it nothing was lost. Core motifs and elements were continually replicated, subdivided, differentiated, and reshuffled, simultaneously conserved and expanded. Presumably using pattern books and other methods (see Chapter 5), the academy succeeded in keeping the total repertory available for use, although some sectors of the repertory probably did become "archaic" and others seemed for a time "up to date." Strong transformations through reversal or negation were not canonical procedures, being too disruptive; dialectically they generated the unacceptable possibility of an entirely different system of representation. In the sense that the vast majority of images were intelligible to a viewer who understood a single system of motifs, equivalences, and rules of transformation, canonical iconography was highly invariant.

Needless to say, maintaining invariance in the sense that I have been considering was not the same thing as being inflexible. In logical terms, transformational principles like the additive modification of a core element are almost infinitely productive. A relief sculptor could add as many captives to the victory scene as his wall space permitted. Artists did not hesitate to rearrange units of compositions, like building blocks, to arrive at a satisfactory alignment of forms on a particular surface defined by architectural elements. The

problems of finding suitable space could be severe, and problems of expression, visibility, the patron's individual demands, and so on had to be considered in each instance. The
very possibility of expanding, dividing, and otherwise modifying a core motif provided the decorator with enormous
flexibility in mediating the canonical image in or, more precisely, into its specific architectural context.

If typical motifs could be inserted easily into many contexts
and compressed or elaborated as these contexts required, then
their highly invariant intelligibility should strike us as significant. It is not so much that the production of images
responded to individual problems or expressive purposes –
which will always be complex and various – as that the canonical qualities of the image were preserved, were still intelligible, even in variable contexts of use.

CHAPTER 5

ACADEMIC PRODUCTION

TRANSMISSION OF THE CANON

I<small>T</small> is now appropriate to consider how the canonical principles outlined in preceding chapters were encoded and transmitted from one generation of practitioners to the next. I will distinguish three interrelated factors somewhat roughly. First, the canon necessarily depended upon a fairly unitary theory about the canonical image. The body of interrelated practical procedures and formal principles has already been considered, and later (see Chapter 7) I will examine possible underlying beliefs about canonical images and motivations for producing them. At this point it is important to ask how the practical procedures and formal procedures were encoded, that is, made available for instruction and preservation. Second, systematic instruction introduced new artists to canonical procedures and, perhaps, to canonical beliefs and motivations, in a way that ensured the maintenance of invariance. The encoded canon was employed in an academic setting. The archaeological evidence for the character of this institution requires consideration. Third, mechanisms of preservation – some of them associated with the academy, but some not – ensured that canonical forms survived three thousand years of Egyptian history and were constantly available to new practitioners.

The academic institutionalization of the canon has many implications for the general study of Egyptian art. Two are particularly worth keeping in mind as we review some of the evidence pertaining to the academy. First, the effort to specify completely rules for producing a work of representational art ultimately involved the academy in a contradictory or impossible project. Second, the role of individual artists in an institution that minimized individual creative participation in the making of signs requires cautious evaluation.

Although many of these points may seem relatively straightforward to students of the academic art of later cultures, it would be misleading to present the Egyptian evidence in any other way than the way we have it: It is fragmentary, puzzling, and open to various interpretations. For example, no Egyptian artist has left us a complete written practical or aesthetic treatise. An exemplary work of canonical production could serve as a "textbook," of course, and it is certainly conceivable that most Egyptian practitioners in fact depended upon nothing more than a set of existing models, some of them finished works of art, from which they could copy using simple mechanical devices. Although this possibility is useful in interpreting Egyptian art, how did an artist initially acquire the knowledge to make an exemplar or model work in the first place? The problem of the origins of the canonical conventions cannot simply be waved away (see Chapter 6). In any case, the corpus of practical procedures and formal principles could not all have been equally well embodied in one single exemplary work, nor even in a series of such works. Whatever its physical form, the rule book would have to include an amount of further technical detail or explanation, particularly for problems of proportion.

Assuming an inevitable tendency toward variation in production over time and space, for no two works could ever be made exactly alike, it is a major problem of Egyptian archaeology to show how many individual works could have been made canonically. The apparent completeness of the archaeological record disguises the real extent of our ignorance. For example, although we have many depictions of craft activity and of the manufacture of statuary, these scenes actually tell us rather little about the stages of the craftsmen's work (Vandier, 1964: 4–6), perhaps, as Eaton-Krauss suggests (1984: 38, 43), because the tomb scenes generally show works of art not as unfinished but as completed. We do have many remains of works in progress (Figure 5.1), from which it has been possible to reconstruct the working methods and many of the preferences of Egyptian architects, sculptors, and painters. However, in themselves the remains of works in progress do not tell us why work was being conducted in the way it was or how the methods were initially conceived. Painstaking archaeological scrutiny of production methods may tell us no more than what we already know – namely, that widely shared standards were operating.

As with many ancient arts, our sources simply do not permit us much engagement with the immediate contexts of production and particularly with what participants them-selves believed they were doing. The record is tantalizingly incomplete for key elements of our problem – artistic per-sonalities, teachers, commissions, patronage and a commerce or trade in works of art, workshops, and so on – and requires much more detailed interpretation than I can give here.

INVARIANCE

At the risk of belaboring the obvious, I will begin with what seems most evident. The most important trace of the canon is simply the great similarity between works produced at different times and places. Invariance between works of art was presumably as striking a fact to the ancient Egyptians as it is to a modern historian, although we do not yet necessarily understand their view of this fact. The formal qualities of invariance have been addressed already in earlier chapters; its archaeological character, its character in context, is perhaps less apparent: In archaeological contexts invariance has a sta-tistical meaning. Invariance is a peculiarity, as it is in Egypt, if and when the proportion of objects departing from the norm is extraordinarily low. If the sample of objects is care-fully defined to minimize the inclusion of idiosyncratic var-iations (for instance, defined carefully as the output of a single workshop, over a limited period of time, for a preestablished kind of demand), we will find – if the definition of canonical

Figure 5.1. Unfinished or Incomplete Limestone Seated Figures of King Mycerinus, from His Fu-nerary Complex at Giza, Third Dynasty. Courtesy Boston Museum of Fine Arts.

96

invariance is to have any real power – the proportion of variability approaching thresholds of negligibility.[1]

The striking art-historical facts are still too often taken to be the facts of variability, possibly because normal practices in connoisseurship derive from attributing classical Greek and Italian Renaissance works to the minutest differentiation available, the work of separate individual hands or masters. We tend to take for granted the uniformities that made possible the initial grouping of objects then scrutinized for differences. But in the Egyptian context pursuit of difference essentially amounts either to a truism, demonstrating the obvious fact that things cannot be made exactly alike, or a secondary finding, unintelligible without a secure understanding of invariance, that some anomalies are occasionally significant; we would need, for example, an independent argument that locating "individual hands" is significant. Such arguments are available (the best being the technical point that at some limit in production the artist has no rule) but the unargued pursuit of difference is seriously misleading.

If a canon is characterized visually and archaeologically by the standardization of features, then we might convert this description into an analysis of the production, administration, and economy of art in Egypt. Standardization in the product requires standardization in production. Evidence for the practical means of standardizing production is somewhat meager, in part because the mechanisms were not preserved as assiduously as completed works or were actually consumed in the process of production itself. It is therefore important to stress that the primary evidence for the institutional standardization of artistic production in ancient Egypt is simply the standard appearance of the final product. In the remainder of this chapter, I will simply assume the overwhelming significance of this evidence.

THE ENCODING OF THE CANON

In the general history of art, the production of canonical works has been specifically characterized by the use of pattern or copybooks and models. Little material of this kind survives from Egypt in a pure, fully developed, or easily recognizable form. Furthermore, even when we have these aids, they might not be very useful to us (Schäfer, 1974: 62–3): They might tell us how certain effects were achieved, but nothing about underlying purposes or preferences. At some point an original designer had to work out the standards for the models themselves, but the models may not reveal his intentions explicitly; his ambitions must be inferred from the appearance of the models. In fact, formal description of the Egyptian canon (see Chapters 2, 3, 4) is founded only upon visual and technical analysis of completed canonical works – whether canonical artists' models and preparatory drawings or "finished" tomb paintings and monumental sculpture.

None of these analytic problems necessarily tells against the possibility that various aids were extremely important in their original cultural context. Although not quite definitive, the Egyptian archaeological and textual evidence can be interpreted fairly convincingly in this light. A papyrus in Berlin in poor condition, dated to the Greco-Roman period, apparently bears a plan for sculpting a sphinx holding a human figure between the forward paws (Figure 5.2); the plan includes proportion grids for the front and profile elevations of the sculpture, or copy grids (?), and proportion grids possibly for the plan view as well (Borchardt, 1917; Schäfer, 1974: 328–30, Figs. 325–6). The drawing was probably a sculptor's working scheme. In proportion to the number of projects completed by Egyptian sculptors, the amount of this kind of material that survives is infinitesimal. But the very survival of the sketch, a highly perishable product, perhaps implies that it was preserved carefully in order to teach the method of manufacture or to maintain a record of the pro-

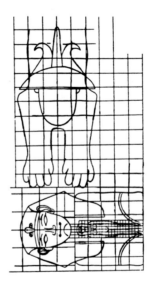

Figure 5.2. Sculptor's Preparatory or Pedagogical Drawing on Papyrus, a Plan of the Top View and Front Elevation of a Sphinx, Greco-Roman Period. After Schäfer, 1974: Figs. 325–6.

duction. The same can probably be said for a proportion of
all such plans dating from earlier periods. Other material
should not always be interpreted this way: Some ostraca with
architects' and designers' sketches were employed for purely
casual calculations and were immediately discarded – only
chance preserving them in the detritus of building projects.[2]

By the Middle Kingdom, we apparently hear very indirectly of the existence of plans, patterns, or other architectural
and technical material stored in written form in the temples.
The somewhat minimal evidence can be summarized rather
briefly. The scribe-artisans occasionally hold the title Master
of Secret Things, like the vizier and royal architect Mentuhotep under Sesostris I in the Twelfth Dynasty[3] and Hatshepsut's architect Senmut in the Eighteenth who, obviously
proud of this aspect of his career, elsewhere claims to have
invented the flying-eye vulture motif (Drioton, 1938). The
"secret things," apparently, in addition to texts of other sorts,
may also have included papyrus or leather rolls and drawings
of technical artistic information.[4]

In the New Kingdom, an inscription from the reign of
Tuthmosis I tells of artisans commanded by the priests to
"conduct the work, causing to come [to attend the project]
. . . every prepared one of [the king's] workmen, the best of
his lay priests, who knows the directions and is skillful in
that which he knows . . . [in order to erect] the monument of
his father, to equip his everlasting statue; execute the very
secret things, no one seeing, no one beholding, no one knowing his body." The chief treasurer who organized the work
replies to the order; a description of the statues follows, and
we are told that the "[carrying-] standards thereof, more
secret were they than the fashion of the nether world"
(Breasted, 1906: II, secs. 92–5; Grapow, 1924: 26). We know
from the Palermo Stone that even in the greatest antiquity
the manufacture of the images of the gods was one of the
principal administrative and symbolic tasks of each monarchy.[5] Various texts detail the enormous quantity and evident expense of these and certain commemorative projects;
for example, the archives of El-Lahun in the Twelfth Dynasty
contain records for statues of the reigning king and his father,
the deceased monarch to whom the temple was dedicated,
along with statues of women of their family, other kings,
and several officials (Kemp, 1983: 89, 92).

What is perhaps the most informative text recounts the
activity of the otherwise rather shadowy ruler Neferhotep of
the Thirteenth Dynasty (Pieper, 1929). Dismayed at the decay

of the Temple of Osiris at Abydos (possibly in existence, in one form or another, since the First Dynasty), the king investigates the proper making of the divine statues:

"My heart has desired to see the ancient writings of Atum [at Heliopolis]," the king informs his nobles, "so open for me a great investigation; let the god [Osiris] know concerning his creation [in a new statue], and the gods concerning their fashioning, their offerings, and their oblations. . . . Let me know the god in his [proper] form, that I may fashion him as he was formerly, when they [the gods] made the statues in their council in order to establish their monuments on earth." "Let your majesty proceed to the house of writings," the nobles advise, "and let your majesty see every hieroglyph." "So his majesty proceeded to the library; his majesty opened the rolls together with these companions," to whom, after inspecting the records, he says that "I will fashion him [the god Osiris], his limbs . . . his face, his fingers according to that which my majesty has seen in the rolls." With this information in hand, the king earnestly hopes that he "may make the god's monuments according to the beginning [the gods' initial plans]"; finally, after all the work has been completed, the king instructs his nobles to "be vigilant for the temple, look to the monuments I have made. I put the eternal plan before me, I sought that which was useful for the future by putting this example in your hearts." (modified after Breasted, 1906: I, secs. 755–65)

Although "restoration" texts of this type cannot always be accepted as reliable documents (Björkman, 1971: 29–38), this text is unequivocal in stating that the king's sculptural project depended on consulting stored written records. It would make sense for the canonical academy to guard its records from casual eyes, partly for the safety of the records themselves and partly, as we will see (see Chapter 7), for purely ideological reasons. We can only speculate on the real source of these books or plans Neferhotep tells us were handed down to man from the council of the gods. We know architects prepared drawings for their great projects – the ostraca plans have been mentioned already – and presumably submitted them to their patrons for review. In the middle of the Twentieth Dynasty, a scribe named as a leading draftsman at tomb projects for several of the late Ramesside kings, an ostracon tells us, "made a written plan of the [royal] tomb" (Černý, 1973b: 131); perhaps some of these plans were preserved and used for study. They may have included more than architectural plans. An inscription at the temple of Ramesses II at Abydos tells us that the *Urgestalt* or basic form for a statue of Thoth could be found specified (drawn or described?) in a great *Inventarbuch* (M. Müller, 1980: 244–5). In the Ptolemaic period at the great temple of Edfu, the list of sacred books included a set of "instructions for the decoration of a wall."[6] After a detailed résumé of the evidence, to which the reader is referred, Bogoslovsky has concluded (1980: 91) that the plans of the royal tombs included "the subjects of the pictures and their composition in general," "well thought out and fixed in the plan." These planning efforts make perfect sense in the light of what we know about the almost para-military organization of artisans and workmen at Deir el-Medineh, the workmen's village, and in the valleys of the tombs themselves (helpful summary in Bierbrier, 1982, and see also Bogoslovsky, 1976; Simpson, 1973b). It is, of course, not completely clear whether written instructions or speci-fications told an artist how to draw in addition to what to draw. For instance, in a Middle Kingdom text about Khufu of the Fourth Dynasty, builder of the Great Pyramid at Giza, we are told that the king sought out sacred understanding he hoped to use in building a tomb (Lichtheim, 1973: 215–22; Simpson, 1973a: 15–30), but it is not specified that he sought out technical information per se. Perhaps due to its material perishability, practically nothing of this work survives for us to assess directly, although evidence for the practice of spec-ifying plans for production may date as far back as the Old Kingdom (Capart, 1941a, 1945).

Full-scale pattern and copybooks, whatever their exact physical form and whether or not the texts I have mentioned are specifically referring to them, would effect a systematic transmission of canonical formulas. Theoretically such "books" would contain accurate drawings, when appropriate with proportional and guiding lines, for every canonical for-mula from the royal head to various animal vignettes. A workshop would maintain such "books" for their practical and pedagogical usefulness. With a stock of plans, the patron or the king directing his engineers and draftsmen would settle upon his specific requests. With a stock of plans all made up, the workshop could immediately begin production. That art-ists and shops often worked under intense pressure is implied by the vast number of projects undertaken and directly visible in the amount of slipshod work that passed inspection.

Sculptures survive which are, on the whole, fairly finished, although the heads themselves have been left roughly worked – waiting, perhaps, for a particular patron to select the "blank," at which time his portrait features could be finished off. (There are many variations in these practices, and some may not be "blanks" but merely unfinished works: Edgar,

1906: iv, CG 33306, where the figure below the head is rough and undetailed.) Many heads survive half-completed. A late specimen now in Copenhagen (Figure 5.3) still bears no less than twelve principal and nine secondary guiding lines (Mogenson, 1930: No. AE634); a work like this may have been waiting for a sculptor to finish it off, although the numerous lines imply it might have been a teaching aid. Blanks which could actually be used are a specialized by-product of a pattern book. We should not expect to find them because they would be consumed in the completion of the work, that is, become completed canonical works. As an efficient rationalization of workshop procedures, using blanks was presumably widespread: Whether or not a patron had come forward, a workshop supervisor could have his team continually engaged in turning out a standardized object.

Late Period relief sculptors and painters visited older tombs and monuments, where their study of traditional formulas remains archaeologically in the various analytic lines they drew over the finished ancient works they examined (com-

Figure 5.3. Limestone Sculpted Head with Remains of Principal and Secondary Guiding Lines, Front and Back Views, Probably Late Period. Courtesy Ny Carlsberg Glyptothek, Copenhagen.

prehensive résumé in Manuelian, 1983). At least some of the lines are proportional, but others are guiding lines drawn to help masters and apprentices copy down a scene. One such examination was conducted by Twenty-sixth Dynasty or later artists of the reliefs at the Fifth Dynasty temple of Sahure at Abusir (Borchardt, 1913: Pls. 28–9). Drawn over the existing paint and bare patches are both proportional lines, superimposed on figures of gods and king, and copy lines, gridded haphazardly over small figures of animals and over hieroglyphs that the later artists wanted to copy for their own use. Presumably artists copied from model onto ostracon or papyrus and then used the copy elsewhere, on location or in the workshop. However sparse the surviving traces, the practice was probably widespread: We must imagine some physical mechanism for the transmission and preservation of canonical formulas.

INSTRUCTION IN THE CANONICAL USE OF ENCODED CANONICAL FORMULAS

The existence of pedagogical studies for the training of young artists has been a source of scholarly dissension. Several different kinds of workshop and nonworkshop production are often indiscriminately classified as *ostraca figurés*, for they all used the ubiquitous medium of a limestone flake as a drawing surface. Painted ostraca turned up as early as the First Dynasty (Emery, 1939: Pl. 19, no. 431). Apart from serving as inexpensive religious images (e.g., Brunner-Traut, 1956: Nos. 7, 80?), painted ostraca seem to copy from existing models in accessible tombs, to bear preliminary sketches for work in progress (e.g., Brunner-Traut, 1979: 7, 17–18), to serve as idlers' sketch pieces, and to hold teachers' assignments for students, either in the form of a drawing to reproduce exactly or a drawing to complete (Figure 5.4*a*), often with various guiding lines added in and sometimes even with the master's corrections visible. The master's firm and authoritative line can usually be distinguished easily from the tentative, faltering efforts of students; the ostraca provide clear evidence of the development of Egyptian graphic skills, or acquisition of conventions, under canonical instruction. Some ostraca must be associated with work in relief, for they are copies after or studies for work on temple walls.[7]

Test pieces for relief sculpture and pattern blocks for three-dimensional (freestanding) sculpture survive among the numerous so-called sculptors' studies – some of which may be votive or magico-religious (like anatomical *donaria* given in search of or thanks for healing an afflicted limb), but some of which are clearly study and trial pieces (Figure 5.4*b*). They bear two or more attempts at the same design, sometimes executed by an exuberant but incompetent student (e.g., Edgar, 1906: CG No. 33477), and, like the painted ostraca, often bear various helpful proportion and guiding lines (*Hilfslinien*) (Figure 5.4*c*)(Edwards, 1969–70, for an early example). The widespread use of three-dimensional models, perhaps to teach apprentices the finer cutting of individual parts, apparently misled the Greek commentator Diodoros (I.98) into believing Egyptian statues were actually manufactured in separate parts (Davis, 1981a: 74–5; Schäfer, 1974: 325, n. 34). The essential preparation for a freestanding sculpture, of course, was the series of frontal and profile sketches applied to the four faces of the roughed-out block; these sketches naturally do not survive, as they were consumed as the work progressed. The "unfinished" seated figures of King Mycerinus from his complex at Giza have been used by modern historians to document the stages of the sculptor's work as he cut in from the four sides of the block and rounded out the figure (Figure 5.1) (Reisner, 1930: Pls. 62–3; Vandier, 1958: Fig. 4). Con-

Figure 5.4. *a*. Painted Limestone Ostracon with a Student's Efforts and Master's Prototypes, from Deir el-Bahari, Eighteenth Dynasty. Courtesy Brooklyn Museum. *b*. Limestone Trial Piece with Figures of the King in Majesty and Various Hieroglyphs (Master's Model and Students' Attempts?), from Sakkara, Third Dynasty (Possibly First). Courtesy British Museum. *c*. Reverse of the Same, Showing Guiding Lines.

a.

b.

c.

ceivably these unfinished works were used by the sculptors themselves to instruct novices in the manufacture of a statue (Liepsner, 1980: 172, and discussion of further possible studies for freestanding sculpture). The earliest datings for painted ostraca and sculptors' studies confirm that these aids were used at all times in Egyptian history and as early as the canon existed.

For historians of Western art, maintaining a canon of form and theme consists in maintaining the academy, that is, the organized methods of transmitting canonical procedures to students and new artists. The academy need not exist in one place as a physical institution (Pevsner, 1940). In Lee's (1940) definition of academic art, a group of artists and patrons base a program of design upon a fairly unitary, well known theory.

In Egypt, the institution is not well described by our sources. Few complete centers of organized artistic production have been found in situ. The workshop of Tuthmosis at Amarna is the most important example (Capart, 1957; Schäfer, 1974: 58; compare Kemp, 1987 for the workmen's village). The tomb of Ankhmahor at Sakkara, decorated in the reign of Pepi I (Baer, 1960: 64), contains a detailed scene often used to reconstruct the setup of an Old Kingdom estate workshop (Figure 5.5) (see discussions in Badawy, 1978: 22–3; Drenkhahn, 1976: 157; Eaton-Krauss, 1984: 44–5, 131–4; Junker, 1959: 35–6). In the New Kingdom, temple workshops produced quantities of goods, presumably in part at the king's orders (Drenkhahn, 1976: 2–3). Prepared models, drawings on papyrus, or stone models, Michalowski has claimed (1969: 171), were "circulated to all provincial centers of government and religion and were faithfully followed wherever temples or tombs were decorated with paintings and reliefs" (see also H. W. Müller, 1973: 29, for the circulation of models in the Ptolemaic period). Perhaps the existence of a central academy should be recognized, although the possibility has never been fully substantiated; it is difficult to think of canonical principles being advised and administered without some sort of central academic control. Michalowski may have been thinking of the possibility that a central scribal school, the so-called House of Life, may have maintained artists in its ranks (Barta, 1970: 85; Gardiner, 1938: 178). Most likely the royal workshops were the centers for the canonical training of artists. In the Old Kingdom, they must have been located at Memphis or in the necropolis. The influence of individual masters from and of procedures specific to these establishments can be traced in innumerable ways (e.g., Smith, 1949: 22, 25).

In part we learn indirectly of the real power of the Egyptian academy. An increase in the variability or individuality of separate works of art seems to vary directly with socioeconomic and institutional stability. For example, in the First Intermediate Period, an era of dynastic and economic upheaval (Kemp, 1983: 112–16), we find numerous departures from the "classical" canonical standards of the Old Kingdom commencing, in fact, with the so-called Memphite style of the Sixth Dynasty (see especially Dunham, 1937; Fischer, 1968; C. P. Peck, 1958; M. M. Saleh, 1977). Intermediate Period artists had many difficulties with the proportional system. Figures were spaced irregularly and sometimes the register lines disappeared altogether. Within a single composition, human figures may appear either short and squat or tall and attenuated. Drastic reduction in the amount of decoration applied to wall surfaces resulted in the presentation of "greatly abbreviated scenes" in small niches and miniature chapels (Smith, 1949: 19; see also Simpson, 1972).

Figure 5.5. Detail of a Register in a Scene of a Craft Workshop, Showing the Making of Sculpted Figures, Etc., Painted Tomb Relief from the Mastaba Tomb of Ankhmahor at Sakkara, Sixth Dynasty. After Badawy, 1978: Fig. 32.

All of these works can be described as loosening canonical definitions or as extending the ranges of variation. (Although certainly conventions changed for the handling of specific details [Schäfer, 1974: 41, 176], it is probably going too far to identify the emergence of a distinctive "First Intermediate Period style," as Smith [1949: 217–34] and Senk [1959] have done, because we are seeing the decay of a production system, not the crystallization of a new one [Davis, 1989].) Some regions of Egypt at this time do give evidence of considerable continuity in workshop production (Smith, 1949: 236–43). Although in local areas a regional overlord may have maintained social order, the arts still may have lost canonical controls; seemingly it was enough that major centers of production and establishments for the education of artists suffered economic and administrative impoverishments.

It is important to be clear about the thrust of this argument. It is not at all to say that an artist could only "know the canon" by being a fully paid-up member, so to speak, of the institutional apparatus with which canonical production was normally associated. The existence of the academy seems to have been necessary for the systematic employment of the canon but not for the mere survival of the forms. Canonical conventions sometimes survive over periods of far greater unrest than ever marked Egyptian history; archaeology offers ingenious hypotheses about the mechanisms of survival. A favorite explanation assumes the continuity of production in the popular, perishable media, bridging chronological or cultural gaps between canonical production in the "high" luxury arts of permanent media. For ancient Egypt, a developed but pre- or noncanonical production in textiles and wall decoration is thought to have existed throughout Egyptian history. Except in a few cases, like that of the prehistoric textiles from Gebelein (Scamuzzi, 1965: Pls. 1–5; and see Williams and Logan, 1987), examples have not survived. Precanonical wall paintings were produced as early as or earlier than canonical production in painted relief and monumental sculpture and are preserved here and there, in abysmal condition, on predynastic and early dynastic brick walls at Hierakonpolis, Sakkara, and Giza.[8] An actual genetic continuity between wall textiles and paintings – paintings being a more permanent version of the portable textiles used by nomadic groups? – has been suggested, although the proposal is difficult to evaluate in the absence of the documents themselves (Schäfer, 1926). Production in wood is also often thought to precede archaic production in stone. Substantial productions in wood were certainly contemporary with early dynastic Egyptian monumental stone sculpture (Eaton-Krauss, 1984: 6, 58–9).

pleted productions of the Old Kingdom academy, the continued activity of some artists (now separated from centers of academic support), and the possible mediation of forms in popular media were enough to ensure that canonical conventions were preserved intact in many cases. Nevertheless, recovery of the refinements and, perhaps, even of fundamental social and metaphysical meanings was still a matter of some research for artisans in the early Middle Kingdom. Khnumhotep tells us that in the early Twelfth Dynasty the king and his builders erected monuments "to restore that which was found obliterated" (Breasted, 1906: I, sec. 632). In the process of such research and restoration, important replacements of Old Kingdom preferences and some novelties were introduced into Middle Kingdom work (Fischer, 1959; Groenewegen-Frankfort, 1951: 67; Kemp, 1983: 112–16; Smith, 1949: 239–43).

ARTISTS AND THE CANONICAL PROGRAM

The didactic transmission of canon has an important corollary: If canonical procedures were learned from teachers who, in turn, relied on standardized aids, then little could have been contributed by any individual artist. What was the relation between canonical authority (in the etymological sense of authorship) and individual knowledge and authority? If we are to have a view of this question, three difficult features of the historical record must be appreciated.

First, study of the formal and thematic principles of canonical art (see Chapters 2, 3, 4) and of the academic institutionalization of these principles should suggest that the Egyptian artist was principally engaged in the reproduction of a program of design that had been precisely fixed before he ever encountered it. If this program was not designed or projected by the individual artist, then, of course in itself it cannot be used as evidence for his perceptions of the world or his beliefs about it. Basing arguments about the Egyptian artist's interests or motivations upon his reproduction of canon will always require supplementary arguments: For instance, that the artist believed the canonical image of the world, that the artist was constrained to reproduce it whether he believed it or not, and so forth.

The artist's private reaction to the existence and authority of the preexisting program, then, is a second and independent question to which, unfortunately, we have not been able to provide definitive answers. We do not know exactly what Egyptian artists felt or thought about their work. On balance, it is probable that artists – or master artists at least – participated willingly in the canonical institution, perhaps originally as a fully rational means of extracting surplus from the economy as a craft specialist (see Chapter 7); this is to say that an Egyptian artist maintained a notion of authority quite different from our own. Analysis of this question must take a roundabout route in the absence of the direct testimonies of practicing Egyptian artists.

Third, variations could have been introduced into the program if artists and their patrons strongly believed that change was worthwhile. Furthermore, variations were introduced more or less randomly as the program was transmitted over a period of time. But we have already seen that these possibilities were held to a minimum. Significant variations can be correlated with perturbations in the fabric of Egyptian life, but these perturbations were not necessarily introduced willingly by the Egyptians themselves. In fact, after the First Intermediate Period the artists and patrons of the Middle Kingdom seem to have made an effort to reconstitute Old Kingdom procedures, and a similar process occurred in the Nineteenth Dynasty after the "revolutions" of Amarna (Groenewegen-Frankfort, 1951: 120–7).

There is a straightforward consequence of these three facts – that Egyptian artists do not represent individual worlds, that they do not speak to us directly about their beliefs or values, and that even merely "archaeological" traces of their individual intentional activities are minimal in comparison to the massive invariance of canonical production. These very facts at least in part are the "worlds" and "values" of Egyptian artists. This would not be an interpretive problem at all, of course, had not the whole structure of Western thinking about art and its history constituted "an individual artist," whose "biography," "intentions," and "style" or "manner" are known and valued, as a fundamental unit of analysis. From a modern historian's point of view, the result of the Egyptian mode of thought about the production of works of art is simply that the individual artist effectively disappears from view.

On the whole, as the literature has repeatedly and almost obsessively stressed, the Egyptian artist accepted anonymity.[9] Of course this need not be an interpretative problem: If they did not design the forms in the first place, then the personal histories or psychologies of artists may be largely irrelevant to the history of art anyway. Egyptian artists reproduced rather than produced culture. Yet as I have argued elsewhere (Davis, 1989), even a virtually invariant replication of a form must irremediably be mediated through an individual's cognitive representation of that form, which will ineluctably incorporate elements particular to that single individual's cognitive history: So even in a society which, as it were, calls for the erasure of individualities in the replication of culture, the success of the project cannot be taken for granted. In other words, it is not that Egyptian art is "anonymous" because Egyptian society had no notion of "individual artist," although it may not have had such a notion, but rather that production deliberately suppresses those replications which would be the inaugural indexes of the presence of individuals in replicatory sequences. The canon was anonymous in spite of the fact that individuals made and continued to make it: And this is a genuine interpretive problem.

Our definitions must allow us considerable room for maneuver. For one thing, we do know the identities of some Egyptian artists: We know the names, titles, and sometimes the projects and life histories of craftsmen connected with the various arts, like the famous architect Imhotep, Master of Works and Master of Sculptors under Djoser and Sekhemkhet in the Third Dynasty (Wildung, 1977). Despite some difficulties in making attributions, the products of different sculptural schools in one era can be identified, like the "idealizing" portraiture of a Sculptor A under Chephren and Mycerinus produced alongside the contemporary and slightly later work of the "realist" Sculptor B (Smith, 1949: 22, 35, 39–40; Terrace, 1961). A number of works from different periods can be identified as the products of an individual artist's labor.[10] Apparently some artists even "signed" their compositions by adding their own portraits to groups of figures (Erman and Ranke, 1923: 503–4; Smith, 1949: 43–4); even written statements of authorship can be found,[11] although Wilson (1947) asks trenchantly whether the artists are really claiming "credit or responsibility" or are merely listed as retainers on the project.

In a fundamental study Junker (1959) tried to prove that Old Kingdom society may have greatly esteemed its artists, although what this meant in remunerative terms still remains obscure (and see Drenkhahn, 1976: 65–9 for criticism of the arguments). There are numerous contradictions in the evidence, which must be drawn, spottily, from different periods and regions. A text like the "advice to young scribes" or *Satire on the trades* (Simpson, 1973a: 329–36), composed in the Middle Kingdom, speaks of the artist's lowly position: Perhaps the standing of the artist had shifted in absolute terms since the Old Kingdom eras reviewed by Junker, or perhaps the texts simply refer to the ordinary manual artisan, a draftsman's assistant or stonecutter, rather than to master workers (the Egyptians themselves distinguished between "officials who controlled the execution of orders" and "men who executed the orders," in Bogoslovsky's [1981] words; see also Drenkhahn, 1976: 133–61). Bogoslovsky concludes (1980: 113, Table 4) that in the Nineteenth Dynasty artists in the necropolis required state support (they were not living independently in any way); but perhaps by definition artists working in this context were state employees and we should not be surprised at their dependence. At any rate, as early as the early dynastic period artists were apparently recognized as an economic and possibly as a social class (Davis, 1983a) – the first step, we might think, in recognizing them as individually different intellects sharing definable economic and cultural interests.

None of this at all implies that the Egyptians themselves regarded their own art history as the history of various artists linked in action and reaction with one another's work over time. Art-historical consciousness in Egypt, as the text of Neferhotep suggests, took a form common to other species of historical understanding in Egypt: In the "first time," the gods established an order, which human generations attempt to protect against the constant possibility of excessive variation or disruption.

Did craftsmen in the immediate work of production think of their work as anything more than technical, like making bricks or pottery? Bogoslovsky (1980: 108) has concluded that among draftsmen in the necropolis of Thebes in the Ramesside period, officeholders – head draftsmen and the title "draftsman" being more senior than "scribe" and laborers – made every effort to ensure that their children also received the professional titles. Their feelings might be associated in part with a devaluation of manual labor at this time. Yet what, exactly, were these men proud of and attempting to guarantee for their children?

As we can see from the work itself, some Egyptian artists cared about the technical skill with which they depicted their subjects and therefore apparently about the qualities of the finished product (see further Schäfer, 1974: 45). Craftsmen may have had a well developed sense of their individual or mutual strengths and weaknesses. By examining the relative importance of the projects assigned to different hands – as Kozloff (1979) has done for the projects of decoration in the tomb of Menna – we may be able to determine exactly what "talent" consisted of. If we assume that experienced and talented artists were assigned prominent passages in a program, "talent" was the ability to reproduce canonical conventions appropriately and to employ canonical rules of drawing with confidence and technical flair. Masters' contributions to teaching exercises also have these properties. The master artist was sometimes the initial draftsman, plotting the way for others, and sometimes the finisher, finalizing the work with deft touches: His work is distinctive.[12]

We hardly know whether and how the Egyptians would have referred to these matters. It may be that certain notions operated at a high level of verbal definition. When Plato speaks of Egyptian music as an art of "intrinsic rightness" (*Laws* 656–7), he may be making an effort to find a Greek equivalent for a well known Egyptian concept of order and rightness, *ma'at* (Davis, 1979b). However, there are no directly revealing texts about artistic order from Egypt itself.[13]

In their funerary and public statements, Egyptian artists generally refer to only two achievements: They were able to master (occasionally to invent) a technique and complete a project, and they found royal favor (excellent summaries in Junker, 1959). These statements do, at least, reflect a crucial association of interests. In the canonical tradition, a judgment on the artistic value of a work was, seemingly, principally a judgment about the artist's canonical competence. Judgments of value must have involved discernment, but taste derived in turn from the canonical education of men participating in, directing, or consuming artistic production. The canonical education of artists and patrons would have supplied them with a strictly empirical test of correspondence between the exemplary work of canon and any particular product.

The archaeological evidence for this essential identity of quality with competence is rather straightforward. The work of highest quality was most expensive, its producer sought out by the most eminent patrons. Rare or hard stones, expensive to acquire, transport, and work, that is, the best materials, were apparently consumed by the most favored artisans; at least in the Old Kingdom, the quarrying of hard stones was a royal undertaking and the materials were employed in royal projects (Helck, 1975: 126–30). Men of less means shifted with second-rate artisans working with imperfect materials, like the discarded or leftover chunks of larger blocks often used by private patrons of the later Old Kingdom for the manufacture of their statuary (Shoukry, 1951: 88–90). Kanawati (1977) has used the size and presumably, therefore, the expense of Old Kingdom mastaba tombs as a reliable guide to the relative economic and social standing of their owners. High quality associates with great expense and so on: These equivalences between aesthetic and material categories are so common among dozens of arts that we tend to forget how entire avenues of productive artistic endeavor have been closed off in the process.

It is more difficult to determine whether Egyptian artists took pride in their expressive or intellectual abilities as well, abilities which could be significantly detached from and not dependent upon technical training or professional skill. In his famous autobiographical text, the artist Iritsen of the Eleventh Dynasty seems to claim an understanding of the position and movement of bodies, perhaps in order to prove that he is a master of expressive, evocative representation as well as of the standard formulations (Badawy, 1961; Barta, 1970); Weeks tentatively suggests (1979: 68) that Iritsen claimed he was able "to represent the divinely inspired ideal" aspects of the world. Certain products of the early New Kingdom or the Amarna period could never have found even limited acceptance if artists and patrons had not appreciated further elements of original expressiveness in the obvious mastery of technique. As I have stressed earlier (see Chapter 4), expressive innovation was stage-managed according to fully canonical rationales in sequences or cycles of iconographic variation.

IMPLICATIONS

Egyptian art has always posed a problem for those whose Romantic or modernist sensibilities place great store by the supposed fact that the visual arts are usually "autographic" – each work individual and nonreproducible – and cannot be prescribed in advance by some systematic, comprehensive notation (Goodman, 1971: 112–21, for the most rigorous analysis from the point of view of a theory of notation). Although intuitions about the nonreproducible, nonnotational, autographic qualities of representation or of the "aesthetic" are not necessarily misconceived (Goodman, 1971, 1978), historically societies have varied greatly in their degree of ambition to produce a reproducible, nonautographic notation for the graphic arts. Such a notation for all intents and purposes would be a set of explicit "plans and specifications" for establishing the "constitutive properties of a work" (Goodman, 1971: 120–1). Strictly speaking, a plan for a canonical work or any exemplary diagram used in manufacture is not a notation, although if it uses script, measurements, or other characters, it may incorporate notational elements. In fact, it is a crucial feature of a representational sign system that it should violate criteria of notational disjunctness and discreteness; many symbol systems violate some but not all of the theoretical requirements for notationality. Nonetheless, a canonical art may be distinguished by its attempt to come close to the impossible standard of precisely prescribing and devising a "textbook" for all practice. As the example of Egyptian art suggests, it is possible to be highly successful. Egyptian artistic practice was of sustainably high quality and cultural consequence as much because of the power of its preexisting plans and specifications as because of the more or less skillful autographing activity of individual producers.

The technological specifications of a notation or notation-like system might be adopted to enhance qualities of "clarity, of legibility, of durability, of maneuverability, of ease of writing or reading, of graphic suggestiveness, of mnemonic efficacy, or of ready duplicability or repeatability" (Goodman, 1971: 154). It is worth keeping these desiderata in mind in considering the origins of canonical conventions or the ultimate rationale for the adoption of various techniques. The advantages of a prescriptive system must have been felt to outweigh the prime disadvantage of the system – namely, the great difficulty in preventing it from collapsing under a pressure generated from within. At the limit, the canonical project was self-contradictory and therefore finally unenforceable. The meaningful units of a representational sign system cannot be arbitrarily separated one from the next; the representational line is continuously varying – that is, potentially every part of the continuum of the line is semantically valuable (Bach, 1970, and see Davis, 1986, 1987, for application to the origins of depiction as such). Therefore in representation the standard of complete notationality cannot be obtained. Moreover, there will always be kinds of reference which can be secured between or outside the lines prescribed in the plan. Within the canon itself, there will always be the possibility of generating a noncanonical image.

Even the most strenuously vigilant prescriptive system could only ever achieve a compromise with the ongoing and inevitable generation of unpredictable variabilities. Yet this is certainly not to say that canonical practitioners simply acquiesced, permitting the survival and reproduction of all and sundry variations. The system prescriptively called for kinds of artistic work that could not be specifically planned in advance; most portraiture was canonical without being worked out ahead of time. The important point is simply that at a definable limit, certain possibilities not planned in advance were suppressed.

In all of this, the artist did not act as "authority" upon his own work.[14] The work was not fundamentally his own to defend, to explain, or to justify. That an academic institution defined authorship and creativity as the mastery of specifiable problems and skills is an absolutely characteristic feature of canonical endeavors throughout the history of art. As these definitions result in a rational, efficient regularization of production – they make good sense to craftsmen and to consumers (see Chapter 7) – we should remember that a society must powerfully enforce and materially reinforce them. They must be imposed upon a preeducated, preacademic, precanonical state of potentially absolute individuality or variability in representational practice.

Collingwood (1958: 5–6, 17–18) notes that the classic Greek conception of *technē*, "art" or "craft," meant no more or less than the technical mastery of the principles and skills of production, in explicit contrast both to *physis*, "natural ability," and *tyche*, "random occurrence." We can imagine, and the history of art offers examples of, various ways in which a society might attempt to maintain and to resolve the different and perhaps contradictory claims of *technē, physis,* and *tyche*. The Egyptian academic solution was quite distinctive: *Technē* defined *physis* and restrained *tyche*; Egypt institutionalized a canon explicitly designed to control individuality and variability.

CHAPTER 6

THE EMERGENCE OF
CANONICAL CONVENTIONS

I T is probably only when a canon is fully formed that we easily recognize it as such. As in the classical architectural orders, not only must each formal element be in place, but it must also bear a particular, fixed relation to all the others in a total system. Despite appearances, canonical artistic practice in Egypt was not entirely a single "invention" occurring in one place at a certain time and to be attributed to the efforts of a single individual or small group of individuals – although this is certainly an important part of the story.

In considering the emergence of canonical conventions in this chapter, I will need to distinguish between the existence of various elements of the canonical program and the synthesis of the canonical system of practice itself. The elements may exist long before the canon is synthesized; they may continue to survive long after the canon is diluted or replaced; in fact, some of them might be used in alternative or rival programs of design. Furthermore, I will stress that the emergence of canonical practice was not as it were the inevitable cumulative result of the preservation of its elements but rather the deliberate choice of these elements for a synthesis from a range of existing possibilities, some of which were not selected for preservation or nominated for canonical regard.

THE PREHISTORIC ORIGINS OF THE EGYPTIAN CANON

Many elements of the Egyptian canon were rooted in prehistoric and predynastic artistic production. From the earliest prehistoric drawings in the Nile Valley to the final resolution of the canon at the beginning of the third millennium B.C., the possibilities for artistic action were gradually narrowing subject to a set of distinct pressures.

The prehistoric development of drawing in the Nile Valley and Northeast Africa reaches back millennia before the formation of the dynastic state (bibliography in Davis, 1979a, 1983c). Although dating is problematic, rock art in several regions of the Nile Valley, like a region around the second cataract of the Nile, may be as early as the seventh millennium B.C. (Davis, 1985; Myers, 1958, 1960). Many questions about the function or meaning of these images remain unanswered, but in principle the drawings can be associated with known late Paleolithic and Neolithic populations. In general, prehistoric rock art produced by indigenous peoples was subsumed into the Upper Egyptian cultural synthesis in the late fourth millennium B.C.

Probably executed by hunter-gatherers who roamed the western Sahara (at this time savannah rather than desert) and frequented the Nile Valley, the earliest drawings (e.g., Figure 6.1a) are geometric or polymorphous designs of concentric circles, parallel and intersecting lines, patterns of unidentifiable shape consisting of curving lines and dots, and simple outline shapes (Davis, 1977, 1985). The first engravers tended to prefer small, horizontal, somewhat rough surfaces for their nonrepresentational markings. Representational images make an appearance slightly later; we find antelopes, various weapons, and perhaps depictions of human figures and animal traps. By the fifth millennium B.C. the repertory had considerably expanded to include drawings of game – antelope, giraffe, elephant – as well as drawings of human figures hunting or capturing diverse animals. These engravers moved to larger, more or less vertical surfaces for drawing; a review of the several corpora of rock art (Davis, 1979a) shows that style varied tremendously. Although perhaps some "compositions" were engraved little by little over long periods of time (e.g., Myers, 1958, 1960), some narratives, including scenes of men hunting animals, giraffes captured by men with lassos, and families or herds of game, were deliberately planned (Figure 6.1b).

Centuries later, in the Egyptian predynastic period, the rocks bear designs of boats and cattle, reflecting the new material culture and economy of the settled villages of the Nile riverside (Trigger, 1983). Designs of this kind are also found on predynastic decorated pottery. Here, animals and men are arranged in compositions only somewhat more simple than the scenes carved on the cosmetic palettes or ivories of the late predynastic period. Style was still quite variable.

The rock drawings closely document climatic, ecological,

and cultural change. Conceivably they recorded information about animal habits and movements, seasonal cycles, and the whereabouts of previous sightings and kills. In a brilliant work of detective ethnography, Hans Winkler (1947) discovered that the Bedouin Arab – who contributed many of the drawings in the Sahara, the Egyptian deserts, Sinai, and Transjordan – used markings on rocks as route, territory, and property marks. We do not yet know how much earlier marking was an effort of this kind as well. A preliterate population may have invested considerable significance in what appear to be aimless, vaguely symbolical sketches. The most detailed studies (e.g., Hellström, 1970) suggest that rock drawings contained detailed information about many species of animal, bird, and reptile, various weapon, trap, costume, and house types, boats of several kinds, and so on. The images were probably embedded in a complex system of representation that mediated knowledge about ritual and sacred practices, out-of-the-ordinary perceptual and environmental phenomena, and adaptively significant features of the world (Davis, 1983c).

Similarly, later canonical art – whatever its narrative or other meaning – served in general as a medium of specialized knowledge; images classified the world according to certain criteria and exerted human control over experience and problematic knowledge. More specifically, as even cursory glances show, in its mastery of line and swift characterization of contour, choice of outline components, and selection of aspect, prehistoric art in the Nile Valley exhibits many of the

Figure 6.1. *a.* Nonfigurative Rock Drawing from a Prehistoric Rock-Drawing Site at Abka, Near Wadi Halfa (Second Cataract of the Nile), Southern Upper Egypt, Probably Eighth-Seventh Millennium B.C. After Myers, 1958.
b. Rock Drawing with Animals and Human Figures from a Prehistoric Rock-Drawing Site near Wadi Halfa, Southern Upper Egypt, Fifth or Fourth Millennium B.C. Courtesy Egypt Exploration Society (Winkler Archive).

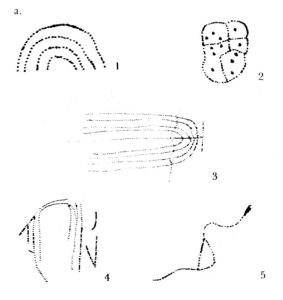

a.

118

preferences later to be exemplified in predynastic, early dynastic, and canonical Egyptian art. These preferences apparently remained relatively constant from the earliest prehistoric to the latest moments of Egyptian history.

PRECANONICAL PRODUCTION

The prehistoric hunting and gathering and village economies of Egypt were succeeded by the nascent state polities of the late predynastic period and by the final emergence of the "unified" Egyptian state under a single dynastic monarchy in the historical First Dynasty (reviews in Hoffman, 1979; Trigger, 1983). For our purposes, the period of precanonical production extends from the beginning of the Nagada culture (Nagada I or Amratian, Nagada II or Gerzean) to the early or middle Third Dynasty, with the most significant developments occurring in the Nagada III/early First Dynasty. Experimental coalescence of the canon, by the end of the Sec- Dynasty, follows upon economic and political shifts of a major order in the late predynastic period and historical First Dynasty. The canon symbolically states certain social

b.

119

achievements that society had recently recognized as significant, potentially unstable, and problematic for its continued reproduction – namely, the stability and validation of a centralized state. The crystallization of the canon by the end of the Second Dynasty immediately precedes the final stabilization of the Egyptian state in the period of dynastic absolutism, the high Old Kingdom – the representational art of which has formed the basis for my outline of canonical principles (see Chapters 2, 3, 4). The canon, then, became a language of an ultimately successful consortium of social interests.

For analytic purposes I will identify four features of precanonical or incipiently canonical production in Egypt, in addition, it should be remembered, to the maintenance of elements from the prehistoric past as early as the eighth millennium B.C. Artistic production at the end of the fourth millennium and into the third was strongly exposed to four extraartistic or extratraditional influences – first, the powerful demands of new functions for objects of art; second, the powerful appeal of foreign novelties; third, the powerful stimulation of contemporary intellectual endeavor in other departments of social life; fourth, and most important, the powerful selection exerted upon available artistic possibilities by artists and patrons closely affiliated with the emerging state authority and seeking above all else the stability and validation of that authority. Although all of these processes could be traced for all phases of predynastic and early dynastic artistic production in Egypt, for analytic clarity I will attempt to provide relatively self-contained examples in chronological or other terms.[1]

THE CONSTRAINTS OF DRAWING ON UTILITARIAN SURFACES

Although rock artists continued to work on the relatively free and unconstrained surfaces of cliffs and boulders from the eighth millennium B.C. through the pharaonic period, in early predynastic cultures of the valley itself (Nagada I/II) artists began to draw or to work in relief on the much more restricted surfaces of objects made for actual use in domestic, military, industrial, and possibly "ceremonial" contexts (fundamental survey in Baumgartel, 1955, 1960). The objects have been found in settlements, cemeteries, and possibly in "palaces" and cult centers. Some pottery types were highly ornamented with paintings or even with plastic additions and may therefore have had more of a decorative or ceremonial than an immediately functional nature, but the vessel forms and even some of the designs often derive from mundane utilitarian sources. For instance, Nagada I or Amratian decorated white Cross-lined Ware (C-Ware) sometimes imitates basket work (e.g., Petrie, 1901: 35, 39; Petrie and Quibell, 1896: Pl. 33 [12, 29]); other forms may imitate stone vessels or gourds (Petrie and Quibell, 1896: 40, Pls. 33 [1], 35 [62, 63, etc.]; von Bissing, 1898).

Whether or not the vessel "functioned" ceremonially, white cross-lined decoration most commonly appears on two principal classes of Nagada I pottery, roughly defined: a "bowl" type, with rim much wider than base and decoration applied to the fully exposed round or elliptical interior, and a "vase" type, often roughly cylindrical, with decoration applied to the continuous tall exterior surface (Figures 6.1a, b). As publication of the designs sometimes involves unrolling or flattening them on the printed page, pottery art of this early period should be consulted in the museum, where the artist's approach to graphic order can be fully appreciated. Decoration of surfaces stresses the natural lines of the vessel and distributes elements evenly, explicitly using the boundaries of the surface as fixed generators of order (Figure 6.2a) (see further Finkenstaedt, 1981). Surface and compositional field, then, are identical: The artist makes no consistent effort to frame part of the surface or to use forms that "look out" from the surface to any imaginary unbounded space. The connections of these habits with canonical compositional schemata have been discussed already (see Chapter 2).

The desire to fill space uniformly usually involved the sequential repetition of a limited number of motifs, often triangles or other geometric units. Sometimes a representational figure was inserted into the decorative sequence as a focal point, as in the case of an animal drawn in the center and bottom of the interior of a bowl otherwise ornamented with geometric figures (Figure 6.2b). In representational designs of the hunt and of what seems to be some kind of dance, artists apparently present half-developed narratives. For instance, in a few cases a little strip of grazing animals is represented immediately above a strip of water, with trees calculatedly drawn to set the scene (review in Kantor, 1974; Vandier, 1952: 264). This tendency was to be considerably elaborated in the Nagada II (Gerzean) period; for example, the triangle, a favored motif of Amratian decorators, became, in Gerzean decoration, a hill or mountain used to set the scene and differentiate the various locales in which events take place (Petrie, 1920: [C], Nos. 27–8, 31, 33–7, 40–3; Petrie, 1921: [D], Nos. 49b, 49f).

The Amratian artist relied on the contrast between the almost sketchy white outline and the reddish ground of the pot. He suggested form with a few strokes: A line defining the backbone sweeps continuously into the back leg or tail, with a few added strokes for head or legs and perhaps some hatching, and serves to represent a giraffe, antelope, dog, or hippopotamus. With a quick flip or short extension of the line, the artist differentiates his subjects: a fat belly line for the hippo, a jagged upward-pointing ear for the dog or hyena, an arching horn for the antelope. With human figures, portrayals can be more detailed. On one intriguing pot (Figure 6.3) the artist evidently wished to distinguish two tribes or classes of people – one a tall, perhaps hairy-legged, short-haired figure, naked except for a dagger in a sheath, the other a shorter, long-haired figure, wearing a penis sheath and carrying a spear. Male torsos consist of a triangle filled in with white paint; the body is more solid and fully conceived than the sketchy animal forms. Women appear generally as hour-

Figure 6.2. *a*. Three Nagada I (Amratian) White Cross-lined Vessels. Courtesy Metropolitan Museum of Art. *b*. Nagada I (Amratian) White Cross-lined Bowl with Central Figures of a Hippopotamus, Man in Boat (?), and Crocodile (?). Courtesy Metropolitan Museum of Art.

a.

b.

glass-shaped figures. (For these conventions and variations, see el-Yakhy, 1981.) Heads are apparently always drawn in profile, although bodies are frontal. Animals are shown completely in profile, with all four legs, both horns, both ears, and so on visible to the viewer ("twisted perspective").

The so-called Decorated Ware (D-Ware) of the Nagada II (Gerzean) period elaborates many of these tendencies.[2] Here a few remarks on decorative style are relevant (Figure 6.4a). The Gerzean potter-artist worked with a vessel very roughly spherical in overall shape. The program of decoration follows this shape and is, as we would expect, more friezelike than Amratian decoration. A few motifs are painted versions of the mottling of stone vases; spirals are also a favorite motif, possibly also related to the texture of stones (Petrie, 1921: Pls. 31 [1b, etc.], 33 [31a, etc.]). The "narrative" efforts in Decorated Ware seem to be confined to a single theme (Figure 6.4b), involving boats (Arkell, 1959; Edgerton, 1923) and standards (Newberry, 1908, 1913) in association with female figures who appear to be dancing or "mourning" with raised arms (Vandier, 1952: 329). Occasionally some attempt was made to indicate the presence of water, trees, and mountains, with the creatures inhabiting them, as surroundings for the action. Conceivably some important ritual activity was represented in these puzzling scenes (Murray, 1956; Vandier, 1952: 329; Williams and Logan, 1987, for various views). Narrative techniques like the differentiation of locales were limited to this single theme, which evidently appears later in the evolution of Decorated Ware than purely ornamental pro-

Figure 6.3. Nagada I (Amratian) White Cross-lined Vase with Human Figures Belonging to Two Social Groups (?) (Tall Figure with Feathered Headdress at Far Left). Courtesy Musées Royaux d'Art et d'Histoire, Brussels.

Figure 6.4. *a.* Nagada II (Gerzean) Decorated Ware Vessels with Scenes of "Mourning" Women, Sacred Boats, Figures of Men and Animals, and "Landscape" Details (Various Collections and Provenances). After Smith, 1949: Fig. 45. *b.* Nagada II (Gerzean) Decorated Ware Vessel with Scenes of "Mourning" Women in a Sacred Boat, Ostriches, and "Landscape" Details, Three Views. Courtesy Metropolitan Museum of Art.

grams. Whatever the precise date of its emergence (probably roughly SD 46?), at this point in the development of precanonical art a standardized theme emerged, repeated over and over again with small variations. Specific rules seem to have governed the details to be included and the methods of arrangement. Apparently the viewer was supposed to understand readily the few laconic details, perhaps suggestive of a well known series of events or a ritual story (Murray, 1956). No doubt the uniformity of the utilitarian context and the homogeneous social identity of the producers of daily and funerary pottery (Adams, Davis, and Hodder, 1981; Davis, 1983a) had a great deal to do with the invariance of the program. It is practically superfluous to say that later Egyptian art embodies many of these tendencies in a highly developed way.

Functional contexts and origins could also be specified for various other kinds of predynastic objets d'art. For example,

a.

b.

predynastic ivory combs and knife handles (Figure 6.5a), although in some cases very skillfully and strikingly ornamented, actually were or were derived from routine functional items. For lack of space, I will not be able to consider these fascinating artifacts in any detail (bibliographies in Asselberghs, 1961), especially their role in the evolution of register composition (Davis, 1976). Again, the earliest cosmetic palettes manufactured in slate/schist and graywacke, found in the extensive predynastic cemeteries, were simply rhomboid in form, but some took the shape of animals, occasionally with insets (Figure 6.5b), or had incised designs (Figure 6.7). The genre culminated in the great series of late predynastic cosmetic "ceremonial" palettes, apparently not ordinarily functional, worked in relief on an impressively

a.

b.

Figure 6.5. *a*. Ivory Knife Handle with Carved Rows of Animals, from Abu Zeidan, Late Predynastic Period (Nagada III). Courtesy Brooklyn Museum. *b*. Slate Palettes in the Forms of an Elephant, Hippopotamus, and Lion, from Nagada(?), Late Predynastic Period (Nagada II or III). Courtesy Boston Museum of Fine Arts.

large scale, to be considered later in this chapter. In the decorative programs of these items, groups of animals appear in
association with one another or with human figures, as they
had in earlier rock art. Evidently the surface shapes and the
uses of these items set limits for which artists worked out
certain characteristic modes of projection or composition.
Serial arrangements, bird's-eye-view compositions, and register composition are all rooted in a desire for ornamental
clarity in a restrictive situation.

If we turn from the effects of functional contexts on composition, a similar effect on the treatment of individual figures
can be observed. In principle, a knife handle (Figure 6.6) or
palette could not be modeled in "sculptural" depth, for the
object had to be grasped conveniently or had to imitate such
a utilitarian object. Ornament was visually legible but phys-
ically unobtrusive. Shallow sculpting added internal details
to the flat contours of the forms (see Chapter 2), reflecting
in turn the flatness of the drawing/carving surface. Even when
images came to fill functions in later dynastic public and
funerary architecture, this "flatness... may have been preserved and encouraged by the ever closer connection between
reliefs and the wall-surfaces of buildings" (Schäfer, 1974: 26).[3]

These investigations of modes of construction, some of
which eventually were to become canonical modes, were
undertaken by craftsmen producing specialized, luxury, "ceremonial" artifacts. The manufacture of the impressive palettes, combs, and knives was made possible by the increasing
technological power and stored wealth of late predynastic
populations; the emergence of stratified distinctions and specializations in late predynastic society, with the attendant
displays of ceremony and luxury; and the increasing
sophistication of patrons (review in Hoffman, 1979). If the
evidence of cemeteries is any guide (Davis, 1983c), late predynastic and early dynastic craftsmen gradually distinguished
themselves from the rural farmers or the "urbanized" towns-
men of low status; they were professionals of some standing,
closely associated with the "elite" of Upper Egypt by Nagada
III. Certainly it would be correct to view the concern for
symmetry, balance, and proportion as a natural response to
a formal problem in composing designs. However, the canonical preferences have a further, more general root in the
discovery – made in all departments of life – that socially
organized technological ingenuity has sufficient power to
master and even increase the regular yield of material things.

Near Eastern (Palestinian, Sumerian, and Elamite) influences were undoubtedly felt in the late predynastic and early dynastic material culture. Early dynastic monumental brick tombs with buttressed facades supposedly reflect Mesopotamian forms and perhaps imply the diffusion of techniques (Frankfort, 1941; Spencer, 1979; but see Kelley, 1974: 6–7). Some late predynastic Egyptian stone palettes and animal figurines find a few parallels in Syro-Palestinian types (Davis, 1981b), although such similarities may not be evidence of diffusion so much as of the existence of a common substratum of material culture throughout Northeast Africa, trans-Sinai, and Syria-Palestine. Individual parallels in pottery form and decoration between various Near Eastern and predynastic vessels can be located (Abu al-Soof, 1968–9; Kantor, 1965).

Most interesting for our purposes, Henri Frankfort argued (1925: I, 93–142, 1941, 1951: 121–37) that a number of particular artistic motifs and mannerisms were imported into Egypt from early Mesopotamian (Uruk) art. This view has been followed in several of its details by a number of scholars (e.g., Helck, 1962; Kantor, 1942, 1952, 1965; Trigger, 1983: 36–8; Ward, 1963).[4] The chronology of the synchronisms and possible diffusions has been greatly refined since Frankfort's initial statements (Boehmer, 1974) – foreign influence from Uruk and Elam is now thought to have peaked in the Nagada IIc–d period – but Frankfort's basic list of contacts remains art-historically important and still well worth reading.

Although certain motifs and mannerisms are certainly common to the art of the Near East and precanonical Egypt, more evidence would be required to prove diffusion from one context to the other. It is not enough merely to cite visual similarities or even the chronological priority of a motif or technique in one "original" context. For example, high-hulled boats depicted on late predynastic portable objects like the ivory knife handle said to be from Gebel el-Arak (Figure 6.6) are sometimes thought to be Mesopotamian (seafaring?) vessels. It is debatable whether Sumerian or Elamite ships ever reached the Red Sea ports of the eastern desert or entered the Nile (Helck, 1962: 6–9; Kantor, 1965: 11–13). Moreover, the representation of high-hulled vessels is much more common in Nile Valley rock art and pottery decoration of the Nagada II period than Frankfort originally believed. Apparently there were several different types of high-hulled Nilefaring vessel and all of them were likely to have evolved indigenously (see Engelmayer, 1965; Kelley, 1974: 5–6; Landström, 1970: 11–25).

To take a second example, serpent-necked felines or "serpopards," a favorite motif of Uruk artists, may have been imported into late predynastic and early dynastic Egyptian art. On the Oxford Palette (Figure 6.9), dated at the earliest to Nagada IId, two appear on one side in "heraldic" confrontation, and on the other a third participates in the hunt of grazing animals by wild and fantastical creatures. Two entwined serpopards subdued by human figures appear on the Narmer Palette (Figure 6.14). Despite having Uruk parallels or even an Uruk origin, the motif may be iconographically disjunct from the Uruk examples, possessing a

Figure 6.6. Ivory Knife Handle Carved with Scenes of the Hunt and Battle and Processionals (?), Said to Be from Gebel el-Arak, View of One Side, Late Predynastic Period (Nagada III). Courtesy the Louvre, Paris.

peculiarly local meaning in and for Egypt: On both palettes, the animals could signify the conflict and/or union of separate social groups in the late predynastic Nile Valley, in compositions which apparently have to do with the early history of the Egyptian state (Gilbert, 1947). On the Narmer Palette, the two beasts probably symbolize the two enemies depicted in their human form on the other side of the palette. Formally, the animals are presented according to Egyptian convention and might derive from the Egyptian funerary palette ornamented heraldically with bird or animal heads in opposed pairs. At most, then, "influence" here amounts to the appropriation of a visually interesting motif for novel Egyptian purposes suitable to an Egyptian artistic context (see also Finkenstaedt, 1984: 107).

As a final example, Frankfort (1951: 124–5) considered the fully developed musculature of the figures on the knife handle from Gebel el-Arak (Figure 6.6), such as the various fighters or a "hero" depicted holding apart two rampant lions, as a foreign feature. This manner of modeling, however, could just as likely be the product of a regional Egyptian sculptural school (see further Bénédite, 1916). As we will see, precanonical sculpture shows considerable variation in the depth and extent of the relief modeling of forms. Although other features of the "hero" figure, including its costume and stance, probably derive from Near Eastern art, the sculptural technique itself cannot be cited as further proof of contact.

These points need not be belabored. The existence of a formal parallel does not document artistic influence, let alone quotation, without further evidence; the representation of novel subject matters does not show Egyptian artists were aware of other representational techniques. If we take a complete view of prehistoric and predynastic production in Egypt, it is easy to see that studies of "foreign influence" in early Egyptian art, said to be distinguishing native from foreign practice, have actually at least in part been distinguishing the variabilities of precanonical Egyptian practice.

Certainly a few definitely un-Egyptian formulas survived in a recognizable form in a process of diffusion from abroad, although there is no guarantee that the symbolic connotations of the motifs were preserved as well as their formats. Initially recognized by Frankfort along with the other, more tenuous examples of "influence" already noted, these motifs include the "hero" figure with two rampant lions (sculpted, on the Gebel el-Arak handle, by a native craftsman) and a griffinlike fantastic winged creature preying on game, such as appears on the Oxford Palette (Figure 6.9). The representation of bearded "officials" in long robes, seemingly driving prisoners, such as appears on the Battlefield Palette and perhaps other works (Figure 6.11) (Asselberghs, 1961: Figs. 151, 181, 183), is potentially a third example; but these "foreigners" may simply be a special group or caste of Egyptian warrior-officials, and their presence in compositions prepared by Egyptian craftsmen does not document foreign artistic influence.

The presence of a few Mesopotamian (?) and Elamite cylinder seals in late predynastic Egypt, although problematic in context (Baumgartel, 1971: 3; Boehmer, 1974), provides supplementary archaeological evidence for the diffusion of these motifs. A few routine parallels in pottery form and decoration between Egyptian and Near Eastern technologies (Abu al-Soof 1968–9; Kantor, 1965) suggest that material contact was mediated through Syria-Palestine, probably in the Nagada IIc–d period.

The possibility of indirect artistic relations with foreign novelties is difficult to document; we can only suppose it played some part in early Egyptian art. Canonical art conceivably found its definition partly in reaction or opposition to major contemporary or preexisting traditions, although we do not know how much precanonical Egyptian artists really knew about them. Certain motifs or techniques could have been picked up or, at least, understood and even resisted on cursory inspection of an item of foreign manufacture; others would have had to have been studied in detail. We do not know the exact whereabouts of the socioeconomic borders between Egyptian, Sumerian, and Elamite spheres of influence in the late Nagada II/Nagada III period. The Eastern Delta, Sinai, and Canaan give evidence of Egyptian penetration in the early dynastic period (Amiran, 1974; Gophna, 1978), but the hypothesis of an Egyptian domination of Canaan (Yeivin, 1960) is entirely improbable; the Red Sea coast came under Egyptian control by the Old Kingdom. All of this is to say that a certain consciousness of being Egyptian could have entered into precanonical artistic experiments. Since part of the argument is "from silence," it is impossible to be sure – but it is my intuition here that Egyptian artists and patrons were aware of other artistic options. The foreign options were probably less important to understand, assimilate, and possibly resist or suppress than options made available in the indigenous traditions.

The relation between precanonical artistic production and contemporary intellectual endeavor offers intriguing possibilities of explanation for much of the formative history of the Egyptian canon. Here I will consider only one example, the close association between graphic art and the invention and swift elaboration of hieroglyphic writing in early Egypt.

The highly formal character of the Egyptian canon often leads commentators to speak of the similarities between Egyptian art and Egyptian writing as if the nature of Egyptian art might somehow be explained by this parallel: We are often told, for example, that a viewer must "read" an Egyptian image.[5] In itself this claim, probably largely figurative, does not prove that the principles of image making were derived from writing; the hieroglyphs present abstract, simplified drawings of objects or figures, stressing the intelligibility, readability, and repeatability of notation, but "as with other scripts outside Egypt, the form of the individual signs, and also the way they are arranged within the lines [of the composition], *follows upon* the pattern of development of the formal sense in major art" (Schäfer, 1974: 258, emphasis mine). Further study would probably reveal the sources in early painting or drawing from which standard hieroglyphs were derived (Arnett, 1982, although it must be used cautiously, collects some pertinent examples and adds the important corpus of prehistoric rock drawing as a possible common point of origin for the forms of both canonical images and hieroglyphs).

Needless to say, one "reads" any graphic or glyphic notation. They are all semiotic phenomena, with arguably well defined paradigmatic and syntagmatic elements, in the case of verbal language the phonemes and syntax and in the case of graphic art the basic plastic means, like lines, points, and fields of color, and the means of combining these in "figures" or "scenes." In interpreting both language and images, one must know a set of rules by which otherwise meaningless marks have representational values. Despite the structural elements shared by all semiotic systems, what lies behind script and endows it with any kind of meaning is speech. A work of graphic art is not a notation for speech but rather, at least in part, for a maker's understanding of some complex set of perceptual and related cognitive experiences. Moreover, notations and images handle the potential or necessary variability of the sign, its discreteness or modulation, in substantially different ways (Davis, 1986; Goodman, 1971). For my purposes, no semiotic or logical argument establishes any necessary points of connection between speech and graphic art and certainly does not show that in Egypt one must have been dependent on the other.[6]

Granting these considerations, there are apparently empirical or contingent points of connection between speech/writing and visual perception/drawing in Egypt. Why should there be a formal similarity between Egyptian writing and the canonical representational conventions? Put another way, what should we make of the simultaneous historical development of two formally similar semiotic systems, hieroglyphs and canonical images?

The early liaison between the canon and archaic writing has a complex and significant legacy. In Egyptian painting and relief inscriptions play an intimate role in composition, filling otherwise empty space with color and calligraphy, assuaging that horror vacui so often said to stimulate the effort toward order and design; indeed, hieroglyphs and images interpenetrate one another almost completely in certain specialized representational contexts, such as the many examples of rebuses and so-called redundant determinatives in Egyptian art (where the whole portrait statue may serve as the hieroglyphic determinative of the name of the portrayed inscribed upon it) (see Fischer, 1986 for full references and many examples; Schäfer, 1974: 256–7). In this book I have not taken up these intriguing intertextual phenomena principally because the main principles of canonical drawing (see Chapter 2) are logically independent of them or, perhaps more accurately, because in the correct drawing of hieroglyphs the Egyptian scribe put to use the canonical principles of drawing: Egyptian writing is a specialized branch of Egyptian graphic art.

We should, in turn, appreciate the dynamic of influence running in the other direction. Common graphic conventions taken up as useful pictographic devices apparently became further standardized under the influence of the regularization necessary for an effective script (Schäfer, 1974: 151–2; Smith, 1949: 148) or, more generally, for the effective administration of knowledge. Formal experimentation narrowed; the invariant component in production steadily gained ground. We do not have enough finely dated evidence to be able to trace this reciprocal evolution for many, perhaps most, hieroglyphic/graphic motifs; illustrations proposed by Schäfer and

Smith will suffice. On early Memphite niche stones of the late Second and Third Dynasty, the seated woman varies considerably in form; for example, on the tablet of Princess Sehenefer in the Cairo Museum (Figure 6.18) (Smith, 1949: Pl. 32a, and compare Emery, 1961: Pl. 32a), canonical proportions do not appear and the artist does not, as later, divide the legs and show both ankles – a slight but telling improvement in legibility. But by the Fourth Dynasty the "seated woman" appears canonically as a hieroglyph determining the name of Queen Hetepheres on her carrying chair and as a relief finely embossed on a thin gold sheet applied to an item of her furniture (Smith, 1949: Figs. 54c, 55). Similarly, in the First Dynasty the flying hawk on the mace head of King Narmer (B. Adams, 1974: 3) differs greatly from the enigmatic outstretched falcon's wings on an ivory comb of Djet (Engelbach, 1930: 115–16; Frankfort, 1948: 47–8; Vandier, 1952: Fig. 566); in the Old Kingdom, on the panels of Djoser or on the gold-covered canopy of Queen Hetepheres, the hawk hieroglyph has been standardized and the conventional canonical formula for this figure entirely fixed (Smith, 1949: 144).[7]

Despite the specific purposes and qualities of canonical representation, art and writing may have played closely analogous roles in the development of the early Egyptian state, the rapid expansion of which at the turn of the fourth millennium B.C. probably depended significantly on the written word. An enormously creative effort in this domain seems to have exerted considerable influence on the formal repertory of the graphic arts (see further Schäfer, 1974: 155–9).

SUMMARY OF PREHISTORIC AND PREDYNASTIC DEVELOPMENTS

Early prehistoric rock art in the Nile Valley is nonfigurative, but representational images appeared by the fifth millennium B.C. Mostly drawings of various animal species, the representational repertory includes some compositions and "narratives" showing human beings in association with animals. Some typical canonical classifications of experience – animals and the hunt, the division of social labor or activity – were probably rooted in this effort to organize knowledge. Similar themes appear on and were developed by predynastic pottery painters and later artists. A strong emphasis on contour line and the rules for outline sections and selection of aspect appear in this prehistoric material and are therefore the most archaic elements of the canonical program.

Other characteristic elements seem to have been worked out in the effort to decorate the restricted surfaces of functional items, such as funerary pottery or toilet objects. These elements include the identity of surface and field, uniform and sequential distributions of motifs, bird's-eye-view composition and awareness of the usefulness of the baseline in orienting figures, outline contrast, the frontal-profile aspect of the human figure, the flatness of relief, proto-narrative iconography, standardized themes with symbolic significance, and stylistic invariance. This artistic work was part of the production of luxury items by a specialist class and reflects the increasing wealth and power of predynastic populations. Whereas symmetry, balance, and proportion are in part responses to formal problems, conceptually predynastic art asserts human control over the material world.

Foreign contacts possibly exerted some influence on the development of the canon, although the temptation to judge predynastic art by later canonical standards sometimes leads to a confusion between foreign and indigenous precanonical styles. Diffusion may not account for some similarities between the arts of early Egypt, Sumer, and Elam, but a few un-Egyptian formulas were indeed taken up by Egyptian artists, including the motif of a "hero" figure holding apart rampant lions and of a griffinlike fantastical creature. Influence from Sumer and Elam peaked in the Nagada IIc/d period, immediately prior to the whole-scale "unification" of Egypt in a dynastic state in the Nagada III/early First Dynasty. Although this final possibility is extremely difficult to document, early art in Egypt may have developed partly in reaction or opposition to foreign styles that led, perhaps, to experimentation or the desire to preserve native standards from pollution.

Late predynastic art seems to have been stimulated by contemporary intellectual endeavors. The close association between graphic art and hieroglyphic writing is a good example; graphic and orthographic conventions were formally similar and intimately linked in many canonical compositions. The development of writing encouraged the standardization of all graphic activity, the regularization of the formats used in both writing and images. The importance of these possibilities and the temptation to analyze the canon itself as a "language" should not lead us to lose sight of representation as a distinctive activity. Even at this level art and writing may have

played closely analogous roles in the administration of the
developing state. As the state invested heavily in the administration of knowledge, both the expansion and regularization
of semiotic systems would have been encouraged.

THE EARLY DYNASTIC SYNTHESIS

The development of Egyptian art from the late predynastic
period to the beginning of the Old Kingdom can be understood as the transition from precanonical variability to canonical invariance. The art of the early dynastic period is visually
characterized by heterogeneity of forms – Smith remarks on
the "wider range of types" and "tendency to experiment"
(1949: 10, cf. 17) in relation to dynastic art – and materially
characterized by heterogeneity in production. In the succeeding era, work of the Third and Fourth Dynasty has the
opposite qualities; dynastic canonical art is largely homogeneous in its sources, forms, and techniques.

Formal, conceptual, and social rationales for increasing invariance can be recognized in predynastic precanonical production as I have sketched it in the preceding pages; yet it is
likely that none of the pressures was sufficient uniquely to
determine a particular technical and formal outcome, namely,
the crystallization of canonical invariance as we understand
it formally (see Chapters 2, 3, 4). This process must be regarded as the further, specific selection of acceptable procedures from the range of formal, conceptual, and social
possibilities available to Egyptian society – and for an "Egyptian culture" – by the end of the predynastic period. The
selection was effected by a well defined group of early dynastic artists, whose preferences gradually took hold over the
whole length of Egypt – leading to the disappearance of pre-
and noncanonical styles and to the artistic homogeneity of
Old Kingdom production. In the remainder of this chapter,
risking the artificiality of pursuing the question as a theme
distinct from those I have already considered, this process of
selection will be documented in a variety of ways.

Illustration of the developments is necessarily confined to
the history of early dynastic relief and monumental sculpture.
Little production in other media has survived. The history
of relief affords the clearest and most comprehensive picture
of the canonical synthesis, for we have little freestanding
monumental sculpture that can be dated reliably to the predynastic period or to the First Dynasty. In fact, monumental

sculpture of the canonical type actually developed using procedures derived from relief sculpture and quite clearly documented in that medium: Canonical selection and definition
occurred first in relief. Therefore I will begin by tracing the
whole development of relief, from the late predynastic period
to the beginning of the Old Kingdom, and then turn to the
history of monumental sculpture.

CHRONOLOGICAL PROBLEMS OF EARLY RELIEF SCULPTURE

Although used as the principal documents of late predynastic
(Nagada IIc/d, Nagada III) and early dynastic (early and historical First Dynasty) Egyptian art, the great "ceremonial"
relief-carved cosmetic palettes – like the so-called Oxford and
Hunter's Palettes and the palette of Narmer, thought to be
an early king of Egypt – must be approached cautiously. If
we want to make sense of the early development of the canon,
it is necessary to have plausible datings for as many specimens
of the series as possible. Unfortunately, only four of the great
palettes possess known archaeological provenances; even
these do not necessarily provide us with precise dates.

The Narmer Palette is a good example of problems with
what seem to be a straightforwardly dated specimen; in order
to dramatize the situation, we may bracket just for a moment
our conviction that this work simply must be early. Because
a personage named Narmer is named and represented there-
upon, the Narmer Palette is often dated to the reign of a King
Narmer, an early if not the first king of the Nagada III/early
First Dynasty (Kaiser's Horizon B), known from other
sources as well as the palette (Edwards, 1971: 6–15; Kaiser
and Dreyer, 1982). The palette was unearthed by Quibell and
Green in the problematic Main Deposit at Hierakonpolis,
traditionally although certainly not impeccably dated to the
early dynastic period (B. Adams, 1975: 3). Strictly speaking,
the archaeological context allows a date for the deposit at
least as late as the end of the Second Dynasty. In art-historical
terms, we know too little about First Dynasty style – on the
basis of dated Nagada III/early First Dynasty material – to
be able to say from its style alone that the palette must be
early; although it has close connections with material thought
to date from the late Nagada period, it is also strikingly
similar to well known reliefs from the reign of Khasekhemuwy at the end of the Second Dynasty (of course, the
similarities are not at all surprising, for Narmer's and

Khasekhemuwy's artists worked in the canonical mode). The palette could have been made years or decades after the reign of a "real" Narmer, perhaps as a commemorative monument. What seems to be a fixed point may be more free-floating. Its date is fixed by close parallels between small emblemata or stylistic details associable with datable early First Dynasty materials; but each one of these parallels could be challenged – admittedly in an overly ingenious way – by supposing a later artist to have been working "archaistically."

It is sometimes claimed we could detect stylistic evolution within the series of palettes. In practice the method reduces to ranging objects as early or late on visual grounds, that is, as primitive or sophisticated according to various stylistic criteria. It would be necessary here to eliminate all teleological criteria, that is, standards derived from the visual appearance of later, canonical art. Nothing essential or ineffable in the history of art, of course, dictates a general evolution from the rough to the perfected: A small, roughly worked piece could be contemporary with a large, finely carved specimen. Variations in the sequence might be due to the differing skills of individual artists, regional preferences, or idiosyncracies in the patron's interests. Some of these possibilities will concern us. Any number of plausible stylistic evolutions can be produced to accommodate various possibilities; how do we choose among them?

Perhaps a stylistic fixed point of sorts is available to us outside the group of palettes in the datable early tomb stelae, the earliest securely datable Egyptian relief work. But here too the root assumptions of comparison should be challenged. Do the early phases of an artistic style really tend toward the consolidation of a succeeding "classic" expression? – permitting us, in this instance, to range palettes as later as they approach the canonical formulations of Old Kingdom tomb relief? Naturally, it is only anachronistically that we call late predynastic or First and Second Dynasty Egypt an early period of Egyptian history and only teleologically that we comb the archaeological record of these eras for evidence of later interests. Should we not rather admit a great variety of experiment in the "early" phases, with no discernible linear evolution in any one direction or another, and only subsequently a much narrower and purposeful selection from the past by classic artists?

Although many of these questions cannot be fully answered here, it would be radically misleading to consider predynastic and early dynastic art in the terms by which we consider later canonical material. Canonical art is firmly locked into an established framework of formal invariance, quotation, and revivification; we have evidence only for the gradual emergence of such a framework earlier. Many early dynastic works are technically, stylistically, and iconographically noncanonical, exhibiting a tremendous variety of individual expression. In fact, the most acceptable nonstylistic datings for individual works belie any characterization of stylistic evolution as a straightforward progression toward the Old Kingdom canon.

In order to establish some fixed points, I will begin with the archaeologically dated specimens. Many undecorated functional funerary palettes, from which the great palettes morphologically derive, are fully datable. Based on Sequence Dates for the graves and their equipment, Petrie (1920: 36–40, 1921: Pls. 52–9) and Baumgartel (1960: 81–105) worked out the morphological history of the functional types, but some fairly subtle refinements needed to be made (Kaiser, 1964: Fig. 6). The earliest palettes are rhomboid in shape; the latest are polygonals possibly derived from earlier theriomorphic types and a rectangular type often ornamented with a border of some kind.

Incised decoration appears on the earliest Nagada I palettes, SD 33–41 (e.g., Baumgartel, 1955: Fig. 2; Capart, 1905: Fig. 39; Säve-Söderbergh, 1953: 18–19, Fig. 8). The later rectangular type with incisions is well dated in the First Dynasty by specimens from Tomb 3471 at Sakkara (Emery, 1949: 60, Fig. 31) and Tomb 1579 at Tarkhan (Petrie, 1914: Pl. 6). The incised decoration on all of these specimens (Figure 6.7) makes an elementary accommodation to the nature of the surface, although the designs actually resemble nothing so much as earlier or contemporary rock art.

The great ceremonial reliefs are not derived simply from such rough markings on functional palettes, many of which are contemporary with the relief-carved specimens. Instead, the carvings seem to be linked with functional palettes that create a highly sculptural effect, namely, a series of "double birds'-head" palettes, well known from many excavations. Like the relief series, the double birds'-head series tends to be quite large in size (often eight inches or more in height), with pointed or slightly squared bottom; the birds facing outward in the two upper corners are very similar in effect to the heraldic treatment of flanking animals on the ceremonial palettes. In fact, one datable relief-carved palette, a specimen in the British Museum with a carving of the Min sign (Figure 6.8a), also has a double birds'-head crown. This example was discovered in Grave B62 at el-Amrah, assigned by Baumgartel (1960: 90) to SD 56–64; the excavators dated the grave in the latter half of this period (MacIver and Mace, 1902: 38), and Petrie (1920: Pl. 51[B62]) opted for SD 58.[8] The sculpted birds' heads on the crown of this palette have been summarily treated, but are closely paralleled on a number of other large but otherwise undecorated palettes of double birds'-head type classified by Petrie (1921) as Type 80 in the *Corpus of Predynastic Palettes*. For a variety of reasons Petrie's typology is difficult to use; nonetheless, a slightly rationalized version makes some sense of the material and of the available sequence or other dates according to the adjusted chronology (Kaiser, 1956, 1957). As far as can be made out from somewhat contradictory reports, Type 80 and a closely similar type, Type 76, date to the late SD 50s, with some possible earlier examples. Type 76 has a rounded or pointed bottom, summarily treated out-facing birds' heads with eyes usually not indicated, and a squared-off hump between the heads, elaborated by two or more deep notches. It is distinctive and defined by more than two individual traits. Dat-

CHRONOLOGICAL
PROBLEMS

Figure 6.7. Slate Palette Incised with Animal Figures and Other Marks, from Hu-Dendereh, Front and Back Views, Late Predynastic Period (Nagada IIc/d). Courtesy Ashmolean Museum, Oxford University.

able examples are at SD 57 and 58 (Nagada IIc).[9] The notches between the heads were sometimes developed into long pointed radii, as on an otherwise undated palette belonging to the ceremonial series now in the Manchester Museum (Figure 6.8b) bearing a relief of a man and three ostriches and probably SD 57/58 (Nagada IIb/c) (see Crompton, 1918 for a description).[10] (The scene itself is puzzling; as we will see, the close association between animals and human figure – note the similarities in the heads of flanking birds, ostrich, and disguised "hunter" (?) – is typical of late Nagada II and Nagada III conceptualizations.) In Petrie's view, the radii are highly evolved morphologically; he suggested that the type must go back as far as SD 40, but this seems to be purely speculative. The dated examples are, again, at SD 57/58 (Nagada IIb/c) and later (Petrie, 1920: Pl. 44 [75c]). The squared-off hump is not always elaborated with radii; many examples only groove or striate the hump without cutting into it entirely. These examples also cluster at SD 58 and later.[11]

In sum, the double birds'-head type (not limited to Types 76 and 80) ranges widely throughout the Nagada II and III. Although it may have first been elaborated in Nubia, c. SD

Figure 6.8. *a*. Slate Palette Carved with the Emblem of the God Min, from el-Amrah, Late Predynastic Period (Nagada IIc/d). Courtesy British Museum. *b*. Slate Palette Carved with a Man and Three Ostriches and Double Birds'-head Elaborations, Late Predynastic Period (Nagada IIc/d). Courtesy Manchester Museum.

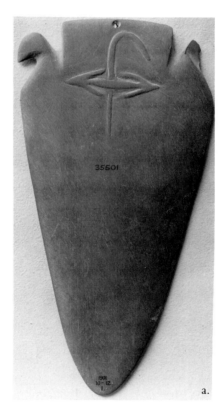

a.

b.

46, deep notching and radii – as on the Manchester relief palette – do not show up until SD 57/58, when Types 76 and 80 appear, the types most like the relief-carved Min palette at SD 56–64. On archaeological grounds it is not possible to assign other material to the early period of the Manchester and Min palettes,[12] but these two examples are enough to offer a definite chronological point of reference. The carved forms are extremely flat and close to the surface, cut very low, with no interior detail to speak of, slightly irregular in contour and positioning on the surface.

Other carved palettes elaborate the double birds'-head format, replace the birds with other creatures, and bring them into the frame of the palette; the crowning elements on the palettes become totally incorporated in the program of symbols and signs (see Kaiser, 1964: Fig. 6). Fischer (1958) has proposed that the sequence develops toward the complete envelopment of the animals. The later, complex stages of the sequence, however, are not easily distinguished in an evolutionary line; once the medium has acquired a developed iconography, it seems that sculptors felt free to devise various suitable formats according to a complex representational mechanism and symbolism I cannot treat in detail here. Nevertheless, the Nagada IIb/c date for the earliest relief-carved ceremonial palettes seems to be confirmed in a variety of other ways[13] and will be accepted here as an established *terminus ante quem* for the great series.

VARIABILITY IN THE SERIES OF PALETTES (NAGADA IID– NAGADA III/EARLY FIRST DYNASTY)

One iconographically well-defined subgroup of the series of great ceremonial relief-carved palettes presents desert animals and imaginary creatures in scenes of the chase or the hunt, the palettes often ornamented with flanking heraldic animals. The most important work in this series is the Oxford Palette from the Main Deposit at Hierakonpolis, now in the Ashmolean Museum (Figure 6.9) (Asselberghs, 1961: 286, Figs. 127–8; Petrie, 1953: 10, 13, Pl. F; Quibell and Green, 1900–1: II, Pl. 28; discussion of composition in Davis, 1976). Although no archaeological date is available (the context, as we have seen, permits an early dynastic date), on typological grounds the palette should be a generation or more later than the Min and Manchester ostrich palettes, that is, Nagada IIIa. With its birds'-eye-view composition (Davis, 1976), relative profusion of figures with little differentiation of scale, and unique depiction of the subject, not easily relatable to royal symbolism of later times, the Oxford Palette cannot be much later (see Finkenstaedt, 1984 for an important interpretation). On the Manchester ostrich palette of Nagada IIc/d (Figure 6.8b) and the Oxford Palette of IIIa (Figure 6.9), human beings are shown to participate intimately in this animal world, almost as it were in a nonviolent dance involving animal "masks" (note the puzzling figure with human limbs and jackal's head/mask piping a flute in the lower left of the reverse of the Oxford Palette); although these people may be hunters, here they are not depicted as hunting; they are part of the wild itself.

The series of hunt palettes also includes smaller or fragmentary works like the gazelle palette fragment in the Louvre

Figure 6.9. The Oxford Palette. Slate Palette Carved with a Wild Animal Hunt Scene and "Jackal"-headed Man Piping a Flute (?) (Reverse, Bottom Left), from the Main Deposit, Hierakonpolis, Front and Back Views, Late Predynastic Period (Nagada IIIa). Courtesy Ashmolean Museum, Oxford University.

(Asselberghs, 1961: Figs. 145–6), the wild dog fragment in Brussels (Asselberghs, 1961: Figs. 133–4), the Four Dog Palette (Asselberghs, 1961: Figs. 129–30), the White Oryx Palette fragment (Asselberghs, 1961: Figs. 131–2), the palette fragment from the Michailides Collection (Asselberghs, 1961: Figs. 141–2), and the Munagat and Brooklyn palette fragments (Asselberghs, 1961: Figs. 137–8, 135–6). Although I will not attempt to date each one of these examples, the Four Dog and White Oryx Palettes are typologically later than the Oxford Palette in the shrinking and schematization of the out-facing sculptural knobs at the upper corners and in the squaring of the shape, certainly Nagada IIIb. They have a number of features – increasing regularization of form, greater emphasis on bilateral symmetry, restriction of the number of figures, along with the more emblematic quality of the presentation and insertion of vividly realistic effects – that associate them with works like the Battlefield and Bull Palettes (Figure 6.11, see Figure 4.11) of the early First Dynasty. Despite the discovery of new examples, Bénédite's (1905, 1916, 1918) early and perceptive discussion of the distinctive style of this group of relief-carved palettes still applies. Eyes are geometrical, circles or squares, the hands and torsos of figures are summarily treated, no knee protuberances are shown (a feature generally marked carefully in canonical drawing), feet are "comb"-like, certain details (horns, hooves) are greatly exaggerated; most important of all, perhaps definitive in the conceptualization of this iconography, no groundlines or baselines are used in composition. (Further discussions of the form, style, and technique can be found in the many individual analyses of these works – basic bibliography in Asselberghs, 1961; Vandier, 1952 – and I will not repeat it here. A full discussion of the representational mechanics of these works will be offered by me in another study.)

In a second group of relief-carved palettes, the artists present scenes of victory over human enemies or scenes apparently depicting the "unification" of Egypt, various early conflicts, and rituals connected with the celebration and renewal of pharaonic kingship. The series includes the Narmer Palette (Figure 6.14), fragmentary Bull Palette in the Louvre (see Figure 4.11), a fragment in Cairo known as the Plover Palette (Asselberghs, 1961: Fig. 159), and possibly the palette fragment in Cairo with rows of animals and town signs known as the "Libyan Booty" or Tjehenu Palette (Terrace and Fischer, 1973: 21–4). Very closely associated in style and technique with the Narmer Palette are three carved mace heads in the Ashmolean Museum (Asselberghs, 1961: Figs. 172–80), one of them generally known as the King Scorpion mace head (Figure 6.15): Along with the Narmer Palette, this object is probably the most important document for the earliest embodiment of canonical representation, and I will turn to it later in more detail. A small fragment of a palette in the Metropolitan Museum of Art bears the upper half of the torso and head of a warrior (Figure 6.13a); the so-called Beirut Palette in the Louvre (Figure 6.12) bears six figures apparently being supervised or led away by a seventh, larger, official figure. These last two works possibly concern battles or ceremonies connected with the dynastic state, although on stylistic grounds they may not be associated with the main body of this group. Stylistically all of these works rely on many similar procedures, to be noted when I turn to the principal work in the series, the Narmer Palette.

In the first and prescient examination of the carved palettes, Steindorff (1897) recognized that all of these works, from both groups, could have been produced in a single century. Nevertheless, the "unification" group is sometimes thought to be stylistically later than the hunt group; certainly in its use of register composition, the proportional canon, and other effects, the Narmer Palette relies upon effects the artist of the Oxford Palette did not use. But placing the hunt group earlier than the unification group as a whole does too much violence to the material. Despite the distinctive technical and stylistic qualities of each group, both clearly belong to the same overall class of artifact, with a common origin in the double birds'-head funerary palette. Furthermore, there is hardly enough room from SD 57/58 (Nagada IIb/c) to Nagada IIIc/d or the early First Dynasty for us plausibly to stretch out a unilinear stylistic evolution from predynastic noncanonical "chaos," as in the composition of the Oxford Palette, to dynastic canonical order, as on the Narmer Palette, especially if sophisticated examples of the hunt group, like the Oxford, Four Dog, and White Oryx Palettes were themselves made in the Nagada III/early First Dynasty, as their morphology suggests. An extremely worn palette now in the Metropolitan Museum of Art (Asselberghs, 1961: Fig. 170; Hayes, 1953: I, 29, Fig. 22), in fact, proves definitively that at least for a time both groups of palettes were being manufactured simultaneously, in this case in the Nagada III/early First Dynasty (Kaiser's Horizon A). Like the Four Dog and White Oryx Palettes, animals ornament the palette in heraldic arrangements (here facing outward rather than inward); conceivably echoes of the mysterious hunt on the Oxford Palette are present (note the serpent-necked feline at the base), but the object also bears a royal *serekh* like those to be found on objects of the unification series. Several objects show that the celebration of kingship and its ritual renewal, presented in the unification series, had important formal antecedents in the Nagada IId and earlier, when chieftains or what might be regarded as proto-pharaohs depicted the victorious smiting, sacred bark, and other paraphernalia of what would later become pharaonic symbolism (for Tomb 100 at Hierakonpolis, the incense burners from Qustul, and other materials, see B. Williams, 1986: 138–47; Williams and Logan, 1987).[14] Conversely the hunting theme, presented on the allegedly earlier late predynastic palettes, continued to be depicted in dynastic times with precisely that freedom of aspect and composition it had attained in predynastic contexts (see Chapter 4). Finally, a close study of the representational mechanics of the best-preserved palettes from both groups (Oxford, Battlefield, and Narmer Palettes) and of a palette not easily fitted into either group (the Hunter's Palette) would show that they all depend upon essentially similar depictional devices and a single coherent symbolic program, despite stylistic or expressional differences in each rendition. These figurative preoccupations are not canonical; they are ancestral to the canonical image. A full discussion of the complex imagery of the carved palettes is reserved for another study. Here and below, I stress the variability of the renditions in relation to the invariance of the canonical image resulting from them.

In sum, the class of late predynastic/early dynastic relief-carved palettes, manufactured from the Nagada IIb/c at the earliest into the early First Dynasty, exhibits considerable technical, stylistic, and iconographic variability; at least two major groups can be distinguished with at least some period of overlap in their history of manufacture. Typological and stylistic classification will always be able to break a larger class of artifacts down into smaller groups on the basis of individual features of examples not shared by all in the class. Although this procedure presumably isolates real degrees of variability in the sample, we have already seen that the vast proportion of variability in Egyptian art was well within the technical, stylistic, and iconographic framework of canonical representation. Therefore it is important to stress that only some aspects of some of the early palettes can be regarded as canonical; other aspects are pre- or noncanonical.

To underline this point, we should recall two palettes made slightly earlier than or at the same time as the Narmer Palette in relation to that palette (Figure 6.14). Technically and conceptually these works are intermediate between the two loosely defined groups of palettes I have mentioned; in real terms, they suggest that sculptors were aware of and could draw upon complementary coexisting traditions of relief sculpture.

The largest of all the great carved palettes, the so-called Hunter's Palette (Figure 6.10), probably dated no earlier than Nagada IIIa,[15] represents a group of hunters and dogs setting out to hunt desert animals and to do battle with a desert lion. The human figures are arranged in file – almost in register fashion, although no groundline is included – along the two long edges of the palette. Pursued by hunting dogs (and perhaps one wild dog or jackal), the fleeing animals are shown in the remaining central band of space on either side of the cosmetic saucer. Each human figure, carefully separated from the next, displays head and legs in profile, the torso frontally, and both arms outstretched with hands holding weapons (such as curved throw sticks) or standards (perhaps identifying the "hunters" as members of the king's army?). Yet there are several notable exceptions to this familiar treatment. Wounded and apparently goaded on in an effort to save its cub, the lion mauls one hunter, shown sprawling on the ground as the beast pounces. Although the lion is rearing up over its victim, the two figures are separated in the manner of predynastic and later representations of the desert hunt, as on the Oxford Palette (Figure 6.9). (Compare the treatment of physical contact on the Louvre Bull Palette, see Figure 4.11, most likely produced by the same sculptor as the Battlefield Palette, Figure 6.11: Here the two figures are fitted together seamlessly and a touch of striking realism is inserted as the sculptor depicts how hoof presses into flesh; this mode of presentation was never to be pursued in canonical art.) The artist emphasizes the death throes of the fallen hunter. In an attempt to save their companion, other hunters attack the lion; one leans forward to fit an arrow to his bow (revealing his right shoulder in profile and the quiver on his back, details not shown in standard aspect). Apparently the rescuers are successful. At the bottom of the palette, the lion has been pierced with six arrows: He is shown "upside down," his head dropping forward in defeat or death. In the central band, otherwise unusable blanks of space are filled with small figures of a running dog and a fleeing rabbit. One

Figure 6.10. The Hunter's
Palette. Slate Palette
Carved with a Lion Hunt
and Wild Animal Chase,
Said to Be from Abydos,
Late Predynastic Period
(Nagada IIIa). Courtesy
British Museum.

147

of the hunters in the file lunges forward with a lasso to rope
in a stumbling gazelle cornered by a leaping dog while, behind, another hunter (standing where the palette is now broken) seems to jump forward as well. The group is brilliantly
but unconventionally inserted into the overall plan of the
action, for it violates the frieze of human figures by opening
it out into a differently conceived spatial field. The sculptor
combines and experiments with a variety of procedures developed in other contexts and reapplied here in a novel narrative presentation.

In his interpretation of the palette, Tefnin (1979a: 221–9)
de-emphasizes narrative elements in favor of a "structural"
reading. He sees the palette as an analysis of two modes of
hunting, "la chasse à l'herbivore, alimentaire et sans danger,
et la chasse au lion, rituelle et dangereuse, donc socialement
valorisée" (1979a: 229). Certainly the sculptor is "articulating
and combining" various elements or aspects of his knowledge
of hunting; in fact, my description in the previous paragraph
is quite consonant with Tefnin's in showing that the sculptor
distinguished these elements by employing different modes
of presentation. It also seems that the play with different
modes constitutes a metaphorics in which the "given" roles
of animals and human beings in the hunt are rhetorically
equated: The group of hunter lassoing gazelle and the group
of lion mauling hunter are clearly meant to be perceived
together or at least in relation to each other – for the sculptor
neatly interpenetrates the two groups and adds the small figures of rabbit and dog below in order to create a large "triangle" of forms echoing, as it were, the triangle of the palette's base. The hunter's capture of the gazelle has its equivalent in the lion's attack on the hunter: human success
matched with human defeat. On the Manchester ostrich palette (Figure 6.8b) and the Oxford Palette (Figure 6.9), both
slightly earlier than or roughly contemporary with the Hunter's Palette, human beings exist in the animal world not as
hunters taking control of that world but as celebrants or even
as semianimal themselves. On the Hunter's Palette – the metaphorics of which must be understood in part in relation to
these other works – human beings have left the animal world
and are arranged in neat rows, still echoing, I suspect, the
rows of animals on contemporary ivory combs (Figure 6.5a)
(there is some equivalence between the king's kine and the
king's army): They now confront the animal world as that
which might still defeat human authority but must be mastered. The lasso snaking out from the file of hunters is the

very groundline of canonical representation appearing and beginning to take possession of the world of the represent-able, while that world, in the figure of the lion, still threatens violence to the repetitive regularity of human order as it tears individual figures from the groundline and spins them into irregular places. As a work translating the representational universe of the Oxford Palette into that of the Narmer Palette, the Hunter's Palette figures the very arrival of canonical representation in a world that it had yet completely to dominate.

The less completely preserved Battlefield Palette (Figure 6.11), is iconographically almost canonical, although in using

Figure 6.11. The Battlefield Palette. Slate Palette Carved with the Scene of a Triumphant Lion on the Battlefield, Prisoners and Officials, Early First Dynasty. Courtesy British Museum.

a pair of mirror-identical giraffes flanking a tree on the reverse of the work the sculptor may be evoking the heraldic animals of the hunt series. No archaeological date for the work is available; on various technical and stylistic grounds it is to be assigned to the early First Dynasty, in the time of Narmer (Asselberghs, 1961: Figs. 151–4; Harris, 1960; H. W. Müller, 1959; Petrie, 1953: Pl. E (14); A. J. Spencer, 1980: No. 576). The palette evidently depicts a royal victory, with the lion metaphorically representing the king; like Narmer smiting, he is shown in a central part of the composition in large scale, mauling a fallen enemy chieftain while other enemies flee or lie slain on the battlefield (as we have already seen, the motif of fallen enemies can be divided from the victory/smiting scene and has its own independent life in works like the statue bases of Khasekhemuwy, Figure 6.19). Above this part of the composition, on either side of the cosmetic saucer, royal standards and an official in a long robe march off with bound enemy prisoners; above this, at the top of the palette, was apparently another scene of battle or of the battlefield.

Presumably the lion's strength and power made him an appropriate symbol of royalty, and it is quite likely that earlier artists had already made some kind of association, apparently falling short of substitutive equivalence, in our sense (see Chapter 4), between chiefly or royal authority and the great beast. On an incense burner from Cemetery L at Qustul, the lion appears in a composition with proto-pharaonic connotations; it is possible that here the lion depicts the "pharaoh," who actually appears elsewhere in the sequence of images (B. Williams, 1986: 138–45, Figs. 54–6, Pl. 34). In the painting in Tomb 100 at Hierakonpolis and on the knife handle from Gebel el-Arak (Figure 6.6), lions are mastered by a Master of Animals figure (= the chief or king?) and therefore again, as on the Hunter's Palette, stand for some kind of power or authority outside or apart from that of the king; however, it is perhaps as the king's animal favorite that the lion became a metaphor for the king's person and power itself some time in the Nagada III/early First Dynasty. Now it is obvious that the Battlefield sculptor was well aware of earlier depictions of the lion. In the treatment of muzzle, tail, legs and claws ("comb"-clawed), and other details, his lion is almost exactly the same lion that we saw on the Hunter's Palette, produced at least a generation earlier. Although there the lion's fearsome strength was equally important in the metaphorics of the image, the subject of that image was the lion's defeat at the hands of heroic human hunters, perhaps members of the

king's army, who aid their downed companion. Extermi-
nating a fearsome beast or undertaking this dangerous sport
may have been a socially valorized action expected of leaders,
as Tefnin has stressed (1979a: 221–9); perhaps the lion even
symbolized a Lower Egyptian population, as the shrine emblem immediately above him implies. Whatever his particular
connotation might be, at the very least it is quite different
from what he has come to mean on the Battlefield Palette.
In this striking example of iconographic disjunction, at minimum the later artist reverses the valence of the earlier's image: Where on the Hunter's Palette the lion was to be
subdued, now it is to be admired. Perhaps where earlier the
lion was a power outside human authority to be conquered
by that authority, now the lion's natural strength has been
utterly assimilated into the total strength of the king; in other
words, the king's strength has been extended to include natural and cosmic powers. In the metaphorics of the Hunter's
Palette, society (the Upper Egyptian army/hunters) subdues
an aspect of unruly nature; but on the Battlefield Palette, the
king's human power has been naturalized and subdues an
aspect of unruly society. It is typical of state ideology, apparently now in the time of Narmer fully in place, that its
power should be represented as naturally derived and as un-
challengeable: Note that the Battlefield sculptor utterly drops
the Hunter's recognition that both sides lose something before any final victories are had.

The disjunction to be seen between the Oxford, Hunter's,
and Battlefield Palettes (see also and compare Finkenstaedt,
1984) does not imply discontinuity. The rhetoric of the state
requires and reuses the established metaphorics of earlier society to secure its own meanings. The system of canonical
representation, of course, was only strong in relation to the
possibility of other systems, other orders, which it must incorporate and then supersede.

Although iconographically canonical, the Battlefield Palette should be distinguished technically from the Narmer
Palette.[16] The sculptor disposes his figures in the field according to a birds'-eye view of the relative orientation of
baselines, without including groundlines. Furthermore, he
produces a good deal of interior modeling of the forms; the
outline contour of each figure has been elaborated with many
minute, rounded details of anatomy: Incised or sculpturally
picked-out lines depict feathers, hair, eyebrows, claws, leg
muscles, and so forth. Even more important, in the use of
overlaps between figures and the cutting of figure contours,

the sculptor has begun to dissolve the distinction between figure and background. On the Hunter's Palette, as on all of the hunt palettes, the sculptor first sketched his design on the surface, then cut down and around outside the outline of the figures, which were modeled only slightly. Finally he removed the negative area, leaving a characteristic depression where he had first cut in around the outline of each figure and the "flat" raised block of the figure itself, upon which he then incised or "sculpted" a few details. The depression around the figures has been greatly reduced on the Battlefield Palette and the raised figures are not "flat." In other words, after the figures were sketched on the surface, all the negative matter was immediately removed. The trace of the incision was removed in this stage or else in the next, where the remaining raised blocks were worked and the outline contour itself modeled. In this extra deepening of the relief and grading of the contour, the sculptor manipulates several planes of relief and a play of light and shadow at the contours. For the first time, figures in relief are actually conceived three-dimensionally rather than as "flat" drawings set against a flat surface. Although only incipient on the Battlefield Palette, this realization matured brilliantly in what can only be regarded as a later work by the same sculptor, the Bull Palette fragment in the Louvre (see Figure 4.11), in which the sculptor's virtuosity with illusion is on full display.

Despite the Battlefield sculptor's fine workmanship, other sculptors did not follow his technique. Interior modeling was extensively used on the Narmer Palette and carved mace heads, but always as "drawing in stone" (see Chapter 2); outlines are sharp edges, not graded contours. The animation of light and shadow playing on a volumetrically realized form, the constitution of multiple planes of relief, and the appearance of space around the figures rather than as flat background, or, in brief, illusionistic effects, were avoided. The canonical drawing pushed less in the direction of a three-dimensional image and more in the direction of a two-dimensional hieroglyph. We can feel the force of the lion's power as his claw bites into the enemy's flesh on the Battlefield Palette or of the bull's strength as he crushes the enemy's leg on the Bull Palette: These are highly vivid details with the not-so-subtle effect of heightening the realism of the scene as a whole. Once such a realistic anatomical or atmospheric effect is secured, it inherently implicates all figures in the composition: The Battlefield Palette's lion or the Bull Palette's bull must be particular real creatures in order to have particular real effects in the space and time of the composition. But it is precisely this degree of spatiotemporal specificity, of mundane reality, that canonical representation of paramount authorities wishes to avoid. On the Narmer Palette (Figure 6.14), then, the bull's hoof trampling an enemy (on the bottom of the obverse) does no apparent damage, and the king's forward leg passes completely in front of his enemy (in the main scene) because the palette is no longer interested in the ordinary viciousness of an actual battlefield, but rather in the transcendent appearance of the king in and for a history that now exists apart from and below or behind him.[17]

Various factors may account for the range of technical, stylistic, and iconographic variability even among contemporary works (such as the Oxford and Hunter's or Battlefield and Narmer Palettes). A unilinear evolution in style from an earlier to a later mode of representation does not offer an adequate account; as we have seen, two major groups of palettes are at least for a period of time contemporary with one another, and some works like the Battlefield Palette, although chronologically late in the whole sequence of palettes, vary significantly from the canonical mode of the Narmer Palette, itself to be regarded as canonical only by hindsight.

First, the functions of the different palettes may have been different. Unfortunately the four excavated palettes suggest little about the uses that this type of artifact might have had. The Min palette and the palette from Tomb 59 at Gerzeh formed part of the funerary equipment of well-to-do late predynastic graves. The Oxford and Narmer Palettes, unearthed in the Main Deposit at Hierakonpolis, do not have funerary or any original context; they seem to be votive or commemorative, like other material in this odd deposit of "holy rubbish" (B. Adams, 1975: 3). There does not seem to be any immediately obvious connection between the medicinal, aesthetic, or religious uses of cosmetic itself and the representational programs of the cosmetic palettes (Baumgartel, 1960: 81–105 reviews the question of function at length), although the cosmetic saucer plays an important role in the composition of the various depictions on all of the palettes. Insofar as the interests of the patrons who commissioned the works may have been quite individual, we could say that each palette had its own idiosyncratic function; but without archaeological contexts these interests must be inferred from the designs and not from independent knowledge of production. In fact, despite stylistic and iconographic differences among the several palettes, it is likely that all carved palettes served roughly the same representational and "ceremonial" functions, whatever these might have been.

Second, the sculptors of the various palettes may have had slightly or greatly different backgrounds as artists. For example, there is a strong possibility that the Battlefield/Bull sculptor had some experience or interest in the cutting, smoothing, and finishing of hard-stone vessels. Many of these, such as the "Hathor Bowl" (Arkell, 1955), various theriomorphic vessels (Desroches-Noblecourt, 1979; Glanville, 1926; Müller, 1970: Pl. 10a), the fine series of sculpturally worked vessels assigned approximately to the reign of Den (Fischer, 1972: 10), and the disc of Hemaka depicting vignettes of the animals' chase (see Figure 4.4) (Altenmüller, 1974), attained a fully sculptural effect. Other palette sculptors seem to have had the more usual experience of working in ivory; ivory relief carving of the early dynasties exhibits the characteristic outline depression around internally flat figures.[18] Whereas ivory was worked with copper tools, hard-stone vessels were worked with stone tools, using chert or quartz sand as an abrasive; with abrasives, one could grade or round out the hard-edge outlines produced by cutting tools (Lucas, 1962: 50–74). Vase workers were apparently a separate group of craftsmen, even in the early period, and probably one of the most well defined communities of workmen; they produced literally tens of thousands of finely finished alabaster and porphyritic vessels on commission from the artisan class, the nobility, and the king. Occasionally a great master of the craft might have tried his hand at representational relief sculpture;[19] at the least, the unusual palettes seem to reflect the three-dimensional interests of this craft in producing a graded outline, high finish, and multiplicity of planes. I do not wish to draw too fine a distinction between relief in ivory and the working of stone vases. Although by the First Dynasty each craft was highly evolved, all kinds of craftsmen seem to have been concentrated at the centers of court and cult and they must have shared ideas and techniques. Moreover, both pre- or noncanonical and canonical or "pharaonic" iconographies are relatively constant in their various applications in the media of wood, ivory, and stone and for objects as different as incense burners, storage or transport labels, palettes, combs, sealings, and knife handles.

Third, at least some proportion of variability in early relief work must be a product of regional differences. For the group of hunt palettes, generally treated as an earlier group in the sequence of palettes, some commentators have attempted to identify a specifically Eastern Delta subgroup (see Fischer, 1958; Ranke, 1925, for discussion, examples, and references). At least part of the argument hinges on the technical and iconographic distinctiveness of these works vis-à-vis the unification group; no archaeological contexts support the suggestion. Although a strong case has been made for the Nubian origin of some elements of pharaonic iconography (for the incense burner from Cemetery L at Qustul, see B. Williams, 1986; Williams and Logan, 1987), on balance the evidence suggests that the core motifs of canonical iconography, such as the victory/smiting scene, developed in chieftains' centers of residence in Upper Egypt, preeminently Hierakonpolis. Here the painting in Tomb 100 and the objects from the Main Deposit document the earlier and the later, perhaps commemorative phases of the formation of the canonical mode of representation. It is important to note that these centers also presumably supported the production of pre- or non-canonical works, like the Oxford Palette (deposited in the Main Deposit) and the Hunter's Palette, closely similar in small details to the Oxford Palette and probably made in the same place (despite its having been given to the Eastern Delta group in some analyses). In my opinion, it is unthinkable that the makers of works like the Narmer and Battlefield Palettes were unaware of earlier works like the Oxford and Hunter's Palettes. As we have seen, these works are all linked, albeit disjunctively, in a developing metaphorics of canonical representation for the emerging dynastic state, and the state artists required the viewer's familiarity with the other objects in order to make their points vividly. The fragments of other palettes that happen to survive, not discussed here (e.g., Needler, 1984: No. 266), suggest that the Upper Egyptian synthesis was a rich and complex one.

Unfortunately our archaeological documentation is not adequate to any demonstration that work produced further from the Upper Egyptian chiefly, and later courtly, centers was more variable or less canonical. Whether made completely outside Upper Egypt or not, it is at least possible to see that some iconographically canonical works were made by producers distinct from those who made either the Battlefield/Bull or the Narmer Palettes. As they are generally cruder, they may have been made by an emerging school newly learning canonical procedures, implying, in turn, that they document the translation of central Upper Egyptian techniques to another site of manufacture. For example, in its depiction of what appear to be small prisoners driven by a larger, official figure, the so-called Beirut Palette (Figure 6.12) is iconographically canonical but quite distinctive stylistically. Despite the evenness of the negative surface, a marked depression surrounds each figure. Some interior modeling has been attempted, particularly for the calf muscles of the figures and the planes of the foreface. The arms remain flat; apart from an abbreviated differentiation of fingers and thumb, no interior detail of the hand appears. Elementary incisions indicate the striations of the braids or the divisions of the penis sheath. The eye is emphasized by carefully isolating three raised elements, the eyebrow, the upper lid, and the lower lid. Between the two eyelids the eye itself appears not as a hollow (as is usual in earlier late predynastic relief), but as a round, central, "pea"-like pupil. The nose is somewhat bulbous. Unlike the tapering feet on the Battlefield Palette, the feet here are blocklike.

The "pea" eye makes a few appearances in late predynastic and early dynastic relief. Two carved mace heads employ pupils possibly of this kind (Asselberghs, 1961: Figs. 172–80), but the parallels are not compelling. The Beirut Palette has its closest affinities with less accomplished early dynastic works, especially a fragmentary slate palette with a single figure of a warrior now in the Metropolitan Museum of Art (Figure 6.13a), where the style of the hair, eye and eyebrow, bulbous nose, and beard are very similar

Figure 6.12. The Beirut Palette. Fragment of a Slate Palette Carved with a Scene of Prisoners and Officials, Early First Dynasty. Courtesy the Louvre, Paris.

to that of the Beirut figures (Hayes, 1953: I, 29). The figures on both works may be non-Egyptian; possibly Western Asiatics or Libyans (?) (Ward, 1963: 5–6), are depicted. The Metropolitan figure is livelier and the sculptural treatment more three-dimensional; in several details, the Metropolitan sculptor has considered his subject more carefully. These fragments seem to be products of a school also represented by a dark-green schist palette in Cairo, with a smaller joining fragment in the Brooklyn Museum (Figure 6.13*b*) (Bothmer, 1969–70; Needler, 1984: No. 266; von Bissing, 1930). Here the eyes appear with carefully distinguished eyebrow and upper and lower lids and ap-

a.

b.

c.

Figure 6.13. *a.* Fragment of a Slate Palette Carved with a Figure of a Warrior, Said to Be from the Eastern Delta, Early First Dynasty. Courtesy Metropolitan Museum of Art.
b. Fragment of a Slate Palette ("Cairo-Brooklyn Palette") Carved with a Scene of Prisoners and Officials, with the King's Attendant (?) in Ritual Activity (?), Early First Dynasty. Courtesy Brooklyn Museum.
c. Fragment of a Hardstone Vase Carved with the Figure of a Warrior, Early First Dynasty. Courtesy Egyptian Museum, East Berlin.

parently with the eye picked out as a small "pea"-like pupil. The feet are blocklike. The musculature of the figures is sketchily suggested by the same kind of summary incising we find on the Beirut Palette. Some of the men in this composition wear knee-length gowns or kilts; others appear to be naked except for a belt with two hanging loincloths (or penis sheaths). Finally, a fragment of a late predynastic or early dynastic stone vase now in East Berlin (Figure 6.13c) bears a relief of a warrior very similar in treatment to that of the figures on the Beirut Palette, although here his position seems to be reversed, for he carries an ax and drives a prisoner before him (only one arm of this other figure is preserved).

We cannot prove archaeologically that the Beirut, Metropolitan, Cairo-Brooklyn, and Berlin fragments are by the same hand, although on visual evidence an attribution to one school or workshop would not be farfetched. On the basis of generalized similarities with Upper Egyptian work, the group, coherent in itself, could be Upper Egyptian, but we must reserve the option of giving it to the north of Egypt as an example of the penetration of the canonical style, a process to be considered in more detail later in this chapter. In this context I simply want to provide a fairly straightforward example of regional stylistic specialization.

Despite the significance of the different trainings and residences of sculptors responsible for the various works we have reviewed, probably the single most important factor in accounting for variability in the corpus is simply the fact that they worked in and with different modes of representation defined, only by hindsight, as canonical or not. With the Battlefield Palette, we encounter a work that closely approaches the canonical, but as we have already seen it, and its immediate precursors in the Hunter's and Oxford Palettes, remains disjunct from the canonical tradition as such. It is probably best regarded as a sophisticated expression of the late prehistoric tradition of representation. Although many of its elements were available and had long been available as individual motifs, the canonical tradition had not yet fully emerged on the Battlefield Palette; it appeared somewhat later in the few works utilizing the full canonical system as such, to be considered momentarily. Strictly speaking, then, variability in the corpus of early relief is merely a way of saying that at least by the early First Dynasty the tradition of invariance had not yet clearly established its predominance: And our question is not just to explain variability but also to account for the rise of invariance in the face of an existing range of possibilities.

THE NATIONALIZATION OF THE CANONICAL MODE IN EARLY DYNASTIC RELIEF SCULPTURE

As we have seen, the canonical mode of representation does not constitute the single sculptural procedure of the late pre-dynastic and early dynastic period. I turn now to its initial appearance and growth as such; in comparison with earlier and contemporary productions related to one another in complex stylistic and iconographic disjunctions, the development of the canonical mode of representation is quite straightforward. Once system as such had been achieved, it was maintained invariantly. During the early dynastic period, the system became increasingly popular, spreading from Upper Egypt in the Nagada III/early First Dynasty to the whole of Egypt by the beginning of the Third.

Our point of reference, of course, must be the locus classicus of canonical Egyptian art, the great carved palette of Narmer (Figure 6.14), often selected to represent late predynastic and early dynastic Egyptian art and indeed the origins of Egyptian art as such (e.g., Aldred, 1980: 33). Despite its importance for the history of Egyptian art, it would be misleading to credit Narmer's artist with great technical or stylistic innovation. He does not set himself difficult problems and does not resolve them with anything resembling the virtuosity of the Battlefield sculptor. Rather than being a revolutionary statement of hitherto unknown principles, the Narmer Palette consolidates widely understood techniques, remaining faithful to the tradition of decoration inaugurated in the simple incision of early rhomboid slates; decoration is applied to the background and does not emerge from it, as on the Battlefield or Bull Palettes. Although complex in comparison to what had been attempted in predynastic art, the narrative conception is not necessarily more sophisticated than the narrative on the Battlefield Palette or perhaps even on sculptures now preserved only in fragmentary form, like the Bull Palette or the Cairo-Brooklyn fragment.

In brief, the Narmer Palette is conservative and synthetic. Chiefly remarkable neither for the fineness of its technique nor the sophistication of its conception – there are important competitors here – the palette is significant for the consistency of its procedures. From cutting the individual outlines of

159

separate figures to the general organization of his several subjects, the sculptor systematically selects methods for securing
clarity, balance, symmetry, hierarchy, proportional harmony, and intelligible structure (see excellent formal discussions in Aldred, 1980: 33–6; Groenewegen-Frankfort, 1951:
20–1; Meyer, 1974; Schäfer, 1974: passim; Smith, 1949: 113,
126–30, 1981: 34–5). Although many of these elements had
had earlier expressions in Nagada I and later Egyptian art,
their full mutual coordination appears only on the Narmer
Palette, where ideal proportioning of the canonical type
(Meyer, 1974), hieratic scale, hieroglyphic labeling, and so
forth are all used simultaneously. It is crucial to stress the
significance of system as such: This is the first work preserved
to us in the art-historical record which can be correctly de-

Figure 6.14. The Narmer
Palette, obverse and re-
verse, from the Main De-
posit, Hierakonpolis, Early
First Dynasty. Courtesy
Cairo Museum.

scribed according to the canonical rules (see Chapters 2, 3, 4). Representational practice has here achieved an unprecedented degree of legibility, maneuverability, and repeatability; a measure of the conventionalization of the motif, as we have already seen (see Chapter 4), is its invariant repetition in the victory iconography of later kings (e.g., see Figures 4.1, 4.2*a*, *b*, 4.3). The selectivity of Narmer's artist is clearly apparent. I believe we should presume him to have known of the realistic effects obtained by the Battlefield/Bull sculptor; but he himself does not seek out such effects. Or again, a complex hunting and animal imagery, just possibly to be associated with the representation of social authority as late as the Nagada IIIa/b (Tomb 100 at Hierakonpolis, Oxford Palette, Hunter's Palette, and so forth), here drops out of

sight; the artist focuses principally on the figure of the king himself.

We do not yet understand completely why these particular forms, rather than the other technically, conceptually, and socially possible procedures put to use by some competitors, were brought together by Narmer's artist in this way and accepted as exemplary by later practitioners. More must be said about the meaning of the canonical image – about what it was supposed to represent – in order to see why its users might have adopted it (see Chapter 7); and since we have no independent evidence about the canonical "theory of images," we have no choice but to risk the circularity of "reading off" its rationale from the palette itself and the works affiliated with it. The existence of related works does, at least, allow us to develop a specifically archaeological point, namely, that this mode of representation was apparently associated with a relatively well defined group of elite or royal patrons in the early and historical First Dynasty who evidently shared a set of distinctive interests. The point can be confirmed by examining other early canonical material and its dissemination in direct correlation with the nationalization of elite Upper Egyptian authority.

Three carved mace heads from the early First Dynasty are convincingly associated with the Narmer Palette:[20] on the mace head of King Scorpion (Figure 6.15) and the other works, registers organize composition, hieroglyphic labels name the king, and the forms are cut flat with hard-edge outlines and exposed in aspective view in largely canonical proportions. These objects are large – the largest is nearly ten inches high – and apparently therefore ceremonial in function, probably commemorating the kings' great deeds, particularly the *Heb-sed*, the royal jubilee, and irrigation or foundation rituals connected with early canals or shrines. They were probably produced at the same time and in the same place as the Narmer Palette. The mace head of King Scorpion (Figure 6.15) was perhaps the product of the same master sculptor's hand as the great palette itself. The disjunction between this and earlier images of the human place in nature such as the Manchester ostrich palette or the Oxford Palette (Figures 6.8*b*, 6.9) could not be more marked: On the King Scorpion mace head, the king is depicted as taking possession of and working nature, in this case the irrigated fields, in order to build one of the canals or dikes that will make human settlement there possible and productive. In the main image, he wields the adze – used elsewhere in early canonical iconography as the weapon with which resisting enemy towns are subdued – to cut a canal, while a bearer in front carries off the dirt and fan bearers behind shade him from the sun; below and to the right, his sacred bark sails down the river past a palisade or cultivated plot apparently inhabited by enemies he has subdued; other scenes of jubilating female dancers and of procession complement the theme of royal success. The main image (Figure 6.15) is a beautifully composed network of horizontals, verticals, and diagonals. As the somewhat awkward arrangement of the

Figure 6.15. Detail of the Limestone Mace Head of So-Called King Scorpion with a Scene of the Cutting of a Canal by the King, from the Main Deposit, Hierakonpolis, Early First Dynasty. Courtesy Ashmolean Museum, Oxford University.

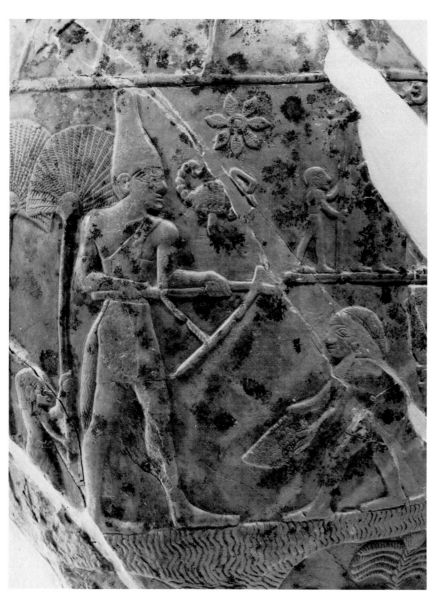

king's two arms, particularly forearms and hands, implies, the artist has sought to have the main handle of the adze remain exactly parallel with the groundline; and indeed it is the groundline which the king wields here – produced by him from the land of Egypt and that which supports the retainers in front of him bearing his standards. It is the king who makes the very order that canonical representation finds in the world.

Although lacking figuration, the royal stelae of the First Dynasty should also be regarded as among the earliest canonical works. What seems to be the earliest royal tomb stela is too poorly preserved for us to assess its significance.[21] For our purposes, the sequence of canonical stelae begins with the round-topped limestone stela of Djer, now in the Cairo Museum (Fischer, 1961: 53, no. 2, Pl. 6), followed by the stela of Djet, now in the Louvre (Figure 6.16), both from Abydos (Bénédite, 1905; Vandier, 1952: 725–6). The succeeding royal stelae from Abydos – those of Den, Merneit, Semerkhet, and two further early kings (Bénédite, 1905: Fig. 3; Fischer, 1961: Pl. 5; Quibell, 1902–4: CG 14632–3; Vandier, 1952: Figs. 484–5) – are far less accomplished but, like the two earlier specimens, with one exception all present the royal name in *serekh* surmounted by the royal falcon. The two best specimens of Djer and Djet substantially raise the figures from the background surface. As on the Narmer Palette or King Scorpion mace head, some internal modeling of the forms has been attempted, and many details are clearly picked out; the remaining surfaces are treated in broad, smooth, flat planes. The extremely high relief of the best specimens allows the sculptor to cut back the outline to some extent; nevertheless, like Narmer's sculptor, he does not pursue the possibility of a deep sculptural relief.

An intriguing feature of the First Dynasty stelae is the raised border around the carved elements; with no evident architectural or iconographic purpose, it was apparently adopted purely for the effect of heightening contrast between figure and ground. Perhaps the technique, in turn, suggested using a grid to position forms in relation to the frame and to proportion them exactly in relation to one another, for the whole design was certainly conceived as a bounded unity and carefully plotted (see further Iversen, 1975: 65–6). The raised border appears on none of the more than 150 stelae of private persons of the first two dynasties recovered at Abydos (Amélineau, 1899; Petrie, 1900–1: I, Pls. 31–6, II, Pls. 26–30; Vandier, 1952: 731–5). Even on the better examples, hieroglyphs are only roughly centered in relation to the rather irregular edges of the stone. It seems likely, then, that the raised border in royal works was an effort at special refinement, of elegantly emphasizing the royal name. The proportional canon and the characteristic canonical procedures of centering were apparently developed specifically for royal imagery and monuments (like the Narmer Palette and tomb stelae) produced in the south of Egypt throughout the First Dynasty. We do not

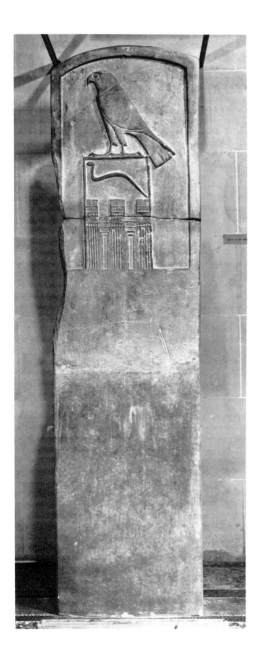

Figure 6.16. Limestone Stela Carved with the *Serekh* of King Djet, from Abydos, First Dynasty. Courtesy the Louvre, Paris.

know exactly what symbolic value the proportional canon(s) may have had but, as the imagery of the Narmer Palette and King Scorpion mace head implies, the king was believed to be one of the sources and guarantors of proper order, perhaps exemplified by proportional perfection.[22]

Scattered material from Sakkara indicates that relief sculpture was produced in the north of Egypt as well. The stela of the official Merka (Figure 6.17) of the mid-First Dynasty, found near the grave below the sixth north niche at Tomb 3505 at Sakkara, has been said to link the royal Abydene round-topped stelae, like those of Djer and Djet, with the later rectangular slab stelae from the Memphite tomb fields in the early Old Kingdom.[23] Since the stela of Merka is exactly contemporary with the royal stelae of the First Dynasty, it does not temporally bridge the gap between early Abydene work and the later stelae. Indeed, typologically it has an entirely different format from the round-topped royal stelae; in its rough carving and awkward composition, it seems closer to the private name stelae discovered by Amélineau and Petrie. Merka's sculptor used a bluntly triangular pillar of limestone and prepared a rectangular raised surface on the

Figure 6.17. Limestone Relief-Carved Tomb Stela of Merka, from Tomb 3505 at Sakkara, First Dynasty. After Emery, 1958: Pl. 39.

smoothest face. At the bottom of the prepared surface, Merka is shown at the left, seated on a low cushioned stool, wearing a long robe and carrying the official staff in his right hand. A groundline is carved beneath him. His name and titles are given in three registers of hieroglyphs above and in front of the figure; an obscure group of signs below the chair refers to the "souls of Buto," a Lower Egyptian town, and the king of Lower Egypt. The entire surface was once painted, a feature consistent with the extremely flat quality of the sculpted forms. These were hammered out in silhouette and the surface actually smoothed flat with hammer or stoneworker's adze rather than incised with details or slightly modeled in interior relief. The chisel was used only sparingly to cut straighter lines (see also Emery, 1958: 84, no. 2, Pl. 96).

The very earliest of the Memphite slab stelae are related to the stela of Merka and Abydene private name stelae. These "primitive niche stones," also prepared for private patrons, were made throughout the Third and Fourth Dynasty (Vandier, 1952: 752–65) and showed the deceased, usually seated at an offering table, with name and titles and lists of goods. The origins of this format seem to be specifically Memphite. Although over a dozen of the slab stelae are thought to date to the Third Dynasty, only one can be assigned with certainty to the late Second Dynasty, the slab stela of Princess Sehenefer from the Archaic Cemetery at Sakkara (Figure 6.18) (Smith, 1949: 142–3, and see Quibell, 1923: Pls. 26–8, for this and two similar stelae, possibly also early). The tablet has been divided into three equal compartments of which only one has

Figure 6.18. Limestone Relief-Carved Tomb Stela (Niche Stone) of Princess Sehenefer, from Her Mastaba Tomb at Sakkara, Second Dynasty. Courtesy Cairo Museum.

any figurative detail, the princess seated on a low, wooden, cushioned throne facing the offering table with its six loaves. Like Merka, the princess' head is much larger proportionally than is usual later and than was established in the canon used on the Narmer Palette; the eye is large and the nose long and, as in the face of Merka, the mouth is placed close to the nose and the chin close to the mouth. Body, arms, and legs are all slender. Later relief sculptors of the seated figure normally divide the legs to show both feet planted on the groundline (rule of fixity); Sehenefer's sculptor adheres to a literal-minded, or less differentiated, interpretation of the profile view of the legs and does not separate them.

The stela of Merka and the earliest Memphite slab stelae of the Second Dynasty, like the tablet of Sehenefer, are technically and morphologically different from the canonical work produced at Abydos in the Second Dynasty.[24] Apparently the two traditions were substantially separate until the early Third Dynasty.

In the south at the end of the Second Dynasty, specifically at Hierakonpolis, material from the reign of King Khasekhemuwy demonstrates that elaborate sculptural programs were undertaken in the mode first explored on the Narmer Palette. Upper Egyptian canonical work of this date includes the reliefs from the statue bases of Khasekhemuwy (Figure 6.19), showing contorted fallen enemies in the manner of similar figures on the Battlefield and Narmer Palettes, the doorjamb reliefs and fragmentary stelae of Khasekhemuwy from Hierakonpolis, and possibly related material from el-Kab across the river from that town.[25] These works seem to have had public architectural settings in temples or palace buildings. As on the Narmer Palette, forms are not substantially raised from the surface but nonetheless have been delicately modeled

Figure 6.19. Incised Reliefs of Crushed Enemies, from the Bases of Statues of King Khasekhemuwy, Relief and Line Drawing, Second Dynasty (See Figure 6.34). After Smith, 1981: Fig 35.

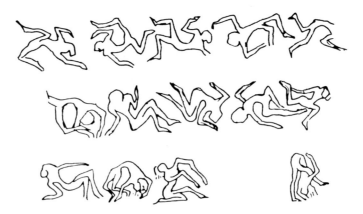

to indicate features like the tendons and musculature of the calf and the cavity of the sternum. The best preserved of the surviving works of this period is one of two reliefs from the Hathor Temple at Gebelein, now in Turin (Figure 6.20), showing the king, a prince, and a sandal bearer as well as other undecipherable figures (Curto, 1953; Scamuzzi, 1965: Pl. 8). Grasping four arrows, the king is represented engaged in a ritual action, perhaps related to the ritual sailing documented in the fragmentary lower register. The relief exhibits canonical compositional preferences for an evenly spaced arrangement of figures on neat groundlines; a grid was probably used to achieve this orderliness.

Like these technically accomplished, compositionally bal-

Figure 6.20. Limestone Relief-Carved Stela with the Scene of a King or Prince in Victory, from the Hathor Temple, Gebelein, Second Dynasty. Courtesy Egyptian Museum, Turin.

Like these technically accomplished, compositionally balanced, detailed representations from Upper Egyptian royal or public contexts, the Memphite work of Djoser's relief sculptors and Hesire's wood-carver (see Figures 2.1, 3.3) from the early years of the Third Dynasty are fully canonical in the treatment of figures, proportions, and composition (Smith, 1981: 53–69 for descriptions). They develop directly from Narmer's Palette, the Hathor reliefs from Gebelein, and related Upper Egyptian material. Evidently they reflect the arrival of Upper Egyptian sculptors at Memphis and Sakkara, where sculptors working for the official Merka and others had been only barely acquainted with canonical procedures, and the importation of the classic canonical mode, now well established in the south, to the north of Egypt at the beginning of the Third Dynasty.[26]

The penetration of the Upper Egyptian style might have been associated with contemporary political events. The reigns of Peribsen and Khasekhemuwy at the end of the Second Dynasty were apparently troubled by unrest in the north (Edwards, 1971: 31–5). Peribsen introduced the cult of Seth to the Northeastern Delta, and royal relations with Syria-Palestine further to the east were possibly reestablished after a period of slack (e.g., Montet, 1928–9: 84, Fig. 1). In Canaan during the Early Bronze IIIa, Egyptian activity at the town of Ai (Level VI) and elsewhere was seemingly intense, possibly implying some political relationship and certainly strong economic ties during the transition to the Third Dynasty (Callaway, 1972: 247–8). The Abydene royal cemetery was abandoned; at the opening of the Third Dynasty, Djoser built his great pyramid complex in the north; Heliopolis asserted itself as the chief religious center of Egypt (Smith, 1971). All of these and other developments imply a shift in the location of the royal court and administrative apparatus from its ancient home at Hierakonpolis or Abydos (Thinis) to the Memphite area. It makes sense to suppose that at this time too a specifically Upper Egyptian style was transplanted to the north, effectively becoming the national canonical style of Egypt.

All individual conventions of the canonical mode did not make an appearance as early as the end of the Second Dynasty. The greatly elongated forms of the earliest flat relief (Figure 6.20), for instance, were replaced at the beginning of the Third Dynasty by more substantial forms, with greater control over contour grading and internal modeling in the best examples, like the reliefs of Hesire (Quibell, 1913: Pls. 29–31). Sophisticated compositional harmony embodying the

interrelated canonical rules and possibly conforming to proportional harmonics (see Chapters 2, 3) was an achievement
of the high Old Kingdom. Fourth Dynasty sculptors developed a bolder relief technique, elaborating further the contrast
between figure and ground. Experimentation continued: To
take one example, the decorated tomb of Meresankh III at
Giza from the end of the Fourth Dynasty (Dunham and Simpson, 1974) contains several noncanonical figures and groupings and seems to experiment, as Smith notes (1965: 139),
with various means of arranging figures on the surface of the
wall.

Nevertheless, all of these later developments took place
within the canonical framework. The principal canonical formulations of components, proportions, aspect, and composition all made an appearance in the early dynastic period and
were synthesized in a system on the Narmer Palette, royal
stelae, and other Upper Egyptian monuments at Gebelein
and elsewhere. Canonical art emerged through the selection
and further regularization of some but not all procedures from
the past and from a range of contemporary alternatives. By
the Third Dynasty, competing traditions or experiments
mostly dropped utterly from sight or were thoroughly assimilated in canonical formats, the outermost limits of which
were only to be approached in occasional episodes of genu-
inely "avant-garde" negation or reversal (see Chapter 4),
themselves never to be replicated as part of the tradition.

VARIABILITY IN MONUMENTAL SCULPTURE OF THE EARLY DYNASTIC PERIOD

Much of what can be determined about the development of
canonical relief sculpture applies to monumental, freestanding
sculpture as well. A small number of monumental productions can be dated to the late predynastic period/early First
Dynasty or to the historical First and Second Dynasty. Although this material is quite heterogeneous, many formulas
and techniques that would later be defined as canonical necessarily appear in it. The canonical synthesis of these procedures was a distinctive occurrence, in this case, the
discovery of a means of extracting the freestanding figure
from a squared-off block of quarried stone. I will first review
the pre- or noncanonical sculptural production of the early
dynastic period, the context within which the canonical se-
lections were made.

Generally identified as the god Min, the three over-life-size standing ithyphallic figures found at Koptos (Figure 6.21) exemplify the problems in evaluating pre- or noncanonical production. The technique of shaping and hammering these pillars is anomalous, as are details like the doubled triangles indicating the knees. Although Smith (1949: 4, 7, 117) tentatively accepted the figures as "early" on the basis of relief carvings below the right hands, in his opinion paralleled by some predynastic carvings on slate palettes and ivory objects, Baumgartel (1948: 533–5) aptly criticized some of these parallels (although her own reattribution of the figures to the First Intermediate Period, on the basis of Mesopotamian parallels of this date, is unlikely). Opinion was equally divided about accepting or rejecting the figures as predynastic or early dynastic at all (Fischer, 1979: 737; Trigger, 1969: 66), until it was recently shown that Narmer's name can be made out in the damaged inscription on one of them (B. Williams, 1988). Now dated to the early First Dynasty, the figures are dramatic evidence of the variability of noncanonical sculpture in early Egypt; probably the colossi were placed before shrines associated with the royal cult (B. Williams, 1988),

Figure 6.21. (*left*) Ithyphallic Limestone Colossus of a Man or Divinity, One of Three "Min" Figures, from Koptos, Early First Dynasty (Time of Narmer). Courtesy Ashmolean Museum, Oxford University.

Figure 6.22. (*right*) Green Schist or Basalt Statuette of a Man, Ex-MacGregor Collection, Perhaps from Nagada, Late Predynastic Period/Early First Dynasty. Courtesy Ashmolean Museum, Oxford University.

but morphologically they are quite unlike the canonical statues that later served in such contexts.

Apart from the Min figures, no other surviving work before the Third Dynasty attains literally monumental scale. But a standing male figure in green schist or basalt from the MacGregor Collection (Figure 6.22), accepted here as a late predynastic work (adding my own inspection to Smith's persuasive comments, 1949: 7–8), is a fully monumental conception, although only a little more than fifteen inches high. The dark green stone has been worked in broad, smooth planes and cylindrical volumes; the figure is rigidly frontal and bilaterally symmetrical. The eyebrows and eyelids have been formed from raised strips of stone circling around the smooth eyes. A similar technique was used on some of the great carved palettes (Asselberghs, 1961: Figs. 171, 181, 183) and is the best evidence for the early date; later, convention isolates a very different formula for this detail.

Similar to the MacGregor statuette in the broad treatment of the planes and volumes is a statue (now missing its head) found just outside the northern gateway of the town wall at Hierakonpolis (Figure 6.23) (B. Adams, 1975: 2; Quibell and

Figure 6.23. Limestone Standing Male Figure, from Near Wall Gate, Town of Hierakonpolis, Probably First Dynasty. Courtesy Ashmolean Museum, Oxford University.

Green, 1900–1: II, 15, 16, 47, Pl. 57), probably a guardian or commemorative figure (Smith, 1949: 7). The arms are hanging down against the back plane of the figure, in a position somewhat reminiscent of the arms of captives represented on predynastic carved palettes. As the right fist is apparently pierced to hold a staff or mace, however, this figure probably represents an official, royal, or divine personage. Unlike the Min colossi or MacGregor statuette, the left leg of this figure is very slightly advanced, but the sculptor has not yet loosed the limbs from the column of stone; in this the work is characteristically precanonical.

A seated man in limestone, supposedly from the Main Deposit at Hierakonpolis (Figure 6.24), can more certainly be called a royal portrait, for he apparently wears the costume of the royal *Heb-sed* jubilee; a similar figure represents a woman, possibly also seated (B. Adams, 1974: Nos. 87–8; Smith, 1949: 8, Pl. 1d, e). Both figures are a little over twelve inches high; they are extremely crude and fragmentary, but in the summary treatment of details and the oddly spherical or cylindrical shape of the block are probably similar to both the MacGregor statuette, which is slightly larger than these, and the Hierakonpolis gateway statue. Despite their uncertain context, they are probably to be dated to the First Dynasty (Murray, 1920: 70–2).

Figure 6.24 (*left*) Limestone Seated Man in Royal Dress, Said to Be from the Main Deposit, Hierakonpolis, Probably First Dynasty. Courtesy Petrie Collection, University College, London.

Figure 6.25 (*right*) Ivory Figurine of a King in Jubilee Dress, from the Osiris Temple, Abydos, First Dynasty. Courtesy British Museum.

Petrie's early dynastic dating for the six-inch-high ivory king found in the Osiris Temple at Abydos and now in the British Museum (Figure 6.25), although possible, is not archaeologically assured (Glanville, 1931; Petrie, 1902–3: II, 23–4, Pls. 2 [3], 13; A. J. Spencer, 1980: No. 483); dating of the piece depends upon technical and stylistic considerations. Strictly speaking, this statuette of a striding king cloaked in *Sed*-festival dress belongs to the history of ivory work, but it is often associated with the origins of monumental stone sculpture in Egypt. Compared with earlier and contemporary figures in ivory, rigid and attenuated, the striding king is naturalistically modeled and proportioned, an element of canonical sculptural procedure.

Other stone works are far too fragmentary to be compared with the little Abydene king. Made before the end of the Second Dynasty, a door socket from Hierakonpolis (Figure 6.26) bears the head of a male figure (B. Adams, 1975: 52; Quibell and Green, 1900–1: I, Pl. 3, II, 6; Smith, 1949: 8); the body is the stone slab itself, into which the door pivot was inserted, although the arms of the prisoner are incised across its top. The sculpture was found in a structure that contained a symbolic deposit, possibly to be associated with the defeat of the enemy represented on the door socket. We are to think of the king himself trampling his enemy as he crossed into this chamber (compare Figure 6.35; see also Fig-

Figure 6.26. Sandstone Door Socket in the Form of a Defeated Enemy, from Hierakonpolis, Before the End of the Second Dynasty. Courtesy University Museum, University of Pennsylvania.

ure 4.11). With high cheekbones framing deep-set eyes, the face of the figure is modeled with great sensitivity, documenting increasing interest in the modification of the core through minutely detailed relief.

Finally, two limestone figures of a man and a woman now in Munich and Lucerne (Figure 6.27) (Seidel and Wildung, 1975: 217, Pl. 114) could conceivably be attributed to the First Dynasty. Almost two feet in height, both figures were cut from cylinders or pillarlike lumps of stone such as might be discovered naturally. Comparatively well-preserved, both originally possessed inset eyes, adding even further emphasis to the proportionally overlarge heads (compare Figures 6.17, 6.18). The man is wrapped in a long cloak, like the gateway figure, and his facial features and the details of dress are worked, like the other sculptures considered here, in broad, smooth planes. He stands on a round base bearing the enigmatic inscription "belonging to the town," presumably naming him as a local god (Hornung, 1978: No. 104). The woman's long tresses hang over a close-fitting robe; perhaps she is a jubilant like the long-tressed dancers on the King Scorpion mace head. Both exhibit the earliest conventions

Figure 6.27. Limestone Standing Figure in a Long Cloak, Probably First Dynasty. Courtesy Egyptian Collection, Munich.

for facial features to be found consistently in Egyptian sculpture, which are most characteristic of Second Dynasty workmanship – broad cheekbones and squat, flat nose, short and slightly receding chin, large eyes, and jutting ears. Lacking archaeological contexts, these figures are extremely problematic. Stylistically they could be placed between the late predynastic and early First Dynasty small figures, MacGregor figure, and other pieces mentioned already and the Second Dynasty funerary portraits. The cylindrical shape is most strongly suggestive of an early date for both figures; the slight lopsidedness shows the sculptor did not work from a squared-off block of quarried stone.[27]

Two possible influences on this precanonical procedure can be noted. First, stone sculptures of the early dynastic period are in some ways only larger, nonperishable versions of the ivory and clay figurines, usually peglike or cylindrical, popular in the Nagada II/III periods and the early dynasties.[28] The craftsmen made no essential distinction between bone or ivory and stone; for example, of stylistically identical figures from Tomb 1392 at Nagada, one is ivory and the other alabaster (Baumgartel, 1955: Pl. 5 [11, 12]). Pottery figurines represent an even older tradition; a group of Badarian figurines is known (Ucko, 1968). Approaching the monumental in scale and conception, stone works still appear to be under the influence of this tradition until the beginning of the Second Dynasty.

Second, and more tentatively, the core shapes of early stone sculpture may reflect an association with monumental work in wood now almost completely lost to us. In the royal tombs at Abydos, Petrie (1900–1: II, Pls. 12, 40 [92]) discovered two fragments of what must have been life-size standing wooden figures. The Boston Museum of Fine Arts owns a wooden face from a similar figure (Figure 6.28) (Smith, 1967). Room 7 of the "funerary temple" of Tomb 3505 at Sakkara, dated to the end of the First Dynasty, contained the bases and feet of two two-thirds life-size wooden statues of striding men (Emery, 1949: 10, 13, Pl. 72). Although not necessarily in costume, in attitude these figures might have resembled the gateway figure from Hierakonpolis (Figure 6.23). The wooden statues were painted and seem to have been built up from separately carved sections. The chief piece was the cylindrical or squared-off timber used for the torso, neck, and head, to which limbs, face, and other details were affixed. Early dynastic sculptors may initially have been concerned mainly to produce a more durable version of a common wooden form, although their product was rather rough and reduced.

"Monumental" works of the late predynastic period or early First Dynasty (Figures 6.21–6.28) seem to have had memorializing or commemorative functions, in which naturalism or realism increasingly seem to have been considered important. The wooden face in Boston is a good example of this interest: It represents a particular ethnic type, with full, fleshy lips; slightly hooked nose; low, broad cheekbones; and elaborately tended hair and beard. If this figure depicted an enemy of the Egyptian pharaoh and his army, was it then part of a larger "group" of statues including sculptures of the victorious king, or did it ornament an architectural complex as a commemoration of the king's campaign successes? We should probably imagine whole palace or temple complexes in the early dynastic period, just as later, serving as monumental three-dimensional versions of exactly the same imagery we find on the small-scale palettes: The king's victories and properties are depicted, with an image of the king or the gods somewhere at the center of the program. Memorializing functions of statuary were not necessarily funerary. Although

Figure 6.28. Carved Wooden Face of a Lower Egyptian (?), from a Wooden Statue, Probably First Dynasty. Courtesy Boston Museum of Fine Arts.

the statues from Tomb 3505 at Sakkara were funerary portraits, other works, like the striding king from the temple of
the god at Abydos and the Hierakonpolitan material in or
near the Main Deposit, were associated with temples and set
up in special public locations.

Monumentality of conception, certain seated or standing
poses (three-dimensional translations of two-dimensional
conventions already developed), various costumes and attributes, and naturalistic conventions for anatomical detail
would all be picked up and developed further by canonical
sculptors. The precanonical works reviewed here were not
systematically produced using a single method. Each sculptor
seems to have started with a suggestive lump of stone suited
to his own particular interests or context. Sculptural production would not become largely homogeneous until the
sculptor's medium and his procedures for working with it
were more rigidly and comprehensively defined.

THE CANONICAL MODE IN EARLY DYNASTIC SCULPTURE

We can easily discriminate canonical sculpture from earlier,
experimental, or noncanonical efforts. Although some precanonical sculptors possessed unparalleled technical ability –
the MacGregor standing statuette (Figure 6.22) exhibits their
mastery of cutting, detailing, and polishing even the hardest
stones – their procedures were not highly systematic. The
discovery of the qualities of the quarried block of stone and
of a way of producing a figure from that block (see Chapter
2) represents not so much a technical as an aesthetic revo-
lution. This discovery was apparently an achievement of the
Second Dynasty. The sculptors must have been thoroughly
familiar with the canonical method of representing the figure
in two dimensions or very low relief, for it was by applying
this schema to the four faces of the squared-off block that
the three-dimensional freestanding sculpture was obtained in
a series of clearly defined stages.

Attributions within the Second Dynasty are difficult to fix;
we have archaeological contexts for only half of the Second
Dynasty attributions to be claimed in the following pages.
Furthermore, the canonical method itself potentially could
have permitted a certain amount of experimentation. For instance, the method of cutting in from all four sides of a block
does not inevitably require that the final form should exhibit
"frontality," although frontality is usual in canonical sculp-

ture. The chronology I will accept here is based primarily
upon dates assigned by epigraphic or archaeological means
to some works, with works not datable in this way placed
with their closest visual parallels in the sequence.

To some extent we can explain the interest in the block
format itself as due to the developing complexity of stone
architecture, making available a suitable material for the manufacture of monumental sculpture. A technology for cutting,
carving, and polishing stone was already widely available to
vase makers. The Min colossi show that by the early First
Dynasty major efforts to transport and work large pillars of
stone were undertaken. Quarried blocks appear architecturally in the First Dynasty; for example, the early mastabas at
Helwan were lined with quarried limestone (Edwards, 1971:
65–6; Wood, 1987). Nevertheless, in both architecture and
sculpture the full utilization of the quarried block did not
occur for generations after the various technologies of masonry and transport were known. On the basis of sculptural
form and what seem to be the principles of its manufacture,
the block does not appear in sculptural use until the Second
Dynasty. Perhaps the architectural location of early monumental sculpture – like the Min colossi set up before a shrine
(B. Williams, 1988) or animal figurines probably used in temple decor (Davis, 1981c) – should also be taken into account,
for evidently memorializing, commemorative, and funerary
sculptures were all made for specific settings. The rectangular
forms and right angles of Egyptian architecture might have
been echoed by sculptors, presumably using the same or
smaller versions of the squared-off blocks delivered to the
building sites.

The Egyptians preserved rather than dissolved the initial
block form so long as the sculptural form was determined
by the drawings on the sides of the block (see Chapter 2).
Why the methods of canonical drawing and relief were applied to freestanding sculpture at all remains an open question.
The result was an extraordinary degree of conceptual similarity between artistic production in various media, sharing
a simple set of rules systematically and comprehensively applied in various contexts. On this evidence, it would seem
that one aim of canonical art was precisely to effect this standardization. The assimilation of freestanding monumental
sculpture to canonical methods is dramatic proof of the growing power of the institution.

The earliest known Second Dynasty work is probably the
limestone seated man in Berlin, thought to come from Abusir

near Memphis (Figure 6.29) (Smith, 1949: 9, 15; Steindorff, 1920). The figure is seated on a low stool, without back support, with the wooden components of the stool indicated separately on the side faces. This format is the best indication that this figure was produced by cutting in from all four sides of a squared-off block. Indeed, the surface of the "throne" is identical with the outermost surface of the block upon which the drawing was made; the sculpture involved the minimum amount of extraction – perhaps, of course, an important labor-saving factor in workshops increasingly loaded with orders. The left hand of this official is clenched across the chest, and the right lies flat on the right knee. He wears a knee-length robe, with right shoulder bare, tied with an elaborate knot carefully incised on his back. His short, full, caplike wig sits low on his forehead, with individual strands of hair represented using parallel incised lines. The head is extremely large in proportion to the body, which is characteristic of most early dynastic work; the eyes, originally inlaid and now lost, were quite large in proportion to the face, with eyebrows shown as raised ridges. The nose, now almost completely broken off, was apparently full and broad at the base; the cheeks are fleshy and the face rounded out, chin and jawline being undefined, with lips protruding substantially. Fingers and toes are small notches on the blocklike appendages of arms and legs, exact transcriptions of the relief cutting of such details on some of the carved palettes. Many of these features appear in other early work and enable us to date more problematic cases.

Succeeding the Berlin statue is the small incised hard stone portrait of Nyneter, third king of the Second Dynasty, from the Michailides Collection (Simpson, 1956). Here the facial type is recognizably early, with full cheeks, protruding lips, broad-based nose, and projecting ears. The brow is somewhat heavy with puffy underlids and deep-set eyes. The king wears the White Crown of Upper Egypt, here without the bulbous knob at the end usual in later examples, and the *Sed* cloak with royal crook and flail. As in the Berlin statue, fingers and toes appear as abbreviated notches. The back support of the throne extends to the top of the crown; perhaps the small size of the block – the figure is only about five inches high – made it difficult to produce a more differentiated format. The side recesses of the throne are now shown. The body contour is closely attached to the throne; body and throne seem to merge around the neck, buttocks, and calves.[29]

At Hierakonpolis, Quibell discovered two life-size kneeling statues, worked in a low-quality white limestone, erected on the east side of the temple at the level of the Main Deposit of "archaic" objects (Figure 6.30) (Quibell and Green, 1900–1: I, Pl. 2, II, 35, Pl. 1; Smith, 1949: 8, 15). Naked except for a narrow belt with a loin tassel, they kneel with left feet under their bodies and right knees raised. Their wigs are parted in the middle and hang to the level of the shoulders, fringed at the level of the ears and curling slightly at the ends of the strands. The striations for braids or strands run parallel with the face rather than circling over it (as on the Berlin figure). The lips are heavy, the eyes prominent, the cheeks fleshy – in the early dynastic manner. Whiskers were indicated in low relief, in effect similar to the wooden face in Boston (Figure 6.28), and the beards were wide and evidently quite

Figure 6.29. Limestone Seated Man, from Abusir (?), Front and Side Views, Early Second Dynasty. Courtesy Egyptian Museum, West Berlin.

different from the short, narrow false beards of later royal statues. As with other earlier statues, the heads are very large in proportion to the bodies.

A soft limestone squatting figure from Hierakonpolis (Figure 6.31) fell apart upon discovery, but the excavators retrieved the head, in facial type similar to the kneeling figures (Quibell and Green, 1900–1: I, Pls. 5–6). Since there is no trace of the cosmetic line at the eyebrow, we should date all three Hierakonpolitan figures to the period preceding the reign of Khasekhemuwy at the end of the dynasty, when this convention appears; the graphic conventions of drawing and relief were only gradually translated into freestanding sculpture. On the limestone head, the eyes were inlaid but for the first time are not large, al-

Figure 6.30. Limestone
Kneeling Figure, from
Hierakonpolis, Probably
Mid-Second Dynasty.
Courtesy Cairo Museum.

Figure 6.31. Limestone
Head from a Kneeling Fig-
ure (Now Destroyed),
from Hierakonpolis, Front
and Side Views, Probably
Mid-Second Dynasty.
Courtesy Ashmolean Mu-
seum, Oxford University.

though again the lips are projecting and the nose broad and full. The brow has now been cut back and the upper and lower eyelids carefully outlined, with the inner corners of the eye picked out. As the canonical tradition evolved, the eye received even more meticulous attention – perhaps for particular symbolic reasons. The hair is short and curly, and the skull seems to swell back.

The Cairo Museum possesses a red granite kneeling man, half–life-size, to be dated after the reigns of the first three kings of the Second Dynasty whose names are incised on his shoulder (Figure 6.32). Borchardt (1911: CG No. 1) gives Mit Rahineh (Memphis) as its provenance and dates it to the Third Dynasty, but an earlier dating is preferable on stylistic grounds (see further Terrace and Fischer, 1970: 25–8). The horizontally straight brow line and broadness of facial proportions are characteristically precanonical features. The cap-like wig, of early type, extends below the level of the ears, apparently also an early dynastic preference. Modeling is highly developed. The cheekbones are extremely high and far out on the face, below the far corners of the eyes. The eyes are wide and surrounded by a raised striplike line draw-

Figure 6.32. Granite Kneeling Man, Said to Be from Mit Rahineh, Mid–Second Dynasty. Courtesy Cairo Museum.

ing them to a point at the corners. The proportions of the face are squat, with the chin under the jaw cut almost flat. The hands are flat and blunt, with the fingers squared off. Peculiar to this work is the remarkable modeling of the breasts as well as the upper dorsal depression, unparalleled in other early works.

On the basis of facial type, Hayes (1945–6) has argued that a seated female figure from Abydos, now in the Metropolitan Museum of Art, is contemporary with the red granite man in Cairo. Archaic features include the proportionally large head and correspondingly squat body, with facial features much more carefully worked than other body features. The face is archaically rounded and full. However, other features of this lady more closely resemble the classic Old Kingdom canonical type. For example, in a manner quite standard in classic work, both hands lie on the knees. The treatment of the eye schematically prolongs the outer corner in a delicate point with slightly down-curving inner corners, surrounded by fluidly modeled upper and lower lids setting off the eye from the planes of cheek and forehead. The eyebrow defines the upper limit of the eye socket and outermost projection of the brow, a definitively canonical preference. She possesses the delicate, thin-bridged, faintly pinched and "patrician" nose of the classic portraits. Although the dress is considerably looser than the tight-fitting dresses of Old Kingdom female statuary, it does reveal underlying anatomy. The breasts are separately and roundly shaped. Still short, the wig parts at the top, with plaits indicated by incisions. The figure may be early dynastic, but it could plausibly also be given to the later Old Kingdom.

A limestone statue head in the Petrie Collection at University College (Figure 6.33) may be placed squarely in the Second Dynasty (Page, 1976: No. 1). Notable here are features that later become absolutely canonical – the treatment of the eyeball as an orb set into the socket, almost squeezing between the tight lids; the complete continuity between the brow line, defined by the eyebrows, and the sweep of the bridge of the nose; the "sharp" cutting of the lips. Older features include the dramatic projection of the ears and the immature full cheeks. The head still displays a broad, flat nose, with only a slight indication for the philtrum; it is about half life size.

The Second Dynasty sculptural style reached canonical expression in the three portraits of Khasekhemuwy from the end of the dynasty, two from Hierakonpolis now in the Cairo and Ashmolean Museums (Figure 6.34) and a third in the Boston Museum of Fine Arts (Figure 6.35) (Quibell and Green, 1900–1: I, 11, II, Pls. 30–41; Smith, 1967).[30] Here we need only note that the body has received as much attention as the face, and its proportions are naturalistically constructed; systematization of proportions has not appeared in freestanding monumental work until this date. The cosmetic line of the eyebrow appears on the limestone portrait in the Ash-

Figure 6.33. Limestone Head from a Statue of a King (?), Probably Second Dynasty. Courtesy Petrie Collection, University College, London.

a.

b.

Figure 6.34. Limestone Seated Figure of King Khasekhemuwy, with Incised Reliefs of His Defeated Enemies on the Base, Front and Side Views, End of Second Dynasty. Courtesy Ashmolean Museum, Oxford University.

molean and is one of the earliest of the important formal conventions for the representation of the face, despite later variations (Smith, 1949: 35). The schist figure in the Cairo Museum and the limestone head in Boston are modeled with eyes and cheekbones placed high on the face, stretching the skin taut from the strong jaw. Judging from the reliefs of slain enemies on the bases (Figure 6.19), the Cairo and Ashmolean portraits commemorate a royal victory. The three different sculptures recognizably "portray" the same individual, but the emphasis is on the majesty and ageless strength of the king rather than on any physiognomic peculiarities. Since we have more than one example of an individual's portrait to consult, here we can clearly observe the regularization of sculptural procedure and the invariance of the final format.

For our purposes, although they differ from high Old Kingdom work in details of dress, anatomy, and attitude, the seated statues of Djoser from the early years of the Third Dynasty stand at the end of the synthetic sequence. They are the first works fully monumental in scale and conception produced by ancient Egyptian sculptors (Smith, 1949: 13–19,

Figure 6.35. Limestone Head of King Khasekhemuwy, End of Second Dynasty. Courtesy Boston Museum of Fine Arts.

188

1981: 53–69) and surviving to us. The further evolution and considerable variability of monumental sculpture in the Third Dynasty has been considered comprehensively by Smith (1949: 13–19). By the Fourth Dynasty, in the portrait statues of Chephren (Khufu) and Mycerinus (Menkaure), "the arrangement of the single figures and the composition of the groups show a culmination of experiment resulting in the ideal type for the representation of kingly majesty" (Smith, 1949: 36).

I have presented the history of monumental sculpture as the gradual emergence of various conventions for facial features, dress, pose, and so forth, accompanied by an overall tendency toward working on larger and larger scales. Initially rather heterogeneous, this tradition was punctuated, at the beginning of the Second Dynasty, by the application of canonical methods of drawing and relief to the manufacture of block sculpture derived from quarried squared-off blocks, which resulted in the rapid systematization of production and the selection of formats and conventions suitable to this procedure. It is not possible to say whether these developments were localized in any region of Egypt. Most surviving large-scale material is commemorative or funerary; there is little or no visible stylistic difference between these functions. The history of early sculpture is chiefly significant in documenting the growth in the power, popularity, and homogeneity of formal canonical procedures from the late predynastic period to the opening of the Old Kingdom.

SUMMARY OF DEVELOPMENTS

The canon certainly did not emerge all at once; despite what appears to be the underlying opinion of some idealist writers (e.g., Schäfer, 1974: 12, 283), it was not a single unitary "invention," "discovery," or "conception." All production before the Third Dynasty is rather heterogeneous and variable relative to dynastic production. The principal elements of the canon all seem to have been in place by the time the reliefs of Hesire and portrait sculptures of Chephren and Mycerinus were produced, but each emerged in its own way and was occasionally used in conjunction or in competition with other, different, noncanonical procedures.

The canonical method of constructing the aspect of the human figure, the so-called frontal-profile view, has the most archaic history. Certain features of composition are also very ancient. Serial organization appears on early pottery, and the groundline was used for limited purposes in the Decorated Tomb at Hierakonpolis. Other features of the canon appear on monuments of the first kings of the First Dynasty. The canonical selection of section contours for the component parts of the figure was achieved at this time, as was the basic calculation of the system of proportions. Register composition appears in a fairly developed form on the Narmer Palette, mace head of King Scorpion, and other works. This canonical material of the early First Dynasty can be distinguished from a great deal of earlier and some contemporary noncanonical material, like relief-carved palettes that employed different compositional principles or different approaches to deriving and modeling contours. The discovery of the sculptural block occurred at the beginning of the Second Dynasty. Canonical sculpture used a canonical drawing to produce a three-dimensional, freestanding, bilaterally symmetrical form. Finally, individual conventions for anatomical details, costume, and complex objects appeared throughout the early dynastic period, occurring with increasing frequency in the Third and Fourth Dynasty. In the representation of the human face in two or three dimensions, in particular, we can follow the gradual crystallization of various conventions – for the eye, mouth, ears, hairstyle, and so on – invariantly associated with one another as the canonical facial type. At the beginning of the Old Kingdom, spacing and other harmonic rules for composition became more secure, although sophisticated compositional harmony was only an achievement of the high Old Kingdom.

In rather uncritical acceptance of the Egyptians' own official ideology, the development outlined here is sometimes regarded as the creation of an artistic "order" from chaos or primitiveness. We have seen that pre- or noncanonical production was often highly sophisticated technically and iconographically. Heterogeneity in production does not necessarily imply primitiveness or lack of formal and expressive controls. Nothing essential or ineffable in the nature of the history of style as such could have determined the inevitable emergence of the canonical ideals. They were selected in preference to equally accomplished and potentially consequential alternatives. In the end, then, it would be more correct to say that Egypt exchanged one form of order for another – namely, the order of the village or chieftain's polity and its representation of its world was exchanged for, was replaced by, the order of the hierarchical state with its representations. As the chronology suggests clearly, the development of the canon coincided with the emergence of the national state, an elite value system, and the artists' own occupational specialization.

CHAPTER 7

THE EXPLANATION OF INVARIANCE: TOWARD A HISTORY OF THE AUTHORITY OF THE CANONICAL IMAGE

IN considering the variability and invariance of the canonical style and iconography, I have placed a good deal of emphasis on core procedures and motifs prepared for use in many, varied contexts and governed by principles of transformation. In a broad sense, the invariance of canonical representation might be attributed to the stability or even unity of this core. In the sense that canonical images are all the products of the same system of core procedures, motifs, and rules of transformation, *they are essentially all the same image*.

However appealing, nevertheless this is still a loose and ambiguous statement. It is not exactly clear what the claim amounts to or what it implies. In this chapter, I will first consider the possibility that Egyptian canonical images were all the same kind of image (Goodman, 1971: 26) – having the same epistemological status or belonging to the same genre. Although modern Western culture uses images that have many diverse statuses, such as news photographs and psychiatric projections, or belong to many and varied genres, such as landscape decorations for a living room or promotional advertising for the television screen, there is no a priori reason why another society or a single system of production within another society should not have restricted itself to the use of images of *one* status or a very few genres.

THE STATUS OF THE IMAGE AS A SYMBOL OF HISTORY

Canonical images generally were not narrative images, at least in the rather precise sense in which we apply this term to the depiction of the unitary, moving anatomy of action, specification of temporal cause-and-effect relations, and so on, most highly developed in certain works of the modern cinema. In those few cases where an Egyptian artist wished to represent events in their actual chronological order, he would prepare a series of separate images – in fact, quite like the frames of an animated film – each depicting the successive stages of a single complex action, like rowing a boat or lifting a heavy load (Schäfer, 1974: 227–30).

Applied more liberally in the everyday sense of "telling a story," it would seem that far more Egyptian images could be interpreted as narrative. Once relieved of the strict logical requirement that he narrate chronologically, obeying temporal cause-and-effect relations, a storyteller is free to employ one of many available narrative genres and his story can be of many kinds. It is important to be precise about kinds of stories and ways of telling them.

Perhaps, as many commentators seem to assume, canonical images represent real historical events in a highly conventionalized way. For obvious reasons, some Egyptologists and historians have been keen to use Egyptian images as documents or evidence for actual events. A biography of an official or king or an account of a battle or expedition is written partly on the basis of what a patron and his artist "tell" us in a tomb painting or temple relief.

Apart from its general assumptions, like its reliance on simple imitation theories of representation or the significance of realism/naturalism, there are several specific problems with this assessment of Egyptian art (see further Hornung, 1973; Schäfer, 1911; Tefnin, 1979a: 219–20; Weeks, 1979). It cannot be reconciled very easily with the nondramatic, nondescriptive character of most canonical compositions and the formulaic, repetitive, rule-governed way in which even innovative iconographic programs were evolved. The literature is marred by minimizing the role of convention, copying, or eclectic archaism in even so "realistic" a "document" as a Ramesside war relief of a campaign we know about from other sources. Furthermore, inscriptions are sometimes taken to be sufficiently corroborative of the "actuality" of content, rather than as yet another kind of representational statement requiring analysis of its status. In fact, a canonical image may just as well be a historical document of an actual event or a fictionalization fulfilling preconceived standards.

The possibility that some images may have a documentary status hardly goes any way toward explaining the invariance of canonical representation as a whole. Many conceivable states of affairs could be documented. Why should these particular documentations have found widespread acceptance? Moreover, on the basis of the images themselves there is no obvious visual means of distinguishing a documentary from a nondocumentary history or narrative. If Egyptian images have a status as history, it still needs to be more closely specified.

The events depicted in an Egyptian representation often need never have taken place, at least in the way the image depicts them as taking place. Just as canonical iconography worked a series of transformations upon a basic core motif, perhaps the canonical image was originally documentary but, through a series of formal and iconographic transformations, gradually became more abstract, generalized, or "symbolic" (see Schäfer, 1957, a brilliant and evocative essay on the victory theme). With certain artistic statements, "one may perhaps say not that they are better than the truth but that the fact was so at the time" (Aristotle, *Poetics* XXV.1451a1). Presumably no original viewer would have confused these symbols with documentary records or matters of fact.

It is worth distinguishing two elements of this persuasive argument and evaluating them separately. First, nothing really assures us that what became a symbol or "myth" in literate, historical times was somehow actuality in prehistoric times. Even if a chieftain really did slay the lion in predynastic times, why should this primordial event have continued to interest later generations? How did the symbol exert its influence on those for whom the event itself was now only a memory or fiction? In fact, we have long since learned to see oral or literary myths as much more than, or quite different from, naive memories of distant events. Why should the visual symbol be treated any differently? It is not helpful to thrust all ultimate explanations irretrievably into the darkness of *Urgeschichte*.

Second, Schäfer (1957) did, however, recognize the potent qualities of symbols as reflections upon or analyses of the ordinary, empirically experienced "facts of life," whether these are the facts of contemporary life or of some long-distant past. A structuralist would say that the image can be the map or re-presentation of constants alleged to be essentially characteristic of the facts of human experience because the human mind organizes its acquaintance with all empirical facts in a particular way. Whatever its haphazard or occasional relationship with history, the canonical image may assume and intend a specific presentation of this more abstract "History."

Let us turn briefly to one of the core canonical motifs. To understand what aspect of History the image of the victorious king represents, we could look to the ideology of divine kingship in Egypt, in which images play a limited role and, beyond this, to complex cross-mappings between the image, the ideology, and the actual person of the king and the many primary daily experiences of all Egyptians (or those Egyptians who saw the canonical image). The image derives a part of its power from and is chiefly intelligible within this symbolic network, some gross features of which Egyptology has enough evidence to sketch.

Even in earliest pharaonic Egypt, the king was the focus of the right order of the universe. The prominence of the victory theme itself suggests this conclusion. Other evidence tends in the same direction. In the Pyramid Texts, which seem to preserve many vestiges of very ancient belief and practice, the king occupies an overwhelmingly important position. Complex systems of metaphor associate him with the stars, with the bull, and with the gods and goddesses of primordial nature (see especially Faulkner, 1966). The existence of royal tombs fully equipped for a hereafter presumes some belief in the divinity of the king and in his continuing life. We know little about the genesis of divine kingship in Egypt in historically exact terms, but apparently in the sociopolitical developments of the late fourth millennium B.C., a great symbol shifted in meaning to accommodate new material circumstances of life: The divine king took on both the social and symbolic role of the local hunter.

Symbolic usages in Egyptian literature, religious ritual, and art suggest that the Egyptians sensed the contrast between society and the world, between man and his environment, to lie in a contrast between the desert, thousands of square miles of uninhabited, inhospitable desolation, and the narrow strip of green cultivated land which, in essence, was only water, that is, made possible by water, served by water, returned to water (see especially Wilson, 1946). The desert was evil; the evil creatures of Egyptian superstition or religion were often creatures of the desert – snakes, scorpions, hyenas, the jackal (see, for example, Habachi, 1939: 771–4). According to popular cosmology, at the end of the desert mountains ringed the world. In the earliest paintings on predynastic Decorated Ware, the ends of the earth may appear as the bands of triangles positioned above and away from the birds, animals, and human beings living at the water's edge (see with caution Murray, 1956; Raphael, 1947). Water, on the other hand, was life. Osiris, one of Egypt's most popular gods, was a god of vegetation, reborn in water; human culture – the possibility of human life – was founded on irrigation, the understanding and manipulation of waters and fertile alluviums (Butzer, 1976); the king was Osiris; the king, as the early carved mace head of King Scorpion reminds us (see Figure 6.15), was also the primal and chief irrigator.

The association between death and the desert presumably extended to the earliest burial practices. These practices must be reconstructed from badly plundered predynastic cemeteries, and their social and religious determinations remain a matter for much further study and interpretation. The desert destroyed bodies; the jackal and vulture scavenged, picked clean corpses, scattered and crushed bones. It is no accident that the late predynastic sculptor of the Battlefield Palette (see Figure 6.11), wishing to show the most horrible of deaths, represents the king's enemies being consumed by scavengers, deprived of proper burial. Nevertheless, men were buried in the "segregated land," the necropolis (Morenz, 1973: 100), away from the land needed for cultivation. The desert preserved the bodies of the dead. Mummification was developed relatively late, and mummified bodies in great stone chambers only further symbolize the original habit of allowing the hot, airless sand to enclose and preserve forever the simply wrapped body of the newly dead. The stones laid down to keep animals out of simple burials in the sand in the great funerary constructions of the later period preserve their original durable and protective qualities. One might go so far as to say – although archaeology cannot keep up here – that the rude early stone markers of a desert grave became substitute people, the magically inhabited portrait statues of the great mastabas (compare Smith, 1949: 23–5). By contrast, water burial destroyed. Egyptian superstition is as populated by horrible water creatures, crocodilian in aspect and behavior, as it is dominated by a desert jackal, lord of the underworld, death itself.

Social man and this terrifying nature come together at many points. In numerous representations of the Egyptian world, it is man who becomes terrifying and the natural world yielding, defeated. On the Oxford Palette (see Figure 6.9), a jackal-headed man, perhaps a hunter wearing a jackal mask, pipes a flute in accompaniment to a mortal battle between a giant winged griffin and other carnivores and a helpless group of peaceful grazing animals. In the village hunt man ventures into the fearsome desert, at first perhaps to bring down game he will use to feed himself or to clear his fields of a troublesome predator (see Figure 6.10); later he participates in the hunt to prove himself worthy, to assert his beauty, grace, and strength. The desert lion, even though a creature of the wasteland, was like the hunter himself mythically valued for its power, becoming a model and a metaphor for the life of the king himself. The king was a lion in trampling his enemies; the lion is his noblest quarry in the hunt. The king also becomes the bull (see Figure 4.11) – associated with the irrigated fields, the fertile agricultural plots maintained by the waters of the Nile. He was also the stars, by which the seasons were measured, by which man gauged the rise and fall and extent of the life-giving floods, and which seemed to regulate the day-by-day existence of man and animals.

In dynastic times the material basis of intuitive equivalences between the king and the hunter had dropped away. Society made over the symbolic function of the hunt to the king alone. At the end of the predynastic period, the Bull Palette fragment (see Figure 4.11) and the Battlefield Palette (see Figure 6.11) represent the affairs of state formation with images associating the king with great animals. The events of political coalescence perhaps gave rise to an image of the king as victorious hunter; in the Cannibal Hymn in the Pyramid Texts, the king eats the gods (Faulkner, 1969: utterances 273–4). The crook he carries as an emblem of royalty appears earlier as a hunter's tool on the Hunter's Palette (Asselberghs, 1961: 258, for this proposal). In fact, the early dynastic patrons and artists took over popular motifs with an ancient tradition in the Nile Valley. In this rhetoric, the new kings were represented as simply reproductions of the successful hunters and masters of ritual who had in turn legitimated their own status in neolithic kin lineages in the rock art, pottery decoration, and so on, intrinsic to *their* culture. As we have seen, the rhetoric of the state requires and reuses the established metaphorics of earlier society to secure its own meanings (recall the sequence of disjunctions from the Manchester ostrich and Oxford Palettes through the Narmer Palette and King Scorpion mace head).

This dense texture of symbols only suggests what kind of History the canonical image of the victorious king might represent, namely, *the king's place in the structure of Egyptian historical experience*. Although the image may end by constructing History – a mental map or image – part of the conviction it carries derives from its dependence upon real, lived orders of historical experience, namely, the established symbolizations of the king as a hunter, as partner of the gods, and so forth.[1] Yet as a re-presentation in the strict sense, respecting only certain relations of similarity between sign and its "symbolic" object, the image is necessarily *selected* or *proposed* as a view of History. In effect it creates the very History it symbolizes; knowledge of the king's place in the structure of Egyptian historical experience is *only available in and through representation itself*. As we will see in more detail, the image must be constituted as a form of knowledge *essentially different from* ordinary perceptual knowledge of empirical experience: In part History has been constituted by the symbol. Phrased in this way, we can see that there is still a need to focus on the ideological operation of image making itself. There must be an active force at work in the determination that the image should be of a certain kind at all.

THE EXPRESSIVE FUNCTION OF CANONICAL IMAGES

Although the canonical image has a generalized status as a re-presentation of History, in itself this does not explain exactly in what way the re-presentation was effected. Certainly images could not automatically symbolize the constants of History, even presuming such constants were naturally there to be found; the image constructed a symbolization. One interpretation has largely dominated art historical and Egyptological considerations of this problem. According to this view, canonical images invariably *expressed a particular ideology*, namely, Egyptian magico-religious doctrine. This invariant expressive function accounts for the stability of canonical representation.

This approach has three critical limitations. First, the doctrine supposedly expressed in canonical art has never been very clearly specified. Second, emphasis on this doctrine fails to make sense of some obvious historical facts about Egyptian image making. Third and most important, the reductive and mechanical conceptions of expression and ideology inherent in the analysis are unsatisfactory. I will take up these points briefly in an effort to understand and move beyond the traditional analysis.

It is often said that in Egypt the act of representing the world in images was actually believed to reproduce the world itself "magically," in another sphere of existence. According to this view, a tomb painting presents a record of those activities the patron wished to continue in his next life in the hereafter, a wish satisfied by the act of representation and by

certain rituals of "animating" the image (see especially Morenz, 1973: 6; Wolf, 1957, for strong and influential statements
of this analysis).

This general account of the magico-religious function of
canonical images has always been variously interpreted.
There may be important differences between an image that
duplicates, that perpetuates, that reproduces, or that otherwise extends and renews the depicted world. For example,
if an image perpetuates the world, it may depict a world that
has many of the properties of the real world but exists somewhere else, that is, in the hereafter. An image of this world
will perhaps have visionary, utopian, or idealizing connotations. By contrast, if an image reproduces the world, it might
picture the real world or record some world that obtained in
the past life of the patron. An image with this kind of meaning
will have historical, autobiographical, or documentary connotations. Because such symbolic connotations cannot always
be easily perceived "in" the primary subject matters of images, there may be no direct visual means of distinguishing
between these possibilities.

The traditional analysis stated in the literature has actually
maintained contradictory specifications of the underlying
magico-religious doctrine. For instance, some writers suppose that in representation a tomb owner stated his "hope"
that his earthly activities might be carried on in the hereafter.
Moreover, Kees (1926: 50) suggested, "scenes of daily life"
may have compensated him symbolically for his death and
departure from the world of his affairs, family, and friends
(compare Wolf, 1957: 258–62). By contrast, it is sometimes
argued, a tomb picture might merely present a commemorative, ostentatious, biographical memoir of the deceased's
life on earth (Groenewegen-Frankfort, 1951: 28–36, develops
the point at length). Joachim Spiegel, the great historian of
Egyptian religion, concluded that many "scenes of daily life"
intended no depiction of the life hoped for in the hereafter:
They offer a record of the past life, interests, and activities
of the patron (1936: 6). It has even been proposed that funerary scenes represent the dead man passively "watching"
or visiting the land of the living (Groenewegen-Frankfort,
1951: 40, and seemingly Montet, 1925; on the whole literature, see Weeks, 1979).

Before the New Kingdom, pictorial references to the hereafter – if this is what they are – "utterly lack the concreteness"
one would expect if the image secured the continuity of human affairs in the next life (Groenewegen-Frankfort, 1951:

29). If the image really functioned in this way, every tomb owner would surely wish to represent only what he, individually, wished to perpetuate. In practice, magico-religious functions should have resulted in an ever-diversifying representational practice in which every patron presented personal preferences. Instead we find only a few themes presented selectively with little variation. In other words, the "ideology" expressed in canonical images did not permit the expression of individual hopes, beliefs, or wishes. Religious doctrine must have offered only a conventionalized picture of eternal life and those aspects of the "good life" on earth one should seek to perpetuate.

In the New Kingdom, patrons began to use scenes representing their activities in different public offices and rather personal, private activities (Groenewegen-Frankfort, 1951: 85–8). These images raise converse problems. Did the variations reflect individual biographies and preferences? Should we understand these more or less "realistic" and extraordinarily detailed depictions of the world to reflect the religious man's hopes about his life in the hereafter? If general states of affairs are represented by the canonical image – the deceased's general prosperity, health, and happiness – what was the point or function of the variable descriptive details?

It is often said, as well, that the Egyptians believed a record of a man's life perpetuated on earth – by building and maintaining a tomb with its preserved corpse, inscriptions, statues, and wall decorations – would contribute to the eternal happiness of the soul; earthly memorialization would secure eternal survival.

The Elder Judge of the Hall, Hetep-her-akhet [Fifth Dynasty], says: I made this tomb on the west side (in the necropolis) in a pure place, in which there was no tomb of anyone, in order to protect the possession of one who has gone to his *ka*. As for any people who would enter this tomb unclean and do something evil to it, there will be judgment against them by the great god. I made this tomb because I was honored by the king, who brought me a sarcophagus. (Lichtheim, 1973: 16; for the "classic" decoration of this tomb, see Mohr, 1943)

In this general context, images and inscriptions appear to memorialize the past life of the *ka*, the earthly life of the deceased, freezing a picture of a man's time for all of his time, a justified soul, a living *ka*. True enough as far as it goes, this analysis still does not account for the criteria by which the picture's forms and subjects were determined: We need to know what it was about a man's life that he wished to "freeze" or secure as the image.

Before proceeding with this question, note that even if it is possible to specify the magico-religious doctrines about an ideal life supposedly expressed in Egyptian funerary art, the account is necessarily somewhat limited. For one thing, private patrons probably borrowed some motifs for their tomb pictures from royal, public monuments, where imagery was not necessarily funerary in significance – for example, the entire program of Hesire's offering chapel was "probably based on a royal program in the Step Pyramid complex" (Wood, 1978: 19–20, and see Junker, 1938: 61; other examples in Smith, 1949: 153–5, 1965: 147). Furthermore, private painting in domestic contexts probably contributed to the decorative program of the tombs. Did these original but now lost cycles of images somehow magically perpetuate what they represented in another world? Or did they have other functions?

In addition, historically we cannot easily explain prehistoric art in the Nile Valley by any magico-religious functions it might be thought to have had. Although a picture of animal prey might have had a magical value, other rock pictures cannot be interpreted in this fashion. The rise of canonical image making in the early dynastic period seems to have had more to do with the ideological projects of the elite, who were concerned with forging a successful state, and hence "the rise of the various crafts was largely independent of funerary custom" (Smith, 1949: xii; see also Schäfer, 1974: 60). Moreover, many of the formal properties of the canon were already significantly evolved in the prehistoric, predynastic, and early dynastic contexts (see Chapter 6), before the formation of an imposing, complex thanatology, cosmology, and politico-religious ritual.

In brief, although in ritual use an image might have been taken as a magically effective instrument in some sense and a viewer could maintain a cultic relation with it (Morenz, 1973: 88, 106–8, 150–2), the plain fact is that not all images were used magically, ritually, or in funerary art. In nonfunerary and nonreligious contexts, the canonical image exhibits almost all of the features familiar to us in the funerary setting. When a leader represents his military campaigns or when a temple column presents a scene of the king worshipping the gods, representation seems to be less "magical" than generally symbolic in status. What one artist put forward as a historical biography could be used by another as an emblematic gesture of royal power. Since the visual difference between images having these different expressional functions may be quite negligible, an explanation for their formats in terms of one or the other possible function is necessarily insufficient: Many expressive functions were well served by a single set of canonical principles.

The attempt to account for the invariance of canonical imagery as the expression of magico-religious doctrine typically relies upon a problematic conception of expression in representational art – namely, that in some sense art is the "expression of ideas." For our purposes, an account of this kind is necessarily idealist, reductive, and overly general; it fails to explain either the specific character of representation or its invariance in its many contexts of use.

First, we do not necessarily have independent evidence for or of the beliefs that canonical representation is supposed to express. They are apparently conceived by some writers as having been preexisting, even largely nonartistic or nonaesthetic ideas (that is, magico-religious doctrines). In a very loose sense, they may be found in other media of knowledge, such as magical and ritual texts or funerary custom. Nonetheless, to be consistent, these other media would also have to be conceived as "expressions" of belief. Unless we wish to say that one medium of knowledge is especially privileged, then the other media also could not be identified with belief itself. In fact, we can never know what an Egyptian believed "in his own mind" except in so far as he expressed himself publicly in words, images, or other behavior. For these and many other reasons not considered here, the idealist component in the expression account can be regarded as superfluous at best.

Second, to reduce representation to an illustration, an "expression" or "embodiment," of ideas maintained in other media of thought prevents us from seeing why a society should have devised the separate modes of knowledge that it did. The image loses its force and vividness, its status as a medium of significant knowledge, its very raison d'être, if it is regarded merely as a reflection of "deeper" cultural concerns. Images exist alongside other symbol systems as a further self-sufficient form of knowledge. Moreover, it would be radically misleading to suppose that the themes or symbols of image making were synonymous with themes or symbols appearing elsewhere: They have their own specific character and connotation by very virtue of being image themes and image symbols and not a theme or symbol in some other medium.

Third, it follows that if it answers any coherent question at all, the expression theory answers too general a question. Rather than asking what ideas are expressed in a canonical image, we should ask how ideas are expressed in an image – which is another way of asking simply what kind of ideas the images are and not what kind of ideas magico-religious or other doctrines might be or what kind of ideas a textual or ritual theme or symbol might be.

The force of this distinction comes out most clearly when we consider that the expression account, unless very substantially modified, fails to help us with the particularity of canonical imagery. If a funerary image memorialized an ideal life (about which magico-religious doctrine did certainly have a good deal to say in other contexts), how were these ideals ever selected and others dropped from view altogether? For instance, "scenes of daily life" remain remarkably reticent about sexual pleasure (Buchberger, 1983) and other activities that we could plausibly regard as part of an ideal life and were in fact celebrated by the Egyptians in other media. If the image was an idea of an ideal life it was a specifically different idea than the ideal life in love poetry, wisdom literature, or legal judgment.

These three considerations jointly suggest that we must simply make a stronger claim for canonical representation than the usual "expression" theories allow. It is important to recognize the status of canonical representation as *a complete, self-sufficient, and particular kind of idea*. Representation is no more and no less than a specific doctrine or belief *in itself*. We do not find the canonical theory of image making formulated in religious texts or manuals for aesthetic production, whose doctrines it "expresses," because the canonical theory of image making is not anything but image making itself. Only a consideration of this theory in itself – that is, of the organization and principles of image making itself – provides us with an account of *all and only* the invariances of canonical representation.

WHAT THE CANONICAL IMAGE REPRESENTED

Briefly, in all of its contexts of use, the canonical image *represented the same subject*. Complete, self-sufficient, and particular, canonical representation made knowledge of this subject possible in many functional and expressive contexts. The invariance of the canon can be attributed to the fact that all canonical images represented a single, fixed aspect of or truth about the world; moreover, and equally important, it was a truth not subject to criticism or change. Egyptian art was made at the edge of a logical paradox: It attempts to represent what exists outside representation because it cannot be altered by human knowledge.

A few Egyptian representations, of course, attempted a specific spatiotemporal analysis of their subject matters. I have not given systematic attention to these efforts at Amarna and elsewhere. For example, with what looks like documentary accuracy and clarity, some hunt and battle reliefs stress the actuality of space and time by using topographical indications, conventions for the depiction of swift action, and other markers (see Chapter 4). However, we have seen that such images were derived from a core motif through particular principles of transformation, governed by rules above all preserving stabilities rather than by a demand that the motif resemble anything in the world as perception knows it.[2]

What, then, did the canonical image claim to represent? Speaking loosely, the image offers a "typical" or "universal" view. When called upon to be more precise, within certain limits the artist could add any amount of particularizing detail. As the canonical system generally resists such additions, it must value the universal over the particular as pictorially and logically more adequate (versions of this argument, central to the Egyptological conceptualization of Egyptian art, in Frankfort, 1929: chap. 1; Groenewegen-Frankfort, 1951; Scranton, 1964; Smith, 1981: 15–23; Wolf, 1957).

Although helpful as far as it goes, this account is incomplete. It does not in itself identify the typical, universal view's subject. Indeed, the dichotomy between universal and particular is not fully intelligible. The "particular" image – an image that attempted spatiotemporal differentiations – was not a different kind of image from other canonical images, for particularizing detail must be regarded as potentially available to a "typical and universal" representation. In fact, logically there could never be an image offering no particulars; an image necessarily depicts an entity in some respects, in some of its individual properties – but perhaps it depicts few particulars of the kind we know in ordinary experience.

What, then, are the criteria, respects, or qualities of the

"typical and universal" view? In a canonical Egyptian representation, as Plato rightly saw (*Laws*, 656–7),[3] the particulars of the typical and universal view are not unreal but most real. Access to this order was available through attention to certain features of the world, but in the process it was necessary to move away from phenomenological experience. Like Plato or Plotinus, canonical image makers evidently did not consider that our visual perception of the world – the wholeness and continuousness of our experience – tells us what the world *is*, as a continuous whole.

The canonical image represents certain features of a viewer's experience as particularly stable and invariant, as most real, most meaning-full. Specifically (and this will be my organizing hypothesis), of all conceivable respects and qualities of experience, it claimed to be *the most neutral conceivable specification of encompassing, secure, and significant qualities, those most effective, necessary, defining, and bounding for human knowledge, those with generative and founding ontological status.*

As we have seen, Egyptian art avoids detailed specification of locality in the spatiotemporal plane. In more positive terms, the canon selects the most neutral point for depiction, the spatiotemporal coordinates (0, 0) – that is, it attempts to represent an entity in no place at no time. This task is certainly as difficult as the "realist's" ambition to represent the utterly particular form. Although various local spatial and temporal qualities of a subject are not depicted, this does not imply that no qualities at all are depicted: In the very act of depicting the subject, some qualities are given substance, are visualized, are revealed or "realized."

The spatiotemporal plane we begin with in our private, ordinary experience, what we believe we know, is not necessarily all there is. Things exist above and beyond what an individual human being, looking straight forward and sometimes revolving on his upright axis, generates as the particular spatiotemporal plane of his own existence. Things represented as existing at the neutral coordinates of no time and no place exist at the charged coordinates of all times and all places.

Canonical representation depicts the *encompassing and constant* qualities of the world, what is supposed to be everywhere and always the case. The king is always victorious; the desert lion is always brought down by the hunter; the captive is always abject; the official is always broad-shouldered, graceful, healthy, well proportioned. Nevertheless, as hostile viewers rightly remind us (Worringer, 1928), in its search for the encompassing and constant Egyptian canonical representation risks realizing only the ludicrously trivial: The constant would be merely the obvious facts of experience. To circumvent this vulnerability, canonical representation must be extraordinarily selective. In the selection of conventions for an adequate art, the all-encompassing picture identifies an order of *secure and significant* value in what is otherwise the banal chaos of immediate experience – continuousness, variability, featurelessness, boundlessness.

Although official ideology may claim value is transcendent or immutable, we should note that values must be specified from a particular point of view. They can be no more and no less than the values of certain makers and users. There will always be grounds for dispute about the security and significance of values; therefore there will always be grounds for dispute about the adequacy of an art or language. The key question will be how these grounds are defended intellectually and institutionally in particular cases. In canonical arts it seems to be distinctive to found claims of value on extraauthorial or extraindividual grounds, which are peculiarly resistant to the expression of authorial or individual disagreements and particularly hard to refute from the standpoint of authorial or individual knowledge. I will come back to these issues shortly.

An artist does not have an absolute choice between representing all or representing nothing of the continuousness of experience. Gross configurations of the particular can be isolated and classified; indeed, a conventional "notation" for continuous experience is the very concern of representation. The canonical image claims to provide fully effective knowledge of the continuousness of experience; insofar as the continuousness of experience is ultimately featureless and unbounded and therefore ungraspable, the image provides *necessary* knowledge – knowledge the viewer cannot do without and which he would not otherwise possess. Contour absolutely defines forms, isolating a shape the viewer focuses upon closely. The artist and viewer hereby come to know and control a thing; the canonical method provides for the object's very existence, for one's knowledge of its existence, by labeling it graphically. Precisely outlined, formalized, repeated over and over again, the image *defines and bounds* human knowledge.

The order represented in the canonical image is a *generative and founding* order. Not only describing our world, the image also aims to show how our world, our ordinary perceptual and historical experience, is part of an encompassing and constant world of secure and significant values and can be seen to subtend from this world. Constant and significant qualities are "realized" in the here and now, always and everywhere, pictured as true of events and objects in daily life as much as in the superhistorical realms of cosmogeny or mythology. Representation is a "revelation," an order that one must be shown before one can see it or know it. Our uneducated intuition, our immediate perception, our knowledge of historical particulars must be supplemented by this knowledge of Being: This knowledge is a fundamental condition of our experience. The image pictures the transcendent as it is fully immanent in human experience: It represents what one can correctly know in history as the transcendent.

Something invariably and uninterruptedly occurs in this transcendent world: The king of Egypt – and by extension all components of Egyptian society as Egyptians historically knew it – triumphs over chaos or nothingness. This is the subject identified by the image in all of its functional and expressive contexts; it is what the canonical method is designed to picture. Out of all the possible lines depicting possible orders of experience, the canonical artist draws all and only those lines of identity or transparency between the world of phenomenal, historical experience, our world, and the scheme of universal divine being.

It is important to distinguish the claimed from the real sources of authority for this image. Canonical representation claimed that an individual's ordinary knowledge of the world is imperfect, variable, or uninformed, replacing it with an account of a world already made, a fait accompli – complete, ordered, and rational, fully effective and sufficient for individual knowledge. This world could not be grasped without the canonical image. A canonical composition presented a view that the viewer could not possibly acquire from any vantage point he might adopt. Likewise, section contours – the basis of figure construction – could not be derived immediately from a viewer's inspection of surfaces as encountered in real experience (see Chapter 2).

Moreover, the image suppressed evidence of individual authorial participation, of a sense of the individual's construction of the world, of a critical intelligence narrating its ongoing concerns, of a mind identifying new realities with new signs. In these various senses an individual's knowledge of the world was claimed to be inconsequential in comparison with the authority of the traditional, fixed canonical image made available to individual consciousness.

The canonical image presented a viewer with the authoritative codification of completed analyses – that is, a construction of the world *by someone else never explicitly identified as the maker of signs*. The image claimed to lead the viewer through his world to a world he could never grasp without the image and claimed that he could not do without this knowledge, for it pictured his world as subtending from a greater world of constant and significant values. Successful or not in working practice, the canonical hope was an authoritative naming, we might say a "rigid designation" (Kripke, 1980).

Needless to say, a viewer can interpret an image in any number of ways, whether they be acceptable or unacceptable to the maker of the image, and certainly these are not fully predictable in advance. That the canonical image should seem to possess one single received meaning – for forms and themes were held steadily invariant in many different contexts of use (see Chapters 3, 4) – surely intervenes strongly in the flow of free, loose, individual constructions imposed by the viewer on a world of signs. That the image should have such a claim to authority, such sanction on the viewer's freedom of interpretation, is a dominating social fact: The perception and use of images must be powerfully constrained. Similarly, the artist knew one way of drawing the world (see Chapters 3, 5), but it was not essential mentality, natural disposition, or the limits of his individual knowledge that limited him to this mode: He belonged to a dominating social institution.

The institution does not speak its real names. The source of the authoritative image – a source outside individual perception, knowledge, and expression – was claimed to be the tradition, "spoken by the ancestors," in the words of the sage Kha-kheperre-sonbe,[4] and ultimately created by the gods in "the first time," "when the name of any thing was not yet named."[5] We have examined many aspects of this tradition. Most important is simply that "the tradition" – however it presented itself – had a specific social identity as the selection of early dynastic Upper Egyptian artists and patrons, which was swiftly nationalized as the "Egyptian" style (see Chapter 6). The interests and aims of these patrons were undoubtedly structurally perpetuated in the very fabric of Egyptian society until its disintegration after the conquest of Alexander the Great.

In practice it is unlikely that in the Old, Middle, and New Kingdoms the tradition was viewed in this way by individual living participants; however, the "perspective of the actors" is virtually lost to us except in the images they happened to make. In works like the Battlefield and Narmer Palettes or the mace head of King Scorpion (see Figures 6.11, 6.14, 6.15, and see in detail Chapter 6), the tradition mythologized both its origins, by "inventing" its own tradition selectively in relation to the art of the past (e.g., see Figures 6.9, 6.10), and the inherent character of the alternatives to it. In practice, then, the source of canonical authority at any given moment in later history was simply its hegemonic status. There were no observable or creditable alternatives: The tradition could not be recognized as anything other than "the way things are," "the way things have always been," reality itself. When an image is recognized as a selection, as representation or re-presentation, it will fail to contain the viewer's ability to distinguish his own personal knowledge from its authoritative provisions and to devise his own new signs. Therefore Egyptian art fundamentally aimed to establish the clarity and interpretability of the tradition in relation to the ambiguity and strangeness of any new individual image, to ratify knowledge of the one proper image and refute, suppress, or co-opt knowledge of alternatives. The fearsome lion who manages to disrupt human society on the Hunter's Palette (see Figure 6.10) becomes part and parcel of the king's great power as pictured on the Battlefield Palette (see Figure 6.11); the hunter/warrior who had his own independent, dominating status in a neolithic village (see Figure 6.3) or chiefly polity, acting as military leader and Master of Ritual (as in the Tomb 100 painting and possibly on the Gebel el-Arak knife handle and in other early scenes), becomes not someone who might have resisted the expansion of a neighboring polity but rather someone whose way of life and values are reproduced by the leaders of the ultimately successful polity (see Chapter 6).

Egyptian canonical art does, of course, proceed from the life of man in the world. It depicts man coming to control otherness, the success of the hunter, master, or king against animals, the desert, alien or barely human enemies, the domination of man over the land and people, over food, production, and enjoyments, over death and life equally. What is immanent in this life is what the canonical image leads its viewer to know, what he might never know in all of his particular encounters with the world: The canon reveals "the transcendent significance of human action" (Groenewegen-

Frankfort, 1951: 22). However, only certain human beings, engaged in certain activities, are represented as having this status. The canon has found a social ideology as the immanent truth of historical experience and represents a story that never happened.

The corollary is equally important for our purposes. The canon excluded representation of a range of knowledge about the world, preeminently knowledge of sexuality and of certain uncomfortable consequences of social difference and domination. Potentially a viewer could have understood these matters equally well if he could ever have successfully seen beyond the images offered to him by cultural authorities. But canonical practice disputed the adequacy, self-sufficiency, or authority of any such noncanonical representation – of the individually expressive work of art, of variable private thought and variable personal practice. The very possibility of another practice was not even recognized officially: The traditional word or image was contrasted to an unknown Otherness. As a member of the canonical academy (see Chapter 5), the artist's real choice was between making the one proper image or making nothing at all. The "unknown" or Otherness was mythologized as precisely that, utterly empty (Hornung, 1982: 168–9, 175–7) – rather than as what it really would be, another actual mode of life, another actual form of society.

In sum, the canonical image, at once a systematic definition and a thoroughgoing manipulation of an individual's identity as a knowing maker of choices about the adequate representation of his experience, proposed a set of restricted possibilities for individual knowledge. The image rewrote, refuted, or replaced the worlds constituted by ordinary perception or experience or established in modes of representation articulated by competing classes or cultures. The voice of an elite group attempting to define and maintain a very particular representation of the world, the tradition reinforced the initial choices through systematic repetition. In the end alternative choices could not be conceived as possible.

LEGITIMATION AND THEODICY

In *Wirtschaft und Gesellschaft*, Max Weber used Egypt as "the historical model of all later bureaucracies" (1978: 964). The statement was rhetorical, for Weber recognized many of the unique features of the Egyptian hierocracy – especially, as he put it, the "tradition-bound" and "irrationally oriented" aspects of Egyptian culture, which he distinguished from modern "technological-rational" bureaucracies willing to dispense with traditional symbols or customs like a canonical artistic style (1978: 1401–2). For Weber (see also 1976: 105–33), Egypt serves as a test case of "patrimonial feudalism . . . with a significant servile component" (1978: 231–5, 1044–7, and see also Janssen, 1978: 224, Kemp, 1983: 83).

In the Old Kingdom, Weber noted, a complex and powerful bureaucracy composed of privileged and often literate priests and officials came to administer most economic distribution and acquired private estates and benefits (1978: 460, 1030, 1089). This official status group ("class," in non-Weberian terms?) espoused an identifiable "ethos" of its own, "always aristocratic and anti-plebeian" (1978: 508, 1050). In its individual policies, the elite might be highly pragmatic, rationalistic, or intellectual, tolerating, for instance, some degrees of private enterprise or "capitalism" (1978: 1102).

Yet in its iconography, ritual, and official statements, the elite publicly adopted a metaphysical or transcendental language. Most important for our purposes, this language incorporated a theodicy specifically designed to account for or even to deny the obvious, observable imperfections and injustices of the social order (1978: 519). If my reading of its fundamental subject is at all correct, canonical imagery clearly presented such a theodicy. "It may be said," Weber wrote in his remarkable pages on the "social preconditions of hierocratic domination," "that the rise of transcendental speculation" – like the transcendental aesthetic of the canon – "resulted at least in part from the rational development of the hierocratic system" (1978: 1177), for at the head of the elite, at the head of state, was the divine king who officiated "by liturgical methods of meeting public needs" (1978: 1023). Cloaking itself in traditional and transcendental authority, this power had its real origin in society's need and in its capacity to manage large-scale irrigation works, monumental constructions, and transport (1978: 113, 120, 972, 1155, 1261). The *Einheitskultur*, the "unified culture" of Egypt – including its canonical religion, art, and law – is to be attributed to the stability of a "single tremendous *oikos* ruled patrimonially by the pharaoh" (1978: 1013–14).[6]

We owe the most systematic exposition of the sociology of "agromanagerial bureaucracies" on the Egyptian scale to Karl Wittfogel (1957). His notorious "hydraulic hypothesis" (Haas, 1982: 146; Mitchell, 1973) suggests that "individuals depending on a limited and single water supply" like the Nile inundation "may reproduce a limited tribal or national culture for a long period of time" (1957: 163). In the effort to undertake, unify, and regulate massive irrigation projects, an elite acquired its first powers and prestige, including "such fundamentals of effective organization" as "counting and record-keeping," writing, surveying, and mathematical notation (Trigger, 1983: 40, 58). When not performing primary agricultural labors, the "government-directed work teams" were employed on monumental building projects that aided the development of other technologies like quarrying, metallurgy, or transport engineering (Wittfogel, 1957: 41). Whatever its complex internal divisions or differences, a privileged, hereditary, educated elite maintained its fundamental investment in control of technological information and activity – irrigation itself, accounting and recording, writing, and so forth. Ultimately the elite established itself not only by its efficiency in action but also by its monopoly on real and symbolic force. "The agromanagerial sovereign cemented his secular position by attaching to himself in one form or another the symbols of supreme religious authority" (1957: 92). The agromanagerial elite required a metaphysical theodicy.

Weber and Wittfogel put forward a very simple if nonetheless plausible picture of Egyptian official representation in various media. It has its origins in the ritual formalization of skills acquired by the technocrats of irrigation, but even in its furthest elaborations it continues, poetically or symbolically, to serve elite designs.

Like any dramatic anthropological thesis, this interpretation, in its sheer generality, omits much. Weber's terminologies must be provided with specialized, debatable definitions.[7] Wittfogel's hypothesis has its own problems in this case: The Nile Valley, in fact, is not a unitary hydrological entity (Butzer, 1976), so the material basis for political unification or cultural coherence must be sought in a very complex combination of environmental and historical factors.

Nevertheless, the direction of explanation inaugurated by Weber and Wittfogel is well worth preserving. There is less a need to dismantle than to supplement it. Most important, we should recognize how modes of representation participate intimately in the very construction of the social system itself. "There is a danger of making believe that . . . ideology legitimizes, after the fact, a dominance already existing in reality. In fact, this dominance would not exist without this ideology, because this ideology is not only a 'reflection,' an elaborate expression, but one of the *internal components* essential for this dominance" (Godelier, 1982: 237).

The monolithic coherence of the ancient *Einheitskulturen*, enforcing invariance in discursive and representational practice, was not, or at least not only, structural. It is easy to assume that an authoritarian state will necessarily maintain an official ideology with no serious competitors as a structural element of its internal organization. That authority should be so successful is often held to be unsurprising. After all, since in the last analysis the authority commands the power of physical coercion, of terror, its subjects cannot have it otherwise: "Total terror – total submission – total loneliness" (Wittfogel, 1957: 157).

In the evolutionary transition from small-scale hunter-gatherer or village societies to "ranked chiefdoms," such as we apparently find in the Nagada II and possibly in places for the Nagada III (Hoffman, 1979), and finally to stratified states, emerging elites at least initially did not necessarily wield any monopoly on force.[8]

Once a system of mechanisms has been constituted capable of objectively ensuring the reproduction of the established order by its own motion (*apo tou automatou*, as the Greeks put it), the dominant class have only to *let the system they dominate take its own course* in order to exercise their domination; but until such a system exists, they have to work directly, daily, personally to produce and reproduce conditions of domination which even then are never entirely trustworthy. (Bourdieu, 1977: 190)

Even in its moments of greatest security, an authoritarian state must work ferociously to maintain any substantially impressive levels of invariance in the thought and work of its subjects. On what basis does the merely aspiring authority proceed?

Answering this question, at least in some of its aspects, as I have attempted to do in this book, will not be easy. The historical record is not complete; moreover, it may be critically deceptive. For obvious reasons, we do not know much about the experimental or unsuccessful policies or statements of the emerging elite; yet I have interpreted an image like that on the Hunter's Palette (see Figure 6.10) as an experimental "translation" from an earlier into the approved canonical mode and metaphorics which, insofar as it was replaced by an image like that on the Battlefield or Narmer Palettes (see Figures 6.11, 6.14), might even be regarded as partially unsuccessful. We know virtually nothing at all about the activities of opposing or oppressed social groups, such as the peoples depicted as "fallen enemies" in canonical scenes of the king's victory. The "historical record" traditionally consulted by Egyptologists – the official words and canonical images handed down by the Egyptian elites to their posterity and their population – seldom makes reference to the "direct, daily, personal" struggle for social solidarity and for a "trustworthy" internal dominion. (Again, we may see signs of the difficulty of securing such an aloof representation in the appearance, on the Bull and Battlefield Palettes, see Figures 4.11, 6.11, of "realistic" effects depicting the hard, gory realities of conquest and battle.) Canonical images themselves do not explicitly represent the precariousness or the arbitrariness of the "transcendent significance of human action" (Groenewegen-Frankfort, 1951: 22), and we will probably never be able fully to reconstruct the noncanonical voices "stifled and reduced to silence, marginalized, . . . or reappropriated in their turn by the hegemonic culture" (Jameson, 1981: 85).

With these caveats in mind, supplemented by the archaeological record (far less susceptible to the filters imposed upon discourse and representation), the utterances of the hegemonic voice itself can be interpreted as a "symbolic move in an essentially polemic and strategic ideological confrontation between the classes" (Jameson, 1981: 85). The constitutive strategic value of canonical representation can be evaluated along with other parallel elite policies for acquiring "trustworthy" authority.

Late predynastic "chieftains" seem to have involved themselves in long-distance exchange (e.g., Kantor, 1965), in specialized technological activity like the processing of copper ore (Edwards, 1971), in the storage and redistribution of local products, and in the military defense and aggrandizement of territories brought under cultivation. The old centers of Upper Egypt at Abydos and Hierakonpolis came to paramount authority in all Egypt in a development involving many further projects. The monarchs of the first two dynasties continued to promote long-haul exchange with Canaan and Palestine. If the funerary hoards are any guide, kings and high officials accumulated quantities of valuable flint and copper implements. Exploratory, punitive, or commercial expeditions were carried out in the deserts and to the south. Monumental walls, temples, and palaces were put in place, apparently at an early date, at Nagada, Hierakonpolis, El-Kab, Abydos, Gebelein, and elsewhere (see generally Hoffman, 1979; Trigger, 1983).[9]

Late predynastic chieftains and early kings did not automatically command great territories or a traditionally sub-servient laboring population. They were not necessarily sole masters of technological knowledge. However, there were many means by which they could improve their hold upon the minds and the work of their potential subjects. They could nominate and prove themselves masters of the knowledge by which the natural and social universe was systematically made available to its inhabitants in mythological, poetic, artistic, and other symbolic representations.[10]

In order to perpetuate their authority, the seniors must extend their knowledge beyond fundamental subsistence skills to new fields (social learning, knowledge of customs, genealogies, history, the rules governing marriage) and even further to artificial fields (magic, divination, religious rituals, etc.). They will try to make this knowledge their exclusive province by setting up barriers to regulate its transmission: institutional barriers like initiation which in its most elaborate forms defines the individual's rank until a very advanced age; and esoteric barriers which are placed around mag-ical, ritual (or medicinal) information so that it is only transmitted to chosen individuals. The adoption by "wise men" of young men who show great interest or inclination for their skills helps to neu-tralize further possible rivals by creating an artificial link of filiation and hence of dependence. Later the granting of titles or rank to individuals versed in certain "sciences" will also identify them with the senior group which possesses authority. (Meillassoux, 1978: 138)

In this project, the elite as much invented as discovered the technical means and the subjects of representation. They at-tempted to appoint themselves *sole guarantors* of activities of representation that had been central to the life and production of prehistoric cultures in the Nile Valley since the eighth millennium B.C. (see in detail Chapter 6). It was never a foregone conclusion that any one social group should succeed in this project. In fact, succeeding as the nominator of rep-resentations taken to be consequential by society at large was one of the very criteria for becoming elite in the first instance.

ACCUMULATING OUT-OF-THE-ORDINARY OBJECTS

Elite "seniors" of a group could attempt to compensate for their physical disadvantage or small numbers by controlling ritual knowledge through hierarchies of instruction and ini-tiation and by regulating the supply and redistribution of the most valuable goods – including, for instance, stored grains or other foodstuffs, raw or luxury materials obtained through long-distance trade, and "ceremonial" objets d'art symbolizing the out-of-the-ordinary status of those who possessed them – "the objects become the attributes of 'social age' " (Meillassoux, 1978: 141). Apparently it was in the manufacture of these "ceremonial" objects, like the palette of Narmer, that the canon was devised (see in detail Chapter 6).

Unfortunately, as we have seen, we do not often know exactly who did manufacture or possess many of the surviving objects of the earliest period. We have no archaeological access to the specific facts of production or patronage and to that extent our accounts of the process must be speculative. Moreover, we have hardly any data concerning the use of the earliest canonical works after manufacture and therefore little to go on in assessing their place in any system of gifts, exchanges, or displays. The Oxford and Narmer Palettes (see Figures 6.9, 6.14) were discovered in the Main Deposit at Hierakonpolis, seemingly a collection of treasured ritual or ceremonial implements manufactured over a period of time and deposited as late as the Middle Kingdom in a cache of heterogeneous but perhaps "sacred" material (B. Adams, 1974: 3). Our evidence about the significance of the objects reduces to the mere facts of their survival (deliberate preservation?) and of the invariant repetition, in later contexts, of their style and motifs. To take a second example, the upper class or royalty using the early dynastic tomb field at Sakkara evidently valued the copper tools and weapons found hoarded in the tombs (Emery, 1949: I, 19–20; Petrie, 1900–1: II, Pls. 41, 65). In more specific terms, however, it is not clear what the elite valued here: Did ownership of a certain kind of object have a certain symbolic value, or was the raw metal itself, however worked, a highly valuable possession, or both, or neither?

Despite such problems of evidence and interpretation, for some classes of artifact some plausible inferences can be made. In the early dynastic period the technology for the manufacture of full-size and miniature stone vases was highly elaborated (el-Khouli, 1978). Many vases embody a tremendous amount of labor and time. Moreover, some of the most exquisite were clearly not intended for mundane use. The product was not uniformly distributed. Vases were acquired and hoarded in the greatest quantities by upper echelon patrons: In fact, it is in part by the great quantity of their vases that we recognize the status of the grave owners. The magazines in the early dynastic tombs at Abydos (Petrie, 1900–1, 1902–3) and Sakkara (Emery, 1949, 1954, 1958) contained huge collections of vases, representing quite astounding levels of consumption. A full time work force would have labored for years to produce the contents of a royal magazine.

Although we cannot prove archaeologically that all high-quality, labor-intensive craft products and objets d'art served directly in this fashion, the distributions imply that the social territory – a territory of diverse statuses, powers, and privileges – was marked publicly and with great nuance by complex patterns of ownership and consumption. The system of display may, of course, have had ancient roots in the prehistoric cultures of the Nile Valley, where neolithic leaders, hunters, or Masters of Ritual devised their own insignia of rank and status (see Figure 6.3). Once it was established, an aspiring elite could attempt to monopolize the most prized items, which, it seems, in their very representational programs reflect an increasing affiliation with paramount authorities from the Nagada IIc/d through the early First Dynasty (see Figures 6.8*b*, 6.9, 6.10, 6.11, 6.14).

SUBORDINATION OF THE ARTISAN-SPECIALIST

We can see why a social group attempting to establish itself as the foremost authority would wish to regulate the access of junior, novel, or competing social groups to forms of out-of-the-ordinary knowledge and to resources and objects of out-of-the-ordinary status. *This project required that images be designed as a form of knowledge and objects be manufactured as a kind of material thing to which junior individuals did not normally have access in their everyday experience.* As we have seen, the canonical image was presented as a more adequate depiction of reality than what individual perception and experience could provide. But the production of individual works is potentially highly variable, and so the project also required an effort to control the producers of such works. What, then, of the artisan-craftsmen themselves in the production and dissemination of significant symbols or "symbolic goods"?

Before the establishment of the central state authority, in the Nagada I and II periods, individual kin groups in Upper Egypt probably manufactured most of the objects we find deposited in their graves, a range of tools and other implements associated with agriculture or the private activities of daily life. Some specialized items were acquired from other, perhaps distant producers, and some industries, like the production of "desert ware," were localized "at one or two centers" (Mond and Myers, 1937: I, 50). The graves of some craftsmen probably can be identified even in the homogeneous funerary assemblages of the predynastic period. Nevertheless, the graves of the early artisans were neither richer nor poorer than the graves of other villagers (Davis, 1983a: 121–7). No features in the construction or location of the tombs suggest that their owners were economically or socially distinguished from the rest of the population, unlike the proto-elite or "ruling class" so dramatically interred at Hierakonpolis around Tomb 100 or at Nagada in Cemetery T (Kaiser and Dreyer, 1982).

It has been proposed that an emerging elite, like this late predynastic/early First Dynasty "ruling class," will encourage the development of craft specializations. The elite will guarantee the material support required by specialists if they are to remove themselves from primary production. The elite expects various benefits from this policy. Fostering craft specialization may provide chiefs with a competitive edge in interregional trade for, inasmuch as they are able to command potential exports, they may procure privileged access to imports. Furthermore, labor-intensive objects signified the status of those who owned them; the elite will desire privileged ownership, most easily obtained if the producer is one's own retainer.

In the First Dynasty certain artisans drifted to or were conscripted by the court. They worked as specialists in the full sense of the term, dependent upon agricultural producers and supported by royal patrons (Davis, 1983a: 128–37; Trigger, 1983: 67, for details). Among the burials of the immediate royal circle at Sakkara in the First Dynasty, we can detect the graves of artisan specialists (e.g., Emery, 1954: 29, 31, 143–4, 153–4); a number of the early "tombs of the courtiers" at Abydos, particularly some from the reigns of King Djer and Djet, belonged to artisans (Petrie, 1927). By the Third and Fourth Dynasty at Giza and Sakkara, many of the mastaba tombs belonged to administrators connected with various arts or building projects as practitioners or supervisors.

The specialization of artisans, the establishment of central workshops (see further Chapter 5), and the upward advancement of at least some craftsmen depended upon the growing ability of the central authority to supply and support them materially. An emergent state does not necessarily have this ability automatically (although once in place, of course, it merely commands its artisans to work). From the First through the Third and into the Fourth Dynasty, the Egyptian state in some ways still had to persuade its subordinates and prove its superiority.

Now control over specialists could perhaps have been reinforced by monopolizing consumption. The labor power of craftsmen was conspicuously consumed in the funerary hoards or building projects, holding out a persuasive incentive for all producers to contribute to the supply and to extract regular benefits. Perhaps swiftly, this policy could result in the economic dependence of producers upon the few large-scale consumers capable of managing the work.

Maneuvers of this order, however, required deliberated, rather risky planning on the part of the economic elite. The elite had to finance its attempt to co-opt its service staffs. Here it is not possible to review in detail how the early dynastic monarchs accomplished this feat – apparently nonviolently – of generating resources to pay for those who generated the resources for elite consumption. Acquisition of foreign luxury goods by a small cadre of loyal officials or perhaps through military campaigns in foreign territories was probably part of the story (Edwards, 1971; Trigger, 1983). The specialist service staffs – artisans and artists, engineers and scribes – could be rewarded with rare materials or objects, in turn symbolic of the more intangible rewards of royal favor and social prestige.

More concretely, *the rational interests of artisan-specialists had to be seen to coincide with those of the aspiring elite*. What mattered to the specialists was a dependable supply of raw materials, reliable demand, and reasonable remuneration or security, if the obvious disadvantage of full-time specialization – potentially perilous dependence on primary agricultural producers – was to be minimized. Most important, then, the exploitative interests of the despotic authority (entrenched by the early Old Kingdom) required the authority to guarantee its specialists a stable means of exploiting in their turn the production of surplus by the primary work force. The authority necessarily allowed potentially explosive powers – the power of image making, of writing, and so on – out of its immediate personal grasp, at least to some degree, in order to pacify and reward its service staff. In fact, some stylistic variation in Egyptian art may express social maneuvering, perhaps Byzantine, between prime royal consumers and secondary but influential private consumers, between canonical loyal-ists and innovative experimentalists, or among specialists and their noble patrons jockeying for notice or royal favor (see Chapters 3, 4, although in this book I have not sys-tematically studied the phenomena of variability in Egyp-tian art as such).

Insofar as the paramount authority seemed substantively or even symbolically able to guarantee the security of the specialist classes while providing a maximum of personal freedom or reward (at least in comparison to the alternatives), the interest of these classes lay in maximizing their individual appropriations without disrupting the dominant role of the authority. To be specific, the interest of image makers seem-ingly lay in *producing a high volume of products without an undue expenditure of energy and risk in the manufacture of any individual piece.* The greatest incentive – the most efficient rationaliza-tion of production in the circumstances – lay in striving for striking levels of standardization or invariance using the ca-nonical principles (that is, authorized means of achieving for-mal regularity). Enforced invariance minimized the risk and expense of experiments, novelties, and the constant retooling of the production process to meet unpredictable demands. Moreover, striking exhibitions of virtuosity and an insistence upon difficult *technē* – for of course standardized production does not imply poor production – effectively minimized the risk and expense of competition from outside the system altogether. *Invariance in form and production was the means by which an Egyptian craftsman successfully maintained himself as a specialist.*

Summarizing to this point, those who commissioned and produced canonical images had rational, self-interested, per-haps even fully self-conscious reasons for preferring certain formats and themes and for organizing production in a certain way. First, images depicted the activities of the Egyptian elite successfully conquering chaos, in accord with principles of cosmic order sanctioned by the gods. Projecting an order represented as being always and everywhere constant and true, the image legitimated the present social order and its distribution of resources and rewards. Second, the ownership of certain objets d'art – and, by extension, the power to commission all manner of projects – apparently marked the larger powers and social status of the elite. Third, the stan-dardized production and consequently the invariant form of works of art was intrinsic to the success of this elite in obtaining the cooperation and eventually the subordination of knowledgeable craft specialists.

THE SUCCESS OF CANONICAL REPRESENTATION

So far I have looked at canonical image making from the point of view of the elite and the specialists committed to the survival of elite culture. However, as an elite policy in "essentially polemic and strategic ideological confrontation" (Jameson, 1981: 85), canonical image making was fundamentally intelligible only insofar as it made images succeeding in persuading those who would not have assented to a more naked expression of exploitative aims. Again granting that initially the aspiring elite did not necessarily possess a "trustworthy" dominion, why were the misrepresentations of canonical depiction and the exploitations of the canonical system of production ultimately accepted by the dominated as the one acceptable mode?

Several qualities of the canonical system ensured its success at this level. First, the boundaries of the system were absolute and well patrolled, but within limits the system was flexible, accommodating many forms, themes, and functions. Second, the rules of the system were finite and definite. Third, canonical representation made possible consequent knowledge of the Egyptian world and as such was judged acceptable.

The most effective way to control the possibility that an individual might learn to see, draw, or think noncanonically was probably to eliminate alternatives. All of the canonical rules can be regarded as standards for the correct, well formed image. The program incorporated specific means for assessing the competence and finish of a work of art. An artist could be instructed directly in a finite set of standards of judgment, existing in advance of the production of individual works. Noncompliant works could be discarded easily. We know somewhat less about the responses of Egypt to the influence of noncanonical foreign styles and subject matters, an issue I have not taken up in this book for lack of space (Frankfort, 1951: 121–37; Kantor, 1947; Smith, 1965). As we might expect, Egypt generally resisted the penetration of foreign ideas. Many confirmed cases of foreign artistic "influence" in Egypt can be seen to conform to indigenous canonical expectations about appropriate forms and themes.

The boundaries of canonical practice were not subject to

critical evaluation or revision. Present forms and themes were projected into the distant past: Using a formulaic motif to depict a contemporary event – like a military victory or success in the hunt – implied that the event was fully predictable within a well established order, merely a repetition of what had properly occurred in the past. Mythology usually has it that "if the present reproduces the past, it is because the denizens of this world are instances of the same kind of being that came before" (Sahlins, 1983: 528). The power of the king himself was utterly removed from temporal human history, where it depended upon "direct, daily, personal" struggle for "trustworthy" dominion, and transferred to a divine, infinitely distant past (see especially Evans-Pritchard, 1962; Frankfort, 1948). The will of the superhuman forces that first established the worldly order could not be subject to critical human scrutiny.

But despite canonical ambitions, it would be impossible to eliminate all awareness that images might present other forms and themes than those they are seen to possess (see further Chapter 5). Therefore the canonical program must also seem to put forward the best of all possible alternatives. This was usually accomplished by recognizing – or pretending to recognize – the existence of other modes of representation. The effect of this requirement can be seen at many levels in Egyptian canonical art. For example, the mathematical, idealizing elements of the program (see Chapter 2) contributed to disguising the fact that it was highly arbitrary or personal in its picture of the world; geometrical or numerical order seems neutral. Again, canonical texts and images do include within themselves representations of Otherness, usually depicted in noncanonical style as social disarray and disaster or as the defeat of alien enemies (see, for instance, the Fifth-Dynasty "famine reliefs" of Unas [Smith 1981: 133] or the tradition of depicting fallen, defeated, bound, or decapitated enemies in noncanonical poses, Chapter 4, and Figure 6.19). To take a last example, the canon occasionally permitted highly individualizing, almost "psychological" studies of physiognomies and personalities (see Chapter 3). Nevertheless, even the great "portraits" of the Middle Kingdom or Late Period depict the sitters as worldwise, fatherly, authoritative statesmen. In all of these examples the possibility of a noncanonical order has been neutralized or appropriated: Access to novel alternatives could be controlled by suppressing most and co-opting the rest.

Within its boundaries, canonical practice persuaded viewers of its "intrinsic rightness" (Plato, *Laws*, 656–7) by virtue of its consistency, coherence, and completeness in managing an extraordinarily intricate set of formal and thematic concerns. The system was simple, readable, and repeatable; it had many of the characteristics of a notation or notationlike symbolic system. Flexible but finite, the system was cognitively appealing.

The canonical program identified a limited sector of the wide field of conceivable experience and practice as the most valuable and constituted a metaphysics by which these choices seemed to be justified.

One could say that in Egypt "the non-existent" signified quite generally that which is inchoate, undifferentiated, unarticulated, and unlimited: or, in affirmative form, the entirety of what is possible, the absolute, the definitive. In comparison with the non-existent, . . . the existent is clearly defined, and articulated by boundaries and discriminations. It can be set in order and experienced: there are didactic works (the "onomastica") which teach one to know "everything (or better: every category) that exists" – in fact, of course, only a selection of it. (Hornung, 1982: 183)

Like the cataloguers' analysis of "everything that exists," canonical image making established a well defined domain of common, public, and acceptable meanings in the wide field of vague, random, private, disputed, chaotic, variable, uncertain, and local meanings which chiefly constitute human experience in history. To be precise, it nominated a selection of the latter as worth regarding as the former.

If representation – art, ideology – is to succeed within culture, it should be capable of representing "true" information about the world, however specialized, that is, information upon which an agent could successfully rely in his material approach to his own reality. The image must be a means of representing knowledge of real consequence, otherwise no one would have any at all compelling or constraining reason to attend, to assent to, or to admire its picture of the world. Canonical representation was put forward as more adequate than anything ordinary perception and reflection could provide: It literally represented what otherwise could not be seen or known.

Representational invariance must be imposed upon a preeducated, precanonical state of potentially absolute individuality and variability in representational practice. Invariance is not a subsidiary or unproblematic but rather an intentional and fundamentally problematic characteristic of canonical representation. In effect, the canon is designed precisely to control the potential for variability, which arises from within as much as from without the system – a filter upon the potentially variable and socially threatening expression of individual historical experience and self-consciousness. In a sense, the canonical project seems inevitably bound to fail. Variations always appear, prescriptions can never be complete, the world itself changes, and the definitions of a language or mode of representation finally decay. Nonetheless, in periods of canonical absolutism the image pictured that world in which an elite was materially most secure and from which it claimed to derive its transcendental legitimacy and historical self-confidence – that very world in which the continued reproduction of canonical art as a mode of representation was completely guaranteed. The world depicted is that world necessarily requiring its own representation for its continued reproduction: But keeping the fiction alive is the "direct, daily, personal" work of a real and active power. We have to conclude that canonical absolutism made social stability possible, for the social ambition to secure the invariance of representation and of many other languages of social life provided that very degree of invariance that nature, social life, or language do not naturally provide.

NOTES

1 INTRODUCTION

1   On Plato's text, see Chapter 7, note 3. For the legacy of Egyptian art
    in later art and philosophy, see especially Iversen, 1971a, b. Plato's
    view seems to have influenced Hegel, whose pages on Egyptian art
    as the "abstract form of the Understanding" (1977: 421–4) remain
    compelling and are the ground, often unacknowledged, of many later
    accounts.

2   It would be a monumental but intriguing task to trace all of the art-
    historical interconnections. Important and theoretically self-conscious
    essays by the *Strukturforscher* include von Kaschnitz Weinberg 1933,
    1946–7, 1965a, b; Matz, 1922, 1923–4, 1930, 1934, 1944–5, 1950 (and
    see Hanfmann, 1957), 1964; V. Müller, 1928, 1929, 1938. A view of
    Egyptian art, perhaps partly derived from Schäfer, can be detected
    throughout the work of Rhys Carpenter (e.g., 1960: chaps. 1, 2, 1962);
    it has had tremendous implications for students of form in Greek art.
    See also Arnheim, 1954: 112–16; Gombrich, 1960: 120–5; Panofsky,
    1955, 1956: chap. 1.

2 THE CANONICAL REPRESENTATION OF FIGURES AND GROUPS

1   Out of the abundant literature on the Late Period, see especially Brun-
    ner, 1970, Lloyd, 1983: 288–9; for archaism generally, see Brunner,
    1973. The tomb of Mentuemhet at Thebes (no. 34) provides the best
    examples (Bianchi, 1979: 20, n. 54; Manuelian, 1983). See also Bietak
    and Reiser-Haslauer, 1978–82.

2   Although the view in the drawing – that is, the shape bounded by a
    closed contour – may present itself as being fully frontal, it is not
    exactly clear what this view could be a view of. Normally one does
    not perceive the components of an object in a "frontal image" of
    which the drawn image would be some kind of trace. Only some
    kinds of objects – notably not living things – have flat surfaces; often
    we do not look at an object, whether it has flat surfaces or not, with
    the plane of the object facing us at an absolute perpendicular to a
    monocular line of sight. Furthermore, vision is foveal (with central
    regions of the retinal image in sharper focus). Therefore, only certain
    kinds of objects under very special viewing conditions can actually be

perceived as a complete navigation of closed contours. All of this is only to say that even the "frontal image" – which seems like such a simple matter to draw – is a complex analysis of perceptual experience. We need to know, in turn, the criteria by which this analysis was carried forward.

3   There are many instances in which a view seems not to be that of the most "characteristic" frontal or profile part of an object, as usually adopted; the view seems to suit some particular context or create some decorative effect (see Schäfer, 1974: 100). The "characteristic" view – whatever it is – need not be frontal or profile.

4   Here contour refers only to the outline of shapes – the outline of the hand, the dress, and so on. Contour is a more appropriate term than outline, which has the connotation "schematic" (as in Norman de Garis Davies, 1921: 225). For the importance of contour, see further Frankfort, 1929: 22; Mohr, 1943: 4.

5   I am attempting to be more precise than Schäfer, 1974: 315–16. Scharff (1937: 176–7) points out that description along these lines is already more precise than what is usually meant in art-historical accounts of "frontality" in ancient sculpture (see note 15). In itself, the procedure described here would not necessarily result in an absolutely "frontal" figure; instances of a turning or "offset" shoulder (e.g., Dubrovits, 1959), of a torso in a "torsional" position, or other modifications from the frontal (e.g., Bothmer, 1970; Radwan, 1973, for the block statue) could have been achieved by downcutting from the frontal or profile sketches on the four surfaces to variable depths (nonequal depths). Frontality is therefore one subsidiary by-product of the underlying method. For reasons having to do with the convenience of work and perhaps with the meaning and contexts of images themselves it was the overwhelmingly usual by-product in Egyptian art.

6   The most useful account of sculptural principles is still Schäfer, 1974: 310–34. Aldred, 1973; Lucas, 1962: 50–74, make many important points concerning technique. Somewhat different theoretical treatments of Egyptian sculpture include Badawy, 1954; Dubrovits, 1938; Reisner, 1930: 115–19; von Kaschnitz Weinberg, 1933, all of which merit close attention.

7   Schäfer, 1974: 321–2 rejects such practical explanations for "cubism" in Egyptian sculpture; they would necessarily tell against his view that the form of the sculpture was determined by an underlying "perceptual attitude" (see Chapter 3). The Greeks probably recognized the technical usefulness of the method (Carpenter, 1962: 158–60), and in addition to the requirements of canonical aesthetic theory there is no reason to doubt that the Egyptians also appreciated it. Adam (1960: chap. 1) seems to imply that the use of a proportional system (or, we could add, a nonproportional system like the one considered here) would obviate the need for the sculptor to attend the quarry, where the block was roughed out, a proposal disputed by Harrison (1972: 536). Lauren Adams (1978) offers a clear description of the relation between cube block and techniques of carving in early Greece; Greek and Egyptian practices are comparable at many levels.

8   Sunk relief (*relief en creux*) involves special technical considerations and it is argued that for it we must find "a completely different intellectual

background from true relief" (Schäfer, 1974: 76). Whether the artist raises or sinks the figure in the surface, he still begins with a drawing on the surface.

NOTES TO PAGES 18–27

9   For proportional regularization on the Narmer Palette, see Iversen, 1975: 60–6; Meyer, 1974. There are some unclarities in these accounts, and it is not evident that Iversen's claim to see the eighteen-unit canon in use at this early date can be sustained in every detail. Nonetheless, the Narmer Palette and related works do seem to be differentiated from other early dynastic works by the systematic internal consistency of their procedures; the remarkable "stylistic" uniformity of early canonical material could have been obtained partly by regularization through the use of proportional system(s) (see Chapter 6).

10 See bibliographical discussion in Iversen, 1975: 20–6. A fundamental early study by Mackay (1917) is still essential reading; Mackay seems to have been one of the first to recognize that grid squares on tomb walls were not copying devices.

11 It is not yet clear whether the proportional canon(s) offered several options for the breadth of a figure; height-lengths could have been strictly controlled, whereas breadth-widths may have been left to the taste of the artist. The broad shoulders of Mycerinus and Ra-hotep produce a very different figure, for example, from the portly It-wesh, whose statue was represented in a relief now preserved in the Brooklyn Museum (Eaton-Krauss, 1984: 176; Smith, 1949: Pl. 48a). The width of the shoulders or girth of the waist could both have been regulated conventionally; as corpulence was an attribute of the successful courtier (Fischer, 1963: 26), we would expect it to be represented according to formula. Wolf (1957: 189) recognized two types of statues of standing men, slender and portly (*Schmaling und Dralling*).

12 Iversen 1955/1975 is the fundamental work; Lepsius 1884 was the first and is still a useful treatise. See more generally and for alternative emphases Feucht, 1977; Junker, 1957; Meyer, 1975b; Munro, 1971. See Iversen, 1976; Robins, 1984 on the possibility of a finely tuned proportional system for the representation of the face. The variations in the sets of equivalences quoted here are due, for instance, to debate about the definition of various individual units used in the canon. Iversen's detailed proposals have been subjected to many additions and corrections; throughout this book the overall thrust of his account, in comparison with the two most systematic competing accounts by Kielland (1955) and Lorenzen (1977, 1980), has been accepted. For further study, see Hanke, 1959, who proposes the existence of a Late Period canon of twenty-one grid squares to satisfy a revised metrology, which is accepted by Iversen in his second edition (1975). See Baines, 1978; Vandersleyen, 1978, for important corrections to Iversen; Lorenzen 1977, 1980, for although his alternative is wholly improbable historically, his cautionary remarks on ancient metrology are apt.

13 The German *Abstand*, "standpoint," with the secondary connotation of "standing away" from what is being seen, has the advantage of stressing that aspect is the artist's decision about the position of the observing eye in close, frontal, direct relation or in more distant relation to the object. The English "aspect" is preferable to "viewpoint," often used in art theory, as it does not in-

volve any connotation of belief or opinion and is not easily confused with problems of compositional viewpoint. For unusual figure positions, see especially Senk, 1950, although not all of his broader arguments can be accepted.

14 Schäfer, 1974: 91–2. No English rendering of Schäfer's terminology adequately describes his meaning. Brunner-Traut (1973, 1974a) has coined the term *Aspektive*, "aspective," although English readers are tempted to see this term only as the opposite of "perspective" rather than, as also intended, a substantive derived from the German *Aspekt-sehen*, that is, "to see partial, direct, and close views or images." Further confusion may result from not unjustified conflation with another tradition of German writing on art theory and ancient art, in which a precise contrast is drawn between "hypotactic (perspective) and paratactic (preperspective) representation," most effectively by Krahmer (1931: chap. 1). In my treatment, two separate features of Schäfer's (unitary technique of) *geradvorstellig* representation are taken to be quite different efforts, the first to present any one component of a figure in a particular way (the problem of components), the second to articulate these parts in a particular way (the problem of aspect). The treatment of proportions is a third, related organizational effort. These technical and logical considerations are at the root of my argument, developed later (see Chapter 3), that we cannot take *gerad-vorstellig* representation as the inevitable, uniquely determined product of some single perceptual attitude.

15 This feature was first noticed and explicated by Lepsius (see references and discussion in Iversen, 1975: 33–7). For general theory, see Lange, 1899, where the concept of a rotation toward frontality is introduced (compare Suys, 1935 for helpful analysis). For important discussions of this effect in Egyptian art, see Badawy, 1954; Iversen, 1975: 33–7; Schäfer, 1974: 85, 310–34.

16 Compare Schäfer, 1974: 322–3. An interesting example of ambiguity of this kind, between "standing" and "striding" stances, is discussed at length by Wood, 1978. Schäfer, 1974: 187–8 argues that for groups of figures canonical composition offered two formulas, one for static groups and the other for groups moving in one direction (see further 1974: 294–5).

17 Best published in Duell, 1938: Pl. 7, although sometimes discussed by earlier commentators. For analysis of this image, see Barta, 1971; Schäfer, 1936b. Smith, 1949: 355 remarks that the panel painting is "more in the nature of a temple calendar than it is the execution of a work of art" (see also M. Müller, 1980: 244). James, 1955: Pl. 10 publishes one apparently similar instance from the mastaba of Khentika. Petrie, 1898: 20, 46, and Pl. 26 may have discovered such an easel painting in the tomb of Lady Meri at Deshasheh. The evidence is collected and discussed by Duell, 1940.

18 It is sometimes difficult to know whether the scale of a figure reflects its actual size relative to other objects or whether it has been manipulated according to decorative or narrative considerations. For example, Old Kingdom tombs contain several scenes of the transport of "colossal" statues, although no such colossi are definitely known from this period. Eaton-Krauss (1984: 63–4, 74) has suggested that these scenes actually represent the transport of ordinary (life-size or

half-life-size) statues – for the draftsman has drawn the laborers proportionally smaller in order that the picture of the statue be proportionally larger, that is, the size of the tomb owner, drawn elsewhere in the tomb and always the most important personage represented in the program.

19 Schäfer, 1974: 125–8, 195, but compare 1974: 163, where it seems to be suggested, oddly, that the baseline is "in no way a natural inheritance from the early period." Groenewegen-Frankfort (1951: 8, 16–18) says of the contorted figures on the Narmer Palette (see Figure 6.14) that they "seem to float in a medium which baulks spatial imagination" (and see also Smith, 1949: 128); "floating" or "hovering" figures have been seen in other predynastic compositions and in derived compositions like the canonical hunting scene (see Chapter 4). However, some of these figures are merely and very firmly pinned down to the ground plane; the convention is surely a depiction of dying or dead figures lying stretched on the ground, the surface of the earth (as on the bottom obverse of the Narmer Palette). On the Hunter's Palette (see Figure 6.10), the artist seems to stress this by turning his slain lion upside down; the painter of the Decorated Tomb at Hierakonpolis (Case and Payne, 1962) does the same for the body of a defeated warrior. When "contorted" figures are not twisted from the vertical axis (as on the bottom reverse of the Narmer Palette or the left edge of the Battlefield Palette, see Figure 6.11), they are to be understood as upright but fleeing.

20 Egyptian art does contain devices suggesting to a viewer that his world is continuous with the pictorial world. For instance, the aspect of a figure in a drawing could be a "realistic" depiction of what we actually see from a stationary position. Foreshortening is an effort of this kind as well: The figure is depicted as we would see it from a particular position. A "three-quarter back view" of a serving girl in a well-known Theban tomb painting is often held to be an example of cavalier perspective, although it looks awkward from a conventional canonical and illusionistic vantage point, as only one part of the figure is perspectively drawn; Schäfer, 1974: 264 shows that some "perspective"-like elements in this painting are partly the result of serious error by modern copyists. Overlapping and rare instances of partial foreshortening, as well as false overlaps and "transparencies," are probably attempts to clarify the original spatial position of some element, perhaps too ambiguous if treated in the standard manner (see Schäfer, 1974: 117–18, 172–7, and Chaps. 4.1, 4.2, 5). For the publication and analysis of unusual drawings, sometimes thought to incorporate "perspective" elements or partial foreshortenings, see Borchardt, 1893; Klebs, 1914; Rostem, 1948; Schäfer, 1938, 1974: 259–76 (most reliable); Senk, 1933, with a helpful review in Brunner-Traut, 1982. Many of the cases examined by these authorities are disputable and puzzling; some are noncanonical, but what exactly they may be in positive, particular terms is unclear. As Tefnin, 1979a: 220 points out, using several examples, many discussions of the treatment of space in Egyptian representation approach the problem from the wrong end, that is, as the problem of the "lack of perspective" in Egyptian drawing.

1 For bibliography and further discussion, see Chapter 5, note 7.

2 See generally Schäfer, 1936a, 1974: 17–18, 38; Scharff, 1937, 1939, 1941; Vandersleyen, 1975a, 1982; Weeks, 1979: 69–71. The "objectivity" of Egyptian portraits and the dangers of using them as historical-documentary records are discussed by Tefnin, 1979a; Vandersleyen, 1975a.

3 Wood (1978) makes many interesting observations, with which my account does not necessarily conflict. Apparently Wood feels that the two panels discussed here were made by the same sculptor, although she claims to see differences in quality between these two productions and the other surviving relief panels from the tomb. She discusses the balance of "idealizing" and "individualizing" features in these other reliefs and concludes that they are less successful. In her account of the iconographic program, in which the seated panel is the initial "statement," the sculptor attempted to portray "two phases of one state of being, rather than two mutually exclusive states" (p. 16), phases she describes as "active" and "passive" in relation to the offerings being received and/or given. This interpretation may be complementary to my stress here on the sculptor's differentiation, in separate "portraits," of two different aspects of Hesire's character and position in life, signaled by subtle changes in pose, costume, expression, and modeling of details. However, there may not be only two such phases or aspects. My examination of these reliefs in the original suggests that each one of the surviving specimens is highly individual and, although the decayed specimens are harder to describe, that they were also all produced by the same hand. (At another point in her analysis, p. 21, Wood seems to differentiate between three states, seated, standing, and striding, each with a different meaning.) The claim that the overall program of showing different states is "narrative" (p. 19) is difficult to follow. Although the differences between the portraits are conceivably intended to depict Hesire at various moments, they all seem generally to represent him as a youthful and vigorous man of authority rather than tell a story about his change.

4 Baines, 1985a (with references to relevant scientific and anthropological literature); Reutersward, 1958; Smith, 1949: 257–63; Vandier, 1964: 29–33; C.R. Williams, 1932. For the significance of special colorations for particular figures or objects, see, for example, Brunner-Traut, 1977; Fischer, 1963, and the intriguing proposals by Tefnin, 1979b: 135–7 on the possible political significance of the coloration of Hatshepsut's statues.

5 For instance, it is not true at all that children, untutored adults, or any pre-Greek culture will instinctively adopt the *geradvorstellig* mode of representation, although draftsmen will very often do so. On the basis of his own experiment and before he is trained in perspective, a child will acquire techniques of drawing systematically defined in both "aspective" and "illusionist" traditions (see, for instance, Freeman, 1980; Willats, 1977), and beyond the simplest drawings of the simplest forms (like the boxes and cups that Schäfer's children drew for him) children's compositions and Egyptian wall scenes are quite different. For further consideration of the universalizing aspects of Schäfer's

hypotheses, see Baines, 1985b, although with extreme caution on all general points about the theory of depiction and depictional reference.

For general comments and criticisms focusing on the theoretical orientation of the essay, see Baines, 1974b; Norman de Garis Davies, 1952; Simpson, 1955; Vandersleyen, 1974. Groenewegen-Frankfort (1972) has also produced a more accessible account of the development of Egyptian art; her aim "to make stylistic idiosyncracies appear significant" (1972: 13) is an important counterpoint to the identification of regularities undertaken by Schäfer. Although it would require too much space here, an interesting historiographical analysis could trace the influence of Cassirer and the Warburg art historians on Groenewegen-Frankfort's mature writing.

In 1955: 72, Panofsky seems to say that three-quarter and oblique views cannot enter the drawing. For Aldred (1973: 796), "the hips assume a three-quarter view." For this interpretation of the anatomy, see Schäfer, 1974: 293–4. Schäfer's preliminary discussion of "shifts" in construction (1974: 98, 106, 322) is not significantly helpful. Krahmer's insight (1931: chap. 1, and see Wolf, 1957: 281–4) that drawings combining several views are *wechselseitig*, "side changing," aptly characterizes the common policy of a ninety-degree movement of the viewing eye around the sides (facets, planes) of a complex object (compare Badawy's *rabattement*, 1973: 418–19), but does not apply to the ambiguities here, where no specification of angle, view, or direction and degree of shift is made. Despite his insistence on *geradvorstellig* and "directionally straight" preferences, Schäfer (1974: 89–90, 323) was forced to admit that oblique views of objects "help at a subconscious level" in construction.

4 THE ORDER OF ICONOGRAPHY

See Panofsky, 1939: chap. 1 for his crucial distinctions between types of primary or secondary "meaning" or "content," and, further, Goodman, 1971: chap. 1 (on pictorial denotation) and the text and notes of Wollheim, 1980: Essay V (on seeing the picture in the mark, seeing the mark as an object). Throughout this book, I have often depended upon an implicit distinction between the picture's morphology (the form of the mark) and its meaning (its reference). Because we can say a good deal about pictorial morphology, including statements such as "the mark resembles the face of a human being," it says nothing about whether pictorial meaning has been grasped (for just because the mark resembles the face of a human being does not guarantee that it represents that face) (see further Davis, 1987, 1989). For extremely important considerations on the semiotic identity of the "image" in Egyptian art, see Tefnin, 1981, 1983.

See also the useful classifications of subject matters in Old Kingdom tomb scenes in Porter, Moss, and Malek, 1974: 355–58; in Theban private tomb paintings in Porter, Moss, and Malek, 1960: 463–74; and in Theban temples in Porter, Moss, and Malek, 1972: 542–52.

Baxandall (1972, 1980) has made it abundantly clear that the ordinary perceptual skills and information of members of a culture will be a condition of successful artistic production and interpretation. It is not so clear that these skills are an explanation of artistic practices and preferences. As not all perceptual habits enter into image making, the artist selects to depend upon certain skills, implying, in turn, some specific and specialized theory of making and interpreting images above and beyond the perceptual skills inherently required and employed in so doing. I do not believe (see further Chapter 7) that we should find this "theory" written down in a manual of or for artistic production, nor that it is stated in other media of knowledge; when we ask how the picture represents in addition to asking with what eyes it is seen, we are minimally asking only about the interpretation of the mark's morphology. How the picture represents is in the ordinary circumstance of the social replication of meanings not just a function of what eyes see it, but also a function of how those eyes have come to know that the picture could or does represent something for someone, namely, its maker. The minimal interpretative skill, then, is at least partial knowledge of the "epidemiology of representations" (Sperber, 1985) or "chain of replications" (Davis, 1987, 1989) connecting the picture maker and picture viewer's cognitive representations of the morphology of the mark as having been produced for its resemblance to something or other in the world. Although the picture maker and picture viewer may possess identical perceptual habits, interests, and skills, the picture viewer will not interpret the picture maker's meaning in any strong sense unless and until a causal link obtains between their separate cognitive acts of interpreting pictures – a link *in* which the viewer replicates the maker's "inaugural" act of seeing-as (Davis, 1987, 1989).

4   Williams and Logan (1987) have produced a vigorous and important argument that images like the Decorated Tomb painting (see also Case and Payne, 1962; J. Saleh, 1987) exemplify the "conceptual basis" of "pharaonic civilization." Read loosely enough, of course, the "conceptual basis" of later cultures and societies can always be found in earlier. However, Williams and Logan's thesis is much more debatable if read more literally to assert an important similarity or commonality, if not identity, between the reference, symbolism, and ideology of the earlier and the later images.

It is perfectly obvious that early dynastic royal iconography, as it appears on the works of King Scorpion, Narmer, and the historical First Dynasty kings, has formal antecedents in mannerisms and motifs of art in the Nile Valley as far back as the Nagada I (Amratian) and earlier (see further Chapter 6). Since no artist can fully escape his cultural heredity, just as he cannot escape his genes, we should fully expect to find such lineages. But the mere identification of iconographic lineages (where the term "iconography" is emptied of the "content" or "connotation" each image possesses and reductively regarded merely as a lineage of formally similar traits) is tricky. If by definition an artistic tradition consists of works "made for regard in some way works of art in the past have been regarded" (Levinson, 1979, for an elegant statement), then by definition we will at minimum always find morphological parallels for dynastic motifs in earlier art – but if we can always find them, what have we learned of historical significance? Furthermore, a morphological parallel is not a source, that is, an earlier representation explicitly referred to or "quoted" by a later artist (see Goodman, 1978: 47–50, on the intricacies of pictorial quotation), a representation that serves as the very subject of his conservational or revisionary ambition. In his fundamental doctrine of iconographic disjunction, Panofsky (1960) was quite clear that formally similar motifs undergo constant change in symbolic value. There would be no guarantee that the hunting motifs of dynastic imagery have anything "conceptually" to do with the visually similar hunting imagery of the Nagada I, II, or III, just as the Madonna painted in the style of Raphael by Raphael in 1500 has connotations quite disjunct from the Madonna painted in the style of Raphael in 1988 (Davis 1989). In a sense, the whole modern so-called social history of art has been an answer to the methodological problem of possible iconographic disjunction (see Clark, 1986 on Manet's relation to the past of painting; Michael Fried, 1969). Only careful evaluation of the immediate sociopolitical circumstances of an image maker's activities will tell us what his symbolism amounts to.

Two different social histories, very broadly speaking, can be put forward to explicate the formal iconographic lineages from at least Nagada IIb to the imagery of King Scorpion, Narmer, and the historical First Dynasty kings (lineages we fully expect to find at a morphological level). In one account, the known monarchic/dynastic social structure, ideology, and symbolic ambitions of early dynastic Egypt are projected back into the past. If the chieftain buried in Tomb 100 lived and thought like a petty kinglet or proto-pharaoh, then we can comfortably interpret his scenes of battle, hunting, and so on as the "conceptual basis" of formally similar dynastic images. Iconographic source chasing alone cannot confirm or disconfirm this scenario. A great deal depends upon broader evidence for and theories about the societies of Nagada II and of dynastic Egypt respectively – ranked chiefdoms versus states, local direct redistributive economies versus national economies employing large-scale taxation, dispersed settlement versus a form of incipient urbanism, and so forth. In the absence of convincing archaeological and anthropological evidence that state organization and ideology were in place in the Nagada IIb/c (Hoffman, 1979; Trigger, 1983), this account risks a fatal anachronism and teleology. It is not yet entirely clear whether Williams and Logan wish to find state organization and ideology so early; B. Williams does make a convincing case (1986) that a rich, stratified society buried some of its dead in Cemetery L at Qustul (Nubia), but it is not certain that we should interpret this society as anything more than the familiar "ranked chiefdom" preceding state formation in all known sequences of state development (Haas, 1982). Moreover, pushing the chronological appearance of the state as such back to an earlier date does not in itself suffice to show that any earlier images (say, Nagada IIb or earlier) possessed pharaonic "content" or "connotations" in Panofsky's sense.

In the other account, less dramatic claims are made about the sociology and ideology of predynastic Egypt but a stronger claim is made about the qualities of dynastic (that is, state) iconography. Much more than the mere continuation of a tradition inaugurated earlier, early dynastic iconography (whether or not it is the first iconography of the state in Egypt) is palpably an active quotation from and manipulation of a tradition – and this in spite of substantial sociological and ideological differences between state and earlier society which the very reproduction of tradition has been designed to disguise. There is a formal continuity between proto-dynastic and earlier iconography in Egypt precisely and only because the newly emerging state required it; continuity is less the mere maintenance and much more the invention of a tradition. It is this account I pursue in this book (see further Chapter 6).

5 Found at Abydos, published in Amélineau, 1899: Pl. 33; Spencer, 1980: No. 460. For the iconography of this puzzling and controversial artifact, see Frankfort, 1948: 26, 87, 204–5; Smith, 1949: 116, 121; Vandier, 1952: 859.

6 See above, note 4, and Chapter 6 for further consideration of the Oxford Palette; disjunction does not imply utter discontinuity but (a degree of) symbolic difference.

7 Other captive scenes and the motif studied by Schäfer, 1974: 171 (5); Simpson, 1973c (for Ptolemaic cases); Wildung, 1975. For the "falling" figure in battle and other contexts, see Duell, 1938: Pl. 130; Mohr, 1943: Fig. 25; the most suggestive and sensitive examination of the theme is still Matz, 1923–4, although some examples could now be added to his enumeration. The distinction between "dead" and "falling or fallen" figures, ambiguous in terms of aspect or composition, could be indicated by facial expression, as in the reliefs of Ramesses III (Nelson, 1929: 32).

8 Compared with definitely disjunct earlier images like the Oxford and Hunter's Palettes (see Figures 6.9, 6.10) the Bull and Battlefield Palettes (Figure 4.11, see also Figure 6.11) must be regarded as within the range of canonical iconography; although they may indeed be fully substitutable for other pharaonic images of the victorious king, there are unique features of the two works suggesting they too were slightly disjunct from the absolutely canonical motif of smiting as presented on the Narmer Palette (see Figure 6.14) (see Chapter 6). Needless to say, my rough distinction in these paragraphs between "equivalent" and "nonequivalent" substitutabilities is heuristic only, for no substitution can be absolutely equivalent (synonymous) (see Goodman's classic paper of 1949); which is only to say that the reality of metaphor in human representation "always already" works against the "rigid designation" canonical languages strive toward; "chains of replicating" an image necessarily lead to a continual "fading out" of inaugural reference or even of the morphology of the image altogether (Davis, 1987).

5 ACADEMIC PRODUCTION

1 In practice, of course, all observable characteristics could not be enumerated; we must arrive at some working definition of the most significant features, the traits of the type we are examining. Traits that original producers would remark as such – as perceptible properties of the artifact – are not the only ones coming up for the count.

Typological procedures in modern statistical archaeology employ assumptions of deep interest to our problem (Clarke, 1980, for references; Stiles, 1979: 2). The degree of invariance between instances of a trait that appears in a sample should be clearly distinguished from the frequency of appearance of the trait itself. The traits of "art objects" usually are already specified as a complex of qualities (we examine color, size, material, morphology or "style," and so on). Individually measurable (if sometimes imperceptible) qualities are potentially variable even if the trait invariably appears (e.g., colors are within the range of earth tones); the appearance of the trait is potentially variable within a sample of objects each with many traits (e.g., some objects in the sample are not colored). Intuitively, we might suppose that in a canonical art invariance will be high in either case. In fact, individual qualities can be variable within a significant tolerance without the overall sample of objects with many qualities varying one (randomly specified) whole object from the next. Furthermore, if the initial selection of objects for comparison is controlled, usually by grouping them according to presence/absence of one or more traits, then the apparent overall coherence of the group compared with external groups will often be greater, notwithstanding potential internal variabilities from one object to the next. Informally, although in the sample of objects of a canonical art, one object may appear quite different when more or less randomly compared with another, all objects within the sample, compared with noncanonical objects, are highly invariant; moreover, the presence/absence of a single trait is not sufficient grounds either for including or for excluding the object in the sample or subcategories of the sample. On these and other aspects of the theory of polytypic aggregations or polythetic classifications in stylistic description, see further Davis, 1988a, with full references.

2 Whether preserved or discarded, practical or didactic, we can learn a great deal from these sources, however casually they transmitted information to producers. For example, see publications and discussions by Arnold, 1973; Badawy, 1973; Borchardt, 1896; Clarke and Engelbach, 1930: 48–51; Daressy, 1898; Norman de Garis Davies, 1917a, b; de Cénival, 1964: 145–6; Donadoni, 1982; Gardiner and Carter, 1917 (also in Scamuzzi, 1965: Pl. 87); Glanville, 1930; Gunn, 1926; Lauer, 1962: 39, 163, Fig. 53; Petrie, 1926; Smith and Stewart, 1984.

3 Lange and Schäfer, 1908: CG No. 20539, where his title is "master of secrets (or secret things) of the god's word"; *mdw ntr*), "god's word," seems to have the unspecific meaning of "sacred writings."

4 Using this and other examples, this argument has been made, for example, by Badawy, 1965: 9–11, and Barta, 1970: 82–6, with full references to earlier discussions; Barta takes the "sacred words" (*mdw ntr*) in part as texts on the arts and *Vorbilder*, preparatory drawings or patterns, intended as text illustration, collections of motifs for relief cycles, and other material.

5 Gardiner, 1961: 414; Kemp, 1983: 104–5. On divine images, see especially Hornung, 1982: 64, 107, 117, 124, 135, 140, 153.

6 See Sauneron, 1957: 136, 156, on Chassinat, 1928, 351, lines 8–9; translations and comments in Brugsch, 1871: 44 (6): "Die Vorschrift vom Bemalen einer Wand (und) von der Beachtung der Körperformen"; Barta, 1970: 85: "Die Vorschrift für das Beschreiben der Wand und das Bemalen der Körper"; M. Müller, 1980: 245: "Die Vorschrift für des Bemalen/Beschriften der Wand."

7 Although of great interest for many of the problems I have taken up in this book, the material is widely dispersed and poorly known. In

addition to many scattered references to ostraca in the literature, major published sources include Anthes, 1939; Baud, 1935; Borchardt, 1910a; Brunner-Traut, 1956 (with reviews by Keimer, 1957; Mekhitarian, 1957; Roeder, 1957; Senk, 1958a contributing important ideas), 1974b, 1979; Capart, 1941b; Carter, 1923; Daressy, 1901; Norman de Garis Davies, 1917a; de Wit, 1966; Keimer, 1941; Page, 1983; Peck and Ross, 1978; Peterson, 1973; Schäfer, 1916; Senk, 1958b, c; Smith, 1958; Spiegelberg, 1918; Vandier-d'Abbadie, 1936, 1937, 1941, 1946a (with review by Keimer, 1948), 1957, 1959, 1960 (add now Gasse, 1986); Werbrouck, 1932, 1934; C.R. Williams, 1921.

8 Hierakonpolis: Tomb 100, the so-called Decorated Tomb (Case and Payne, 1962; Kemp, 1973; J. Saleh, 1987); Sakkara: interesting and early examples are the mat-pattern paintings in early dynastic tombs (Emery, 1949, 1954) and the "swamp" scene from the tomb of Hesire (Quibell, 1913: Pl. 7, no. 2); Giza: the so-called Covington Tomb (Smith, 1949: 141) apparently contained a painted wall, dated to the end of the Second Dynasty.

9 A fundamental source for the study of the Egyptian artist is Smith, 1949, with a review article by Wilson (1947, on Smith's first edition). Important further studies include Bogoslovsky, 1980; Drenkhahn, 1976 (especially 69–71, for the names and titles of the painter); Eaton-Krauss, 1984; Forbes, 1950; Junker, 1959; Kaplony, 1966b; E. Schott, 1979; Steinmann, 1980–4; Wolf, 1951.

10 For instance, see Capart, 1957; Junker, 1956; Mekhitarian, 1956, 1957; Spiegelberg, 1918; von Bissing, 1929; Ward, 1977.

11 Discussions of "signing" in Roeder, 1912; Spiegelberg, 1902; Ware, 1927; Wilson, 1947.

12 For an Egyptian painted relief, we know of the outline draftsman, whose initial red outlines on the wall were finalized and sometimes corrected in black, possibly by a second draftsman; of the "wielder of the chisel," who cut the relief outlines and modeled the forms; and of the painter, who may have been the same as the outline draftsman (see Drenkhahn, 1976: 69–71; Smith, 1949: chap. 13, for this terminology). Sometimes preliminary yellow sketches were worked over more carefully in red (e.g., Norman de Garis Davies, 1903–8: III, 28; Quibell, 1913: 17, and Pl. 10), and finalized in black. Occasionally the first sketch is the master's organizational plan, the others finishing efforts by subordinates; in the tomb of Hesire, the first yellow sketch was rough and was corrected in red. A large composition was produced by a work gang of artists, often divided into two teams, under the direction of masters (Bierbrier, 1982; Bogoslovsky, 1980; Černý, 1929, 1973a, b). In a sculptor's workshop many hands were also required – plaster workers, stonecutters, relief sculptors, finishers and polishers, painters, and so on (Montet, 1925: 288–95). Textual evidence suggests the Egyptians differentiated between the master sculptors per se and the assistants responsible for either preparatory work (roughing out the block) or finishing work (polishing) or both (Anthes, 1941: 103–6; Drenkhahn, 1976: 60–71; Eaton-Krauss, 1984: 44–45, 48).

13 In the Greco-Roman foundation texts we do read, but rather unhelpfully, of the "rule," "formula," or "canon" for the laying-out of buildings (Badawy, 1965: 9, with references). Conceivably these texts point to the existence of an elaborate vocabulary for "standards" and "norms" of proportion and construction, as Badawy apparently be-

lieved; however, perhaps the formulas were simple, specific, and relatively uninteresting in themselves. The Egyptians did have a complex
vocabulary for the practical aspects of artistic and architectural work;
for instance, see Černý's study (1973a: 27–33) of the terminology for
the parts of the tomb, reconstructed on the basis of literary evidence and
other sources, and P. Spencer's (1984) lexicographical study of the
Egyptian temple.

14 On problems of authority, anonymity, and creativity, see Borchardt,
1910a, Hermann, 1936; Roeder, 1947; Scharff, 1939; Spiegel, 1940;
von Bissing, 1947; Wolf, 1935, in which Romantic aesthetic philos-
ophy comes to grips with Egyptian art; in the more recent literature,
the introduction of the concepts of particular canons of performance
(e.g., of proportions, Iversen, 1975), of "decorum" in discursive and
representational practice (Baines, 1985b), and of canonical representation as such (Davis, 1982) revise the terms of this debate.

6 THE EMERGENCE OF CANONICAL CONVENTIONS

1 Uninitiated readers may find the literature on late predynastic and
early dynastic Egyptian archaeology difficult to follow due to lack of
scholarly consensus on a terminology for the successive phases of
Egyptian culture and on the recognition of these phases themselves.
Useful discussions of modern chronologies may be found in Kaiser
and Dreyer, 1982; Trigger, 1983; Williams and Logan, 1987; fixed
points are provided by radiocarbon dates from Nagada I through
Second Dynasty contexts (e.g., Hassan, 1980, 1984). Needless to say,
all "phases" or "periods" recognized by modern typologists are arbitrary to some extent and possibly misleading if interpreted as anything more than a strictly "archaeological entity." The grossest
division commonly used in Egyptology – predynastic/dynastic – is
almost impossible to avoid in practice but quite unsatisfactory, especially if the Nagada III is regarded as "pre"-dynastic. Recognizing
that all segmentations of the archaeological continuum will have their
deficiencies, I adopt the following terminology:

Nagada I   (Amratian), Petrie's Sequence Dates 30–38, c. 4700–
                3700 B.C.
Nagada IIa/b   (Gerzean), SD 38–40/45, c. 3700–3400/3300 B.C.
Nagada IIc/d   (late predynastic), SD 40/45–63, c. 3400/3300–.
Nagada IIIa/b   SD 63–at least SD 77/78.

In some writing, Nagada IIIa/b will be called Late Gerzean, Dynasty
0, or "beginning of the First Dynasty." Nagada IIIb certainly overlaps
at least in part with Kaiser and Dreyer's (1982) isolation of the early
generations of the dynastic state:

Horizon A   initial period of the dynastic state, al-
                            though its kings are not named
Horizon B   period of the state in the reigns of Scor-
                            pion, Iry-Hor, Ka, and Narmer
historical First Dynasty   begins with Hor-Aha, c. 3100 B.C.

I refer to both Horizons A and B as "early First Dynasty" and frequently write Nagada III/early First Dynasty to indicate the fact that

the two "phases" of the culture may overlap and that the whole period may be fairly brief. For our purposes the most significant distinction should be drawn, as a rough approximation, between Nagada IIc/d and Nagada III, as prestate ("chiefly") and state societies respectively (Hoffman, 1979; Trigger, 1983).

2   For the types, see Kaiser, 1956, 1957; Kemp, 1982; Petrie, 1920: 16–22, 1921: Pls. 31–37; Vandier, 1952: 329–56. George, 1975 is an exemplary catalogue of Decorated Ware.

3   In 1974: 102, Schäfer goes even further in speaking of the "resistance" of the surface when a draftsman explicitly attempted a foreshortened view. The Egyptians supposedly lacked a "plastic sensibility" that would have directed their interest to fully modeled mass (1974: 75).

4   Von Kaschnitz Weinberg (1965b: 149–54, 190–5) made provocative but in the end untenable comments on the development of relief under Mesopotamian influence. Recently, Baines (1983: 575) has reiterated, as a "widespread guess," the proposal that "the idea of writing was introduced by 'stimulus diffusion' from Mesopotamia" (see also Trigger, 1983: 37).

5   Developments of this theme can be found, for example, in James, 1980; Scranton, 1964. A penetrating study by Tefnin (1983) considers advanced semiotic questions, and makes us aware of the conceptual and logical differences between images and notational characters, whatever their visual resemblances (see the crucial arguments of Goodman, 1971: chap. 4).

6   Perhaps an abstract visual image, Egyptian or otherwise, is more difficult for a viewer to understand than an optically faithful image. The effort involved in the interpretation of such images perhaps has a general similarity with the process of reading a script. This cautious equation has been employed effectively by Schäfer (1974: 110), but can be overdone (Schäfer, 1974: 151, 154–5, seems to be inconsistent).

7   Schäfer, 1974: 11–12 considers other possible examples. On the frontal face in relief work, see for instance Smith, 1949: 140, Pl. 57c, e, and for the full-face hieroglyph, Mysliwiec, 1972b.

8   An iconographic rather than morphological dating, sometimes proposed, is not helpful; the Min standard may have an early appearance in the Nagada I (Baumgartel, 1955: 33), but appears as a pot mark in the Nagada II (e.g., Wainwright, 1963: 16–17) with a late appearance at SD 81 (Matmar: Brunton, 1948: 28, Pl. 22 [28]); we cannot obtain a precise predynastic fix on the symbol itself.

9   MacIver and Mace, 1902: Pl. 10 (9), SD 57, and Pl. 8 (3) = Petrie, 1920: Pl. 44 (75k), SD 58 (discrepancy not explained). Petrie places sub-Type 76r earlier, at SD 45–47; the examples he had in mind are not cited.

10 The date offered here is based on the morphological and iconographic considerations offered in the text; the theme appears in other media, most notably Nagada II Decorated Ware: Fattovich, 1978: 201 attempts a precise iconographic date.

11 The notched or radiated forms seem to be a late elaboration of a more simple and very common birds'-head-palette type, in which a single V-shaped notch appears between the heads. This type ranges throughout Nagada II with many firmly dated instances (see Kaiser, 1956): e.g., Type 67d from Mahasna, SD 38–44; Type 67t from Nagada Tomb 164, SD 42; Type 67d from Nagada Tomb 1433, SD 42–63;

Type 67t from Diospolis Tomb U90, SD 50; Type 72p (square) from Abydos (Peet, 1913: Pl. 3 [2]), SD 57–66; Type 67t from Mahasna, SD 60; Type 69d from Nagada Tomb 161, SD 65.

12 The Manchester ostrich and Min palettes might be contemporary with a palette discovered in Tomb 59 at Gerzeh, vaguely dated to SD 47–77 (Asselberghs, 1961: Fig. 118; Kaiser, 1964: 119; Petrie, 1953: Pl. B5), if we favor the earlier end of this range. Carved with horns and stars in relief, this palette is thought to symbolize the cow goddess Bat of the seventh nome of Upper Egypt (Hornung, 1982: 103). However, its shapeless polygonal form is typologically late, and the decoration closely resembles the signs on the so-called Hathor Bowl of the First Dynasty (Arkell, 1955; Arkell and Burgess, 1958; Quibell and Green, 1900–1: I, Pl. 18 [21]).

13 The winged griffin on the Oxford Palette from the Main Deposit (Figure 6.9) appears specifically at this point in late predynastic history (Boehmer, 1974). The griffin is found also on another sophisticated work of approximately this period, the gold-covered and embossed knife handle said to be from Gebel el-Tarif. The late predynastic date for these objects is suggested by works like the Brooklyn knife handle (Asselberghs, 1961: Figs. 39–40), discovered by H. de Morgan (1908) in Grave 32 at Abu Zeidan, dated in the SD 50s by Kantor (1944: 128–9) and now even thought to be Nagada III, that is, slightly later (Needler, 1980).

14 See Chapter 4, note 4.

15 No provenance; Asselberghs, 1961: Figs. 122–4; Petrie, 1953: 10, 12, Pl. A3; A.J. Spencer, 1980: No. 575; important interpretative descriptions in Ranke, 1925; Tefnin, 1979a. Little can be said about the morphology in relation to the date of the palette. Its great size, 64 cm. in length, perhaps implies that it is a highly evolved form. Conceptually the work is quite sophisticated. Here it will be assigned to the earlier stages of the range for this artifact type (c. SD 57/58–65); although my date is partly a concession to past consensus that the work is stylistically early, I will suggest that iconographically it seems disjunct from and anterior to dynastic canonical iconography. Yet it is not critical to my argument that the Hunter's Palette be chronologically earlier than fully canonical material, only that whatever its date its noncanonical features be appreciated.

16 In seeing the Bull and Narmer Palettes as by the same hand, Aldred (1980: 35) would commit us to seeing the Battlefield Palette as by Narmer's sculptor also, for it seems to me evident that the Bull and Battlefield Palettes are by the same sculptor. Although there is certainly a close relationship between Narmer's artist and the Battlefield/Bull sculptor – as we will see, Narmer's artist had to know the Battlefield/Bull sculptor's images – I doubt, on the basis of technical differences, that the artists were the same individual.

17 Bersani and Dutoit's (1986) brilliant analysis of Late Assyrian relief raises many parallel possibilities of interpretation for early Egyptian art, where occasionally, as in Assyria, sculptors lock together ostensibly separable and opposed figures, creating intimacies reminiscent of erotic entanglements that "decenter" the "anecdotal violence" of the main narrative itself; like some Assyrian sculptors, the Battlefield/Bull sculptor could be said to exhibit "ambivalence" about the violence he has "chosen to love" (Bersani and Dutoit, 1986: 131, and see Davis,

1988b). A consideration of Egyptian art as a figuration of the vicissitudes of Desire would require another book. I am told that in the late nineteenth century the British Museum fragment of the Battlefield Palette (BM 20791) was on display in the Assyrian galleries.

18 For early dynastic ivory carving, see particularly fine examples from the tomb of Ka at Abydos (Petrie, 1900–1: I, Pl. 12 [12, 13]), the tomb of Djet at Abydos (Petrie, 1902–3: I, Pl. 4 [13]), and Hierakonpolis (B. Adams, 1974: Nos. 324–7, 359, 361, 364–5, 367). For lack of space I have not systematically treated ivory carving in this book, but much the same analysis of the selection of homogeneous canonical procedures and motifs from a heterogeneous tradition could be made for it.

19 Vessels decorated in relief are particularly intriguing and document the close connection between vase working and relief sculpture. See especially the stone vase with Hathor relief from Tomb 1449 at Nagada (Baumgartel, 1955: Pl. 31 [1–4]; Capart, 1905: Fig. 88), a limestone vase from Hierakonpolis with several raised relief motifs now in the Ashmolean Museum (Asselberghs, 1961: 76, n. 1, Fig. 29), and three fragments in East Berlin with reliefs of a warrior (Figure 6.13c), boat, and scorpion respectively (Capart, 1905: Figs. 70–2a). Desroches-Noblecourt (1979: 111–12, Fig. 8) has published a miniature stone vase bearing in relief a dog and a falcon ("Horus and Seth"?), dated through parallels with seal impressions and palettes to the First Dynasty.

20 Many descriptions and discussions of the mace heads are available and will not be repeated here at length. See B. Adams, 1974: xii–xiii, 3, Pls. 1–4 (with complete bibliography); Arkell, 1963: 31–5; Asselberghs, 1961: Figs. 172–80 (excellent photographs); Groenewegen-Frankfort, 1951: 19–20; Murray, 1920: 15–17; Quibell and Green, 1900–1: I, Pl. 26.

21 Found by Petrie in Tomb B10 of the early dynastic "royal cemetery" at Abydos, the largest and thought to be one of the earliest of the tombs, the limestone fragment is only about eight inches high (Fischer, 1963: Pl. 6b; Petrie, 1900–1: I, 8, Pl. 13, no. 158). Tomb B10 was assigned by Petrie (1900–1) to Narmer, but in their recent definitive reassessment of the material Kaiser and Dreyer (1982: 213–19) assign the tomb to Hor-Aha, at the beginning of the historical First Dynasty. Part of the stela, it appears, carried a representation of architectural elements (?). Apparently the *serekh* appeared around a royal name.

22 Convention changed somewhat in the Second Dynasty. The stela of Raneb (Fischer, 1961: 45–53, Fig. 2), the two stelae of Peribsen (Petrie, 1900–1: II, Pl. 31; A.J. Spencer, 1980: No. 15; Vandier, 1952: Figs. 487a, b), and an additional royal (?) stela in Leiden, possibly Second Dynasty (Klasens, 1965), are carved in hard granite, rather than limestone or basalt, and lack the raised border entirely. Whereas the *serekh* of Djet had been centered on the plane created within the border and is therefore slightly off center in relation to the actual edges of the block, the Second Dynasty sculptors center the hieroglyphs in relation to the edges. The forms are well carved and carefully balanced, although somewhat heavier and broader than the slender signs on the stela of Djet.

23 Emery, 1958: 30–31, Pls. 23, 39; Smith, 1981: Fig. 21. In Kemp's reassessment of this mastaba (1967: 22), the stela is thought to belong to the major tomb owner himself, rather than to a courtier buried in

the subsidiary grave. Kemp claims that the stela was built into the brick of the mastaba and its rough edges would therefore not have been visible. However, the evidence does not rule out the possibility that the stela was set up in front of the wall, for its triangular base seems designed to be set into a receptacle of some kind.

24 For the "ceiling stelae" from Helwan, not discussed here, see Haeny, 1971 (who questions their function as ceiling stones); Saad, 1957; Weill, 1950: 180–2. These products display similarities with Memphite slab stelae, but are distinguished by peculiarities as well.

25 Statue-base reliefs: Quibell and Green, 1900–1: I, Pl. 40; Smith, 1981: Fig. 35. Stelae: Quibell and Green, 1900–1: II, Pl. 58 (top and bottom). Doorjamb reliefs: Quibell and Green, 1900–1: I, Pl. 2 (3), II, Pl. 23 (bottom), and another block noted, II, 36; also Engelbach, 1934; three fragments of a red granite doorjamb or stela mentioned by Lansing, 1935: 44, Fig. 11; architectural context, Kemp, 1963: 22. The Khasekhemuwy material is summarized by Farag, 1980. El-Kab fragments of relief: Sayce and Somers Clarke, 1906: 239. Of all southern relief work before the Second Dynasty, the stela of the official Sabef from a chamber in the tomb of Ka (Petrie, 1900–1: I, 26–7, Pls. 30, 36 [48], with location marked on plan, Pl. 60) looks most like the contemporary stela of Merka at Sakkara. However, as is clear from Petrie's description, the stela was half-finished.

26 Sculptors who had worked for private individuals like Merka and Sehenefer in the Memphite manner did continue to produce niche stones in the familiar mode throughout the Third Dynasty. However, distinguishing their products – students of the subject tend to call them "poor" or "primitive" – from the more accomplished or canonical work of their (southern, southern-trained) contemporaries is a problem lying outside the chronological purview of this chapter.

27 Although these two works complete the catalogue of surviving First Dynasty sculpture, we know that other works were produced in this period. A cylinder seal dated to the reign of Den apparently represents three gilded standing statues of the king (Kaplony, 1963: 806, 1142, Fig. 364; Petrie, 1900–1: II, Pl. 7 [5–6]; full discussion in Eaton-Krauss, 1984: 89–90); other representations of statues of the reigns of Djer and Den might be identifiable as well (Eaton-Krauss, 1984: 90, n. 471, 92, n. 484). Incised inscriptions on stone vessels of Anedjib document the existence of two statues of this king showing him as ruler of Upper and of Lower Egypt (Eaton-Krauss, 1984: 93).

28 Baumgartel (1948, 1968, 1969–70) has argued that many Abydene and Hierakonpolitan ivories may not be early dynastic at all; she lists the few with definite excavated contexts in the early dynastic period. This is not to say that other ivories are not early; a stylistic study still needs to be undertaken, and in a preliminary survey Legran (1971) argues for the early date of many further examples. The ivories from Nagada, including excavated specimens like the ivory-block figure from Tomb 1583 (Petrie and Quibell, 1896: Pl. 59 [8]), show stylistic and technical affinities with Hierakonpolitan work.

29 A recent discovery of a fragmentary seated "royal" figurine from Elephantine should probably be dated to this time as well (Dreyer, 1981). Smith discusses a statuette fragment in Cairo (JdE 71586) thought to be contemporary with the two seated figures in University College, London (1949: 8, n. 1); Simpson (1956: 47, n. 4) appears to

accept the attribution. I have not been able to locate the piece and cannot form an opinion from the available photographs. It should probably be placed hereabouts in the sequence.

30 The Palermo Stone and associated fragments document the manufacture of a copper statue of Khasekhemuwy, apparently of imposing size (Eaton-Krauss, 1984: 96, with references); the monument has not survived.

7 THE EXPLANATION OF INVARIANCE: TOWARD A HISTORY OF THE AUTHORITY OF THE CANONICAL IMAGE

1 There is no space here to consider in more detail my claim that "established symbolizations" in themselves constitute "real, lived orders of historical experience." For an important assessment of symbolism as the reference of symbol to symbol and not symbol to some underlying "reality" see Sperber, 1975.

2 On Amarna composition, see Anthes, 1940; Davis, 1978; Frankfort, 1929: chap. 1; Nims, 1973; C.R. Williams, 1929–30; Groenewegen-Frankfort, 1951: 110–13 offers the most focused treatment of temporal indication in Amarna and Ramesside art, but see also Smith, 1965: 158–66. For Wilhelm Worringer (1928), Egyptian canonical representation lacks "sensibility" because it failed to depict the nuanced transitions and subtle transformations of things existing in and through time and space. Although Worringer's descriptions are quite useful, he far overrates the confidence we might attach to a "realistic" depiction of time and space, even when, as in the illusionistic traditions of the West, it is systematically employed.

3 There are numerous readings of this famous "conservative" passage in the *Laws* (see Davis, 1979b; Froidefond, 1971: 326–7). Gombrich (1960: 126) seems to suggest that Egyptian art was understood by Plato as a representation of *Eidos*. However, for Plato, Egyptian representation as much as any other is an "art," implicated in all of the failures of art – its fiction, its illusion. Keuls (1978: 51) argues that "iconographical stereotypes (in Egyptian art) constitute the reduction of visual experience to traditional patterns for the purposes of communication." But she suggests, oddly, that "types" are not intended to "incorporate a transmitted insight into the true nature of things." Surely Plato's point is the reverse: As a schema for sensation, always confused and uncertain, stereotyped forms present general propositions about the nature of things, although the effort may be misguided. The Platonic or Neoplatonic description of Egyptian art has had a fundamental influence on our own tradition. The Neoplatonists, especially in Plotinus's writings on the hieroglyphs (*Enneads* V.viii.6), took Egyptian images (pictures or glyphs) to be "endowed with certain symbolic qualities (*sophia*), by means of which they revealed to the initiated contemplator a profound insight into the very essence and substance of things, and an intuitive understanding of their transcendental origins" (Iversen, 1971b: 175).

4 This remarkable text of the Middle Kingdom takes up the popular theme of civil strife and unrest, but includes difficult passages on the nature of traditional language and individual experience in relation to

it. The text is preserved on an Eighteenth Dynasty writing board (references and translations in Lichtheim, 1973: 146; Simpson, 1973a: 230–3).

5   "First time": see Morenz, 1973: 119, and compare Hornung, 1982: 152, 156, 162. "Name of any thing": from the text of the ritual of Seti I at Abydos (Morenz, 1973: 165). The concept of a first, divine order is at the heart of most accounts of Egyptian religion (Sethe, 1929) and recent studies of Egyptian concepts of history and government (Kemp, 1983: 74–76).

6   Weber was as well aware as any Egyptologist that the king's claim to "own" the land of Egypt was principally a symbolic one. "The agricultural resources of Egypt seem to have been divided amongst three classes of estate: owned directly by the crown; belonging to pious foundations whose relationship to the crown was a subtle one; in the hands of private individuals and liable to taxation" (Kemp, 1983: 82). For patrimonial rule generally, see Weber, 1978: 231–5. Although many Egyptologists do not employ Weberian terminology, some have followed him in recognizing Egypt as one of the clearest and most important historical cases of patrimonialism (e.g., Janssen 1978: 224).

7   Some debate centers around the relative usefulness of the Marxist conception of class (employed, for instance, in de Ste. Croix, 1983: 81–98, for ancient Greece and Rome) compared with the Weberian emphasis on orders and statuses (see the clear definitions in Finley, 1973: 35–61). Although Weberian proposals frame my discussion here, I accept a historical materialist approach later: The position of producers and consumers in the social extraction of surplus value from primary producers defines their "class" position and identity (by this measure, artisans and patrons both belong to an exploiting class, which, of course, had its own substantial internal divisions).

An important specific problem concerns Weber's "servile component." Weber himself apparently did not imply that in Egypt slaves were held in the Roman legal sense. Alternative definitions of the "status" of the primary producing "class" are very controversial. The Soviet Egyptologist V. V. Struve distinguished between the exploitation of agricultural producers ("rural communes") and slaves and avoided "insisting on the slave status of the bulk of the exploited immediate producers in Egypt" (Dunn, 1982: 59).

J. Janssen has noted that "the obviously enormous amount of work involved in building the pyramids has led scholars from Herodotus onwards to assume that the workers lived under conditions not essentially different from those of slavery, or at least serfdom. There is no evidence to support this. . . . It is likely that *corvée* for the maintenance of what irrigation works existed at the time, together with the custom of conscripting men for expeditions to quarries and mines, constituted the legal basis for the right to summon laborers for public works, among which the construction of pyramids figured prominently; but this does not mean that the peasants and workmen were legally or socially slaves or serfs" (Janssen, 1978: 227).

We need to know not only what the laborers' position was "legally or socially" but also what their life was like practically or materially; here archaeology supplements the official legal and administrative documents. Non-Egyptological readers will note in much Egyptological writing an amount of wordplay that banishes unfavorable terminologies from descriptions of Egyptian life (read "serf" rather than "laborer," "master" rather than "official"). Much of what Finley (1980) says about classical scholarship applies to Egyptological writing as well. We have been very unwilling to tarnish our idealizations of ancient life by recognizing its basis in the massive exploitation of massive populations, a fact that hardly appears in any of our literary, artistic, or preferred documentary evidence.

De Ste. Croix (1983: 3–4) has insisted that the question should concern not the absolute number of "slaves" in the ancient economy (or whether one was a "slave" only now and then) but whether "the propertied classes derived their surplus above all through the exploitation of unfree labor," an entirely different point for empirical scrutiny. "It is above all in relation to its function of extracting the maximum surplus out of those primary producers who were at the lowest levels of ancient society that I propose to consider slavery and other forms of unfree labor" (1983: 39); "we are perfectly entitled according to common parlance to speak of a society as a 'slaveowning' one even though its slaves constitute much less than half the population and slaveowners are quite a small minority": In the antebellum South, less than 25 percent of Southern families owned even one slave and only 0.6 percent of all families owned more than 50, but nevertheless all historians correctly treat "the Old South as a slave society in the full sense" (1983: 54).

8   My account depends upon the classic treatments of Morton Fried, 1967; Service, 1975; revised and extended in Haas, 1982; and upon recent work by Godelier (e.g., 1978, 1982, 1986), Meillassoux (1972, 1978), and Sahlins (1983). For the role of force or violence in state formation, see the clearly focused treatments by Carneiro, Haas, and others in Jones and Kautz, 1981.

9   It is worth noting that many of these features can be associated with "ranked" societies as much as more complex or larger state formations (see Brown, 1971, Earle and Ericson, 1977; Peebles and Kus, 1977): Again, just because a chieftain can command the construction of a "theocratic public monument" (Service, 1975: 304) does not necessarily mean he rules a state.

10 I would extend a speculation of Michael Hoffman's: "It might well be that, with the increased stress laid on floodplain agriculture with the collapse of the desert ecosystem, those individuals familiar with the hydraulic regime of the lowlands were able to parlay their knowledge into increased power through the medium of their organizational ability" (1979: 312). These individuals' efforts must be much more extensive. "The quantity of vital technical knowledge in this kind of society is limited and can be mastered in a relatively short time. This is likely to put all men above a certain age on an equal footing." Although "the social importance attributed in these societies to 'the one who knows' is easily apparent to all observers" (Meillassoux, 1978: 137), knowledge may not merely be of routine technical information.

ABBREVIATIONS

AA	Aegyptologische Abhandlungen
AfO	*Archiv für Orientforschung*
AJA	*American Journal of Archaeology*
AJSL	*American Journal of Semitic Languages and Literatures*
ASAE	*Annales du Service des antiquités de l'Egypte*
BBM	*Bulletin of the Brooklyn Museum*
Bibl. Or.	*Bibliotheca Orientalis*
BIFAO	*Bullétin de l'Institut français d'archéologie orientale du Caire*
BJA	*British Journal of Aesthetics*
BMAA	*Bullétin des Musées royaux d'art et d'histoire* (Brussels)
BMFA	*Bulletin of the Museum of Fine Arts* (Boston)
BMMA	*Bulletin of the Metropolitan Museum of Art*
BSFE	*Bullétin de la Société française d'égyptologie*
CAH	I. E. S. Edwards, C. J. Gadd, N. G. L. Hammond, and E. Sollberger, eds., *The Cambridge Ancient History*, 3d ed., vol. 1 (Cambridge, 1970–1), 2 pts., and vol. 2 (Cambridge, 1973–5), 2 pts.
CCG	Catalogue générale des antiquités égyptiennes du Musée du Caire
CdE	*Chronique d'Egypte*
FuF	*Forschungen und Fortschritte*
GBA	*Gazette des beaux-arts*
GM	*Göttinger Miszellen: Beiträge zur ägyptologische Diskussion*
IEJ	*Israel Exploration Journal*
IFAO Bibl. d'Et.	Bibliothèque d'Etudes de l'Institut français d'archéologie orientale du Caire
JAOS	*Journal of the American Oriental Society*
JARCE	*Journal of the American Research Center in Egypt*
JDAI	*Jahrbuch des Deutschen Archäologischen Instituts*
JEA	*Journal of Egyptian Archaeology*
JNES	*Journal of Near Eastern Studies*
ʲSSEA	*Journal of the Society for the Study of Egyptian Antiquities* (Toronto)
₋ex.	W. Helck, E. Otto, and W. Westendorf, eds., *Lexikon der Aegyptologie*, 5 vols. (Wiesbaden, 1972–84)
ᴧAS	Münchner Aegyptologische Studien

ABBREVIATIONS   *MDAIK*   *Mitteilungen des Deutschen Archäologischen Instituts Abteilung Kairo*

MIFAO   Mémoires de l'Institut français d'archéologie orientale du Caire

MMJ   *Metropolitan Museum Journal*

Mon. Piot   *Fondation Eugène Piot, Académie des inscriptions et belles-lettres: Monuments et mémoires*

RdE   *Revue d'Egyptologie*

Recueil de travaux   *Recueil de travaux rélatifs à la philologie et à l'archéologie égyptiennes et assyriennes*

SAK   *Studien zur altägyptischen Kultur*

ZAS   *Zeitschrift für ägyptische Sprache und Altertumskunde*

REFERENCES

Adam, S., 1960. *The technique of Greek sculpture*. Oxford: Thames and Hudson.

Adams, Barbara, 1974. *Ancient Hierakonpolis*. Warminster: Aris and Phillips.

1975. *Ancient Hierakonpolis: supplement*. Warminster: Aris and Phillips.

Adams, Lauren, 1978. *Orientalizing sculpture in soft limestone from Crete and mainland Greece*. Oxford: British Archaeological Reports.

Adams, W. Y.; Whitney Davis; and Ian Hodder, 1981. "Comments on the evolution of specialized pottery production." *Current Anthropology* 22: 227–32.

Aldred, Cyril, 1973. "Bild (Menschenbild in Darstellungen)." In *Lex*. I, 795–8.

1974. "Bildhauer und Bildhauerei." In *Lex*. I, 800–5.

1980. *Egyptian art in the days of the pharaohs, 3100–320 B.C.* London: Thames and Hudson.

Abu al-Soof, B. A., 1968–9. "Uruk and later pottery in Iran, northern Syria, Anatolia, and Egypt in relation to Mesopotamia." *Mesopotamia* 3/4.

Altenmüller, Hartwig, 1974. "Bemerkungen zur Kreiselscheibe Nr. 310 aus dem Grab des Hemaka in Saqqara." *GM 9*: 13–18.

Amélineau, E., 1898. *Les nouvelle fouilles d'Abydos, I*. Paris: E. Leroux.

1899. *Les nouvelles fouilles d'Abydos, II*. Paris: E. Leroux.

Amiran, Ruth, 1974. "An Egyptian jar fragment with the name of Narmer from Arad." *IEJ 24*: 4–12.

Anthes, Rudolf, 1939. "Studienzeichnungen altägyptischer Maler." *Pantheon 24*: 300–5.

1940. "Die Bildkomposition in Amarna und die Ramessidischen Schlachtenbilder." In *VI. Internationaler Kongress für Archäologie, Berlin, August 1939*, 273–7. Berlin: de Gruyter.

1941. "Werkverfahren ägyptischer Bildhauer." *MDAIK 10*: 79–121.

Arkell, A. J., 1950. "Varia Sudanica." *JEA 36*: 28–30.

1955. "An archaic representation of Hathōr." *JEA 41*: 125–6.

1959. "Early shipping in Egypt." *Antiquity 33*: 52–3.

1963. "Was King Scorpion Menes?" *Antiquity 37*: 31–5.

Arkell, A. J., and E. M. Burgess, 1958. "The reconstruction of the Hathōr bowl." *JEA 44*: 6–11.

Arnett, W. S., 1982. *The predynastic origin of Egyptian hieroglyphs*. Washington, D.C.: University Press of America.

REFERENCES

Arnheim, Rudolf, 1954. *Art and visual perception*. Berkeley: University of California Press.

Arnold, Dieter, 1973. "Baupläne." In *Lex*. I, 661–3.

Asselberghs, Henri, 1961. *Chaos en beheersing: Documenten uit aeneolithisch Egypte*. Documenta et monumenta orientis antiqui 8. Leiden: Brill.

Bach, Kent, 1970. "Part of what a picture is." *BJA 10*: 119–37.

Badawy, Alexander, 1948. *Le dessin architectural chez les anciens égyptiens*. Cairo: Imprimerie Nationale.

1954. "La loi de frontalité dans la statuaire égyptienne." *ASAE 52*: 275–307.

1959. "Figurations égyptiennes à schéma ondulatoire." *CdE 34*: 215–32.

1961. "The stela of Irtysen." *CdE 36*: 269–76.

1965. *Egyptian architectural design: a study of the harmonic system*. Berkeley: University of California Press.

1973. "Architekturdarstellung." In *Lex*. I, 399–419.

1978. *The tomb of Nyhetep-ptah at Giza and the tomb of 'Ankhm'ahor at Saqqara*. Berkeley: University of California Press.

1981. "Compositions murales à système modulaire dans les tombes égyptiennes de l'ancien empire." *GBA 97*: 49–52.

Baer, Klaus, 1960. *Rank and title in the Old Kingdom*. Chicago: University of Chicago Press.

Baines, J. R., 1974a. "Translator's introduction." In Heinrich Schäfer, *Principles of Egyptian art*, 4th ed., edited by Emma Brunner-Traut, translated by J. R. Baines, xi–xix. Oxford: Oxford University Press.

1974b. Review of Groenewegen-Frankfort, 1951 (reprint 1972). *JEA 60*: 272–6.

1978. Review of Iversen, 1975. *JEA 64*: 189–91.

1983. "Literacy and ancient Egyptian society." *Man 18*: 572–99.

1985a. "Color terminology and color classification: ancient Egyptian color terminology and polychromy." *American Anthropologist 87*: 282–97.

1985b. "Theories and universals of representation: Heinrich Schäfer and Egyptian art." *Art History 8*: 1–25.

Balcz, Heinrich, 1930. "Symmetrie und Asymmetrie in Gruppenbildungen der Reliefs des alten Reiches." *MDAIK 1*: 137–52.

Barta, Winfried, 1970. *Das Selbstzeugnis eines altägyptischen Künstlers (Stele Louvre C14)*. MAS 22. Berlin: Hessling.

1971. "Bermerkungen zur Darstellung der Jahreszeiten im Grabe des Mrr-wj-k3.j." *ZÄS 97*: 1–7.

Baud, Marcelle, 1935. *Les dessins ébauchés de la nécropole thébaine*. MIFAO 53. Cairo: IFAO.

Baumgartel, E. J., 1948. "The three colossi from Koptos." *ASAE 48*: 533–8.

1955. *The cultures of prehistoric Egypt, I*. 2d ed. Oxford: Oxford University Press.

1960. *The cultures of prehistoric Egypt, II*. Oxford: Oxford University Press.

1968. "About some ivory statuettes from the 'Main Deposit' at Hierakonpolis." *JARCE 7*: 7–14.

1969–70. "Some additional remarks on the Hierakonpolis ivories." *JARCE 8*: 9–10.

1971. *Petrie's Naqada excavations: a supplement*. Warminster: Aris and Phillips.

248

Baxandall, Michael, 1972. *Painting and experience in fifteenth century Italy.* Oxford: Oxford University Press.

　1980. *The limewood sculptors of Renaissance Germany.* New Haven: Yale University Press.

Bénédite, Georges, 1905. "La stèle dite du roi Serpent." *Mon. Piot 12*: 5–17.

　1916. *Le couteau de Gebel el-Arak: Etude sur un nouvel objet préhistorique acquis par le Musée du Louvre. Mon. Piot 22.*

　1918. "The Carnarvon ivory." *JEA 5*: 1–15.

Berenson, Bernard, 1953. *Seeing and knowing.* London: Chapman and Hall.

Bernheimer, Richard, 1961. *The nature of representation.* New York: New York University Press.

Bersani, Leo and Ulysse Dutoit, 1986. *The forms of violence: narrative in Assyrian art and modern culture.* New York: Schocken Books.

Bianchi, Robert S., 1979. "Ex-votos of Dynasty XXVI." *MDAIK 35*: 15–22.

Bierbrier, Morris, 1982. *Tomb-builders of the pharaohs.* London: British Museum Publications.

Bietak, Manfred, and Elfriede Reiser-Haslauer, 1978–82. *Das Grab des 'Anch-hor.* 2 vols. Untersuchungen der Zweigstelle Kairo der Oesterreichischen Archäologischen Instituts IV–V. Vienna: Verlag der Akademie.

Björkman, Gun, 1971. *Kings at Karnak: a study of the treatment of the monuments of royal predecessors in the early New Kingdom.* Stockholm: Almqvist and Wiksell.

Blackman, A. M., 1914. *Meir, I.* London: Egypt Exploration Fund.

　1915. *Meir, II.* London: Egypt Exploration Fund.

Boehmer, R. M., 1974. "Orientalische Einflüsse auf verzierten Messergriffen aus dem prädynastichen Aegypten." *Archäologischen Mitteilungen aus Iran (DAI Teheran),* n.s. 7: 15–50.

Bogoslovsky, E. I., 1976. "Artists and soldiers in Egypt in the 14th–10th centuries B.C." (in Russian). Summary in *Annual Egyptological Bibliography*, no. 76–089. Leiden: Brill.

　1980. "Hundred Egyptian draftsmen." *ZÄS 107*: 89–116.

　1981. "On the system of ancient Egyptian society of the epoch of the New Kingdom." *Altorientalische Forschungen 8*: 5–21.

Borchardt, Ludwig, 1893. "Die Darstellung innen verzierten Schalen auf ägyptischen Denkmälern." *ZÄS 31*: 1–9.

　1896. "Altägyptische Werkzeichnungen." *ZÄS 34*: 69–76.

　1910a. "Studien und Entwürfe altägyptischen Künstler." *Kunst und Künstler 6*: 34–42.

　1910b. *Das Grabdenkmal des Königs Saȝhu-Re'.* Vol. 1, *Der Bau.* Leipzig: J. C. Hinrichs.

　1911. *Statuen, I.* CCG 53. Cairo: Reichsdruckerei.

　1913. *Das Grabdenkmal des Königs Saȝhu-Re'.* Vol. 2, *Die Wandbilder.* Leipzig: J. C. Hinrichs.

　1917. "Sphinxzeichnung eines ägyptischen Bildhauers." *Amtliche Berichte aus den königlichen Kunstsammlungen 39*: 105–10.

　1928. "Ein Bildhauermodel aus dem frühen alten Reich." *ASAE 28*: 43–50.

Bothmer, Bernard, 1969–70. "A new fragment of an old palette." *JARCE 8*: 5–8.

REFERENCES

1970. "Apotheosis in late Egyptian sculpture." *Kemi 20*: 37–48.

1982. "On realism in Egyptian funerary sculpture." *Expedition 24*, no. 2: 27–39.

Bourdieu, Pierre, 1977. *Outline of a theory of practice*. Translated by R. Nice. Cambridge: Cambridge University Press.

Breasted, James H., 1906. *Ancient records of Egypt*. 6 vols. Chicago: University of Chicago Press.

Brown, James A., ed., 1971. *Approaches to the social dimensions of mortuary practices*. Society for American Archaeology Memoirs 25. Washington, D.C.: SAA.

Brugsch, Heinrich, 1871. "Bau und Masse des Tempels von Edfu." *ZAS 9*: 32–45.

Brunner, Hellmut, 1970. "Zum Verständnis der archaisierenden Tendenzen in der ägyptischen Spätzeit." *Saeculum 21*: 151–61.

1973. "Archaismus." In *Lex.* I, 386–95.

Brunner-Traut, Emma, 1956. *Die altägyptischen Scherbenbilder (Bildostraka) der deutschen Museen und Sammlungen*. Wiesbaden: Steiner.

1973. "Aspektive." In *Lex.* I, 474–88.

1974a. "Aspective." In Heinrich Schäfer, *Principles of Egyptian art*, 4th ed., edited by Emma Brunner-Traut, translated by J. R. Baines, 421–46. Oxford: Oxford University Press.

1974b. "Bildostraka." In *Lex.* I, 811–13.

1977. "Farbe (*jwn* und *jrtjw*)." In *Lex.* II, 117–28.

1979. *Egyptian artists' sketches*. Leiden: Nederlands Historisch-Archaeologisch Institut.

1982. "Perspektive." In *Lex.* IV, 987–8.

Brunton, Guy, 1948. *Matmar*. London: Egyptian Research Account.

Buchberger, Hannes, 1983. "Sexualität und Harfenspiel: Notizen zur 'sexuellen' Konnotation der altägyptischen Ikonographie." *GM 66*: 11–43.

Butzer, Karl W., 1976. *Early hydraulic civilization in Egypt*. Chicago: University of Chicago Press.

Callaway, J. A., 1972. *Ai*. London: Quaritch.

Capart, Jean, 1905. *Primitive art in Egypt*. Translated by A. S. Griffiths. London: Grevel.

1927. *Documents pour servir à l'étude de l'art égyptien*. 2 vols. Paris: Editions du Pégase, 1927–31.

1941a. "Sur les cahiers de modèles en usage sur l'ancien empire." *CdE 16*: 43–4.

1941b. "Ostraca illustrant des textes littéraires." *CdE 16*: 190–5.

1945. "Sur les cahiers de modèles en usage sur l'ancien empire (suite)." *CdE 20*: 33–5.

1957. "Dans le studio d'une artiste." *CdE 32*: 199–217.

Carpenter, Rhys, 1921. "Dynamic symmetry: a criticism." *AJA 25*: 18–36.

1960. *Greek sculpture: a critical review*. Chicago: University of Chicago Press.

1962. *Greek art*. Philadelphia, University of Pennsylvania Press.

Carter, Howard, 1923. "An ostracon depicting a red jungle fowl." *JEA 9*: 1–4.

Case, H., and J. C. Payne, 1962. "Tomb 100: the Decorated Tomb at Hierakonpolis." *JEA 48*: 5–18.

Caskey, L. D., 1922. *The geometry of Greek vases*. Boston: Museum of Fine Arts.

Černý, Jaroslav, 1929. "L'identité des serviteurs dans la place de la verité et les ouvriers." *Revue de l'Egypte ancienne 2*: 200–9.

1973a. *The valley of the kings: fragments d'un manuscrit inachevé.* Cairo: IFAO.

1973b. *A community of workmen at Thebes in the Ramesside period.* Cairo: IFAO.

Chassinat, E., 1928. *Le temple d'Edfou III.* Cairo: IFAO.

Choisy, Auguste, 1899. *Histoire de l'architecture.* 2 vols. Paris: Gauthier-Villars.

Clark, Timothy J., 1986. *The painting of modern life: Paris in the art of Manet and his followers.* New York: Knopf.

Clarke, David, 1980. *Analytical archaeology.* 2d ed. New York: Columbia University Press.

Clarke, E. Somers, and Reginald Engelbach, 1930. *Ancient Egyptian masonry.* London: Oxford University Press.

Collingwood, R. G., 1958. *Principles of art.* Oxford: Oxford University Press.

Crompton, Winifred M., 1918. "A carved slate palette in the Manchester Museum." *JEA 5*: 57–60.

Curto, Silvio, 1953. "Nota su un rilievo proveniente da Gebelen nel Museo Egizio di Torino." *Aegyptus 33*: 105–24.

Daressy, Georges, 1898. "Un plan égyptien d'une tombe royale." *Revue archéologique*, 3d ser. *31*: 235–40.

1901. *Ostraca.* CCG 1. Cairo: IFAO.

Davis, Whitney, 1976. "The origins of register composition in predynastic Egyptian art." *JAOS 96*: 404–18.

1977. "Towards a dating of prehistoric rock-drawings in Upper Egypt and Nubia." *JSSEA 8*: 25–34.

1978. "Two compositional tendencies in Amarna relief." *AJA 82*: 387–94.

1979a. "Sources for the study of rock art in the Nile Valley." *GM 32*: 59–74.

1979b. "Plato on Egyptian art." *JEA 65*: 121–7.

1981a. "Egypt, Samos, and the archaic style in Greek sculpture." *JEA 67*: 61–81.

1981b. "The foreign relations of predynastic Egypt, I: Egypt and Palestine in the predynastic period." *JSSEA 11*: 21–7.

1981c. "An early dynastic lion in the Museum of Fine Arts." In *Studies in ancient Egypt, the Aegean, and the Sudan,* edited by William Kelly Simpson and Whitney Davis, 34–42. Boston: Museum of Fine Arts.

1982. "Canonical representation in ancient Egyptian art." *Res: Anthropology and Aesthetics 4*: 20–45.

1983a. "Artists and patrons in predynastic and early dynastic Egypt." *SAK 10*: 119–39.

1983b. "Cemetery T at Nagada." *MDAIK 39*: 17–28.

1983c. "Representation and knowledge in the prehistoric rock art of Africa." *African Archaeological Review 2*: 8–35.

1985. "The earliest art in the Nile Valley." In *The origins and development of early food-producing cultures in northeastern Africa,* edited by Lech Krzyzaniak, 81–94. Poznan: Polish Academy of Sciences.

1986. "The origins of image making." *Current Anthropology 27*: 193–215.

1987. "Replication and depiction in paleolithic art." *Representations 19*: 111–47.

REFERENCES

1988a. "Style and history in art history." In *The uses of style in archaeology*, edited by M. W. Conkey and C. Hastorf. Cambridge: Cambridge University Press.

1988b. "Pleasure and its contents." *Art History 11*: 445–56.

1989. *Seeing through culture: the possibility of the history of art.*

de Cénival, Jean-Louis, 1964. *Living architecture: Egyptian.* New York: Grosset and Dunlap.

de Garis Davies, Nina (and Alan H. Gardiner), 1936. *Ancient Egyptian paintings.* 3 vols. Chicago: University of Chicago Press.

de Garis Davies, Norman, 1903–8. *The rock tombs of El Amarna.* 5 vols. London: Egypt Exploration Society.

1917a. "Egyptian drawings on limestone flakes." *JEA 4*: 234–40.

1917b. "An architectural sketch at Sheik Said." *Ancient Egypt*, 21–25.

1917c. *The Tomb of Nakht at Thebes.* New York: Metropolitan Museum of Art.

1920. *The tomb of Antefoker, vizier of Sesostris I, and of his wife Senet (no. 60).* London: Allen and Unwin.

1921. Review of Schäfer, 1974. *JEA 7*: 221–8.

1922. *The tomb of Puyemrē at Thebes.* 2 vols. New York: Metropolitan Museum of Art.

1930. *The tomb of Ken-Amūn at Thebes.* New York: Metropolitan Museum of Art.

1943. *The tomb of Rekh-mi-Rē' at Thebes.* 2 vols. New York: Plantin Press.

1952. Review of Groenewegen-Frankfort, 1951. *Antiquity 26*: 52–5.

de Morgan, Henri, 1908. *Revue de l'Ecole d'Anthropologie de Paris 19*: 272–80.

de Morgan, Jacques, 1895. *Fouilles à Dahchour, I.* Vienna: Holzhansen.

1897. *Recherches sur les origines de l'Egypte, II.* Paris: E. Leroux.

Desroches-Noblecourt, Christiane, 1979. "Quatre objets protodynastiques provenant d'un 'trésor.'" *Revue du Louvre 29*: 108–17.

de Ste. Croix, G., 1983. *The class struggle in the ancient world.* Ithaca, N.Y.: Cornell University Press.

de Wit, Constant, 1966. In *Illustrations pour l'éternité*, edited by M. Heerma Van Voss. Brussels: Musées royaux.

Donadoni, Sergio, 1982. "Plan (architectural)." In *Lex.* IV, 1058–60.

Drenkhahn, Rosemarie, 1976. *Die Handwerker und ihre Tätigkeiten im alten Aegypten.* AA 31. Wiesbaden: Harrassowitz.

Dreyer, Günther, 1981. "Ein frühdynastisches Königsfigürchen aus Elephantine." *MDAIK 37*: 123–4.

Drioton, E., 1938. "Deux cryptogrammes de Senenmout." *ASAE 38*: 231–46.

Dubrovits, A., 1938. "Harpokrates: Probleme der ägyptischen Plastik." In *Jubilee volume in honor of Edward Mahler*, 72–122. Budapest: Hungarian Academy of Sciences.

1959. "Le problème de la frontalité dans la sculpture égyptienne et grecque." *Acta Antiqua Academiae Scientarum Hungaricae 7*: 39–43.

Duell, Prentice, et al., 1938. *The mastaba of Mereruka.* 2 vols. Chicago: University of Chicago Press.

1940. "The evidence for easel painting in ancient Egypt." *Technical Studies in the Field of the Fine Arts 8*: 174–92.

Dunham, Dows, 1937. *Naga-ed-Der stelae of the First Intermediate Period.* London: Oxford University Press.

Dunham, Dows, and William Kelly Simpson, 1974. *Giza mastabas*. Vol. 1, *The mastaba of Queen Mersyankh III*. Boston: Boston Museum of Fine Arts.

Dunn, Stephen P., 1982. *The fall and rise of the Asiatic mode of production*. Boston: Routledge and Kegan Paul.

Earle, T., and J. Ericson, eds., 1977. *Exchange systems in prehistory*. Cambridge: Cambridge University Press.

Eaton-Krauss, Marianne, 1984. *The representation of statuary in the Old Kingdom*. AA 39. Wiesbaden: Harrassowitz.

Edgar, C. C., 1905. "Remarks on Egyptian 'sculptors' models.' " *Recueil de travaux 27*: 137–50.

    1906. *Sculptors' studies and unfinished works*. CCG 31. Cairo: IFAO.

Edgerton, William F., 1923. "Ancient Egyptian ships and shipping." *AJSL 39*: 109–35.

Edwards, I. E. S., 1969–70. "Acquisitions, July to December 1969." *British Museum Quarterly 34*: 186.

    1971. "The early dynastic period in Egypt." *CAH* I, pt. 2, 1–70.

Emery, W. B., 1939. *Excavations at Saqqara, 1937–38: Hor-Aha*. Cairo: Government Press.

    1949. *Great tombs of the First Dynasty, I*. London: Egypt Exploration Society.

    1954. *Great tombs of the First Dynasty, II*. London: Egypt Exploration Society.

    1958. *Great tombs of the First Dynasty, III*. London: Egypt Exploration Society.

    1961. *Archaic Egypt*. Harmondsworth: Penguin.

Engelbach, Reginald, 1930. "An alleged winged sun disk of the First Dynasty." *ZAS 65*: 115–16.

    1934. "A foundation scene of the Second Dynasty." *JEA 20*: 183–4.

Engelmayer, Reinhold, 1965. *Die Felsgravierung im Distrikt Sayala-Nubien, I: Die Schiffsdarstellungen*. Oesterreiche Akademie der Wissenschaften, philosophische-historische Klasse, Denkschiften 90. Vienna: Akademie Verlag.

Erman, Adolf, 1909. "Zeichnungen ägyptischer Künstler griechischer Zeit." *Amtliche Berichte aus den königlichen Kunstsammlungen 30*: 197–203.

Erman, Adolf, and Hermann Ranke, 1923. *Aegypten und ägyptisches Leben in Altertum*. Tübingen: J. C. Mohr.

Evans-Pritchard, E. E., 1962. *Divine kingship of the Shilluk of the Nilotic Sudan*. Cambridge: Cambridge University Press, orig. ed. 1949.

Evers, H. G., 1929. *Staat aus dem Stein*. 2 vols. Munich: F. Bruckmann.

Farag, R. A., 1980. "A stela of Khasekhemui from Abydos." *MDAIK 36*: 77–80.

Fattovich, R., 1978. "Scavi nel Museo di Torino, IX: two decorated vases from Hammamiyeh (Upper Egypt)." *Oriens Antiquus 17*: 139–44.

Faulkner, R. O., 1966. "The king and the star-religion in the Pyramid Texts." *JNES 25*: 153–61.

    1969. *The ancient Egyptian Pyramid Texts*. 2 vols. Oxford: Oxford University Press.

Fechheimer, Hedwig, 1923. *Die Plastik der Aegypter*. Berlin: B. Cassirer.

Feucht, Erika, 1977. "Hilfslinien." *Lex*. II, 1201–6.

Finkenstaedt, Elizabeth, 1980. "Regional painting styles in prehistoric Egypt." *ZAS 107*: 116–20.

REFERENCES
1981. "The location of styles in painting: white cross-lined ware at Naqada." *JARCE 18*: 7–10.

1984. "Violence and kingship: the evidence of the palettes." *ZÄS 111*: 107–10.

Finley, M. I., 1973. *The ancient economy*. Berkeley: University of California Press.

1980. *Ancient slavery and modern ideology*. New York: Viking.

Fischer, Henry G., 1958. "A fragment of late predynastic Egyptian relief from the Eastern Delta." *Artibus Asiae 21*: 64–88.

1959. "An example of Memphite influence in a Theban stela of the Eleventh Dynasty." *Artibus Asiae 22*: 240–52.

1961. "An Egyptian royal stela of the Second Dynasty." *Artibus Asiae 24*: 45–56.

1963. "Varia Aegyptiaca." *JARCE 2*: 17–51.

1968. *Dendera in the third millennium B.C.* Locust Valley, N.Y.: J.J. Augustin.

1972. "Some emblematic uses of hieroglyphs with particular reference to an archaic ritual vessel." *Metropolitan Museum Journal 2*: 5–23.

1977. *The orientation of hieroglyphs*. Pt. 1, *Reversals*. New York: Metropolitan Museum of Art.

1979. "Koptos." In *Lex.* III, 737–40.

1986. *L'écriture et l'art de l'Egypte ancienne*. Paris: Collège de France.

Forbes, R. J., 1950. "Professions and crafts in ancient Egypt." *Archives internationales d'histoire des sciences 3*: 599–618.

Frankfort, Henri, 1925. *Studies in early pottery of the Near East*. 2 vols. Royal Anthropological Institute Occasional Papers 6. London: Royal Anthropological Institute.

1929. *The mural painting of El-'Amarneh*. London: Egypt Exploration Society.

1932. "On Egyptian art." *JEA 18*: 33–48.

1941. "The origin of monumental architecture in Egypt." *AJSL 58*: 329–58.

1948. *Kingship and the gods*. Chicago: University of Chicago Press.

1951. *The birth of civilization in the Near East*. Bloomington, Ind.: Indiana University Press.

Freeman, Norman, 1980. *Strategies of representation in young children*. London: Academic Press.

Fried, Michael, 1969. "The sources of Manet's *Olympia*." *Artforum 7*, no. 7 (special whole issue).

Fried, Morton, 1967. *The evolution of political society*. New York: Random House.

Froidefond, C., 1971. *Le mirage égyptien dans la littérature grecque d'Homère à Aristote*. Paris: Gap/Ophrys.

Gardiner, Alan H., 1938. "The House of Life." *JEA 24*: 157–79.

1961. *Egypt of the pharaohs*. Oxford: Oxford University Press.

Gardiner, Alan H., and Howard Carter, 1917. "The tomb of Ramesses IV and the Turin plan of a royal tomb." *JEA 4*: 130–56.

Gardiner, Alan H., and Jaroslav Černý, 1952–5. *The rock inscriptions of Sinai*. 2 vols. Oxford: Oxford University Press.

Gasse, A., 1986. *Catalogue des ostraca figurés de Deir el-Medineh V (3100–3372)*. Cairo: IFAO.

George, Beate, 1975. *Frühe Keramik aus Aegypten: Die dekorierte Negade-II*

Keramik im Medelhavsmuseet. Bulletin Medelhavsmuseet 10. Stockholm: Medelhavsmuseet.

Gilbert, P., 1947. "Fauves au long cou communs à l'art égyptien et à l'art sumerien." *CdE 22*: 38–41.

Gilderdale, Peter, 1984. "The early Amarna canon." *GM 81*: 7–20.

Glanville, S. R. K., 1926. "Egyptian theriomorphic vessels in the British Museum." *JEA 12*: 52–69.

1930. "A working plan for a shrine." *JEA 16*: 237–9.

1931. "An archaic statuette from Abydos." *JEA 17*: 65–7.

Godelier, Maurice, 1978. "Infrastructures, societies, and history." *Current Anthropology 19*: 763–71.

1982. "Myths, infrastructures, and Levi-Strauss." In Ino Rossi et al., eds., *The logic of culture: advances in structural theory and methods*, 232–61. South Hadley, Mass.: Bergin Publishers.

1986. *The mental and the material.* London: Verso.

Gombrich, Ernst H., 1960. *Art and illusion.* Princeton: Princeton University Press.

1984. *The sense of order.* Ithaca, N.Y.: Cornell University Press.

Goodman, Nelson, 1949. "On likeness of meaning." *Analysis*, 1949. Reprinted in *Problems and projects*, 231–8. Indianapolis, Ind.: Hackett.

1971. *Languages of art.* Indianapolis, Ind.: Hackett.

1978. *Ways of worldmaking.* Indianapolis, Ind.: Hackett.

Gophna, Ram, 1978. "En Besor." *Expedition 20*, no. 4: 5–7.

Grapow, Hermann, 1924. *Die bildlichen Ausdrücke des Aegyptischen.* Leipzig: J.C. Hinrichs.

Groenewegen-Frankfort, H. A., 1951. *Arrest and movement: an essay on space and time in the representational art of the ancient Near East.* London: Faber and Faber.

1972. "Egypt, the ancient Near East, and the Minoan-Mycenaean world." In H. A. Groenewegen-Frankfort and Bernard Ashmole, *Art of the ancient world*, 5–84. New York: Abrams.

Gunn, B., 1926. "An architect's diagram of the Third Dynasty." *ASAE 26*: 197–202.

Guralnick, Eleanor, 1978. "The proportions of kouroi." *AJA 82*: 461–72.

Haas, Jonathan, 1982. *The prehistory of the state.* New York: Columbia University Press.

Habachi, Labib, 1939. "A First Dynasty cemetery at Abydos." *ASAE 39*: 767–81.

1963. "King Nebhetepre Mentuhotp: his monuments, place in history, deification, and unusual representations in the form of gods." *MDAIK 19*: 16–52.

Haeny, G., 1971. "Zu den Platten mit Opfertischszenen aus Helwan und Gizeh." In *Festschrift Herbert Ricke*, 143–64. Wiesbaden: Steiner.

Hagen, Margaret, 1986. *Varieties of realism.* Cambridge: Cambridge University Press.

Hamann, Richard, 1908. "Das Wesen des Plastischen." *Zeitschrift für Aesthetik und allgemeine Kunstwissenschaft 3*: 1–46.

Hambidge, Jay, 1920. *Dynamic symmetry: the Greek vase.* New Haven: Yale University Press.

Hanfmann, G. M. A., 1957. Review of Matz, 1950. *Art Bulletin 39*: 233–40.

REFERENCES   Hanke, Rainer, 1959. "Beiträge zur Kanonproblem." *ZAS 84*: 113–19.

1961. *Untersuchungen zur Komposition des ägyptischen Flachbildes.* Münster: Westf.

Harris, J. R., 1960. "A new fragment of the Battlefield Palette." *JEA 46*: 104–5.

Harrison, E. B., 1972. Review of Adam, 1960. *Art Bulletin 54*: 136–7.

Hassan, Fekri A., 1980. "Radiocarbon chronology of archaic Egypt." *JNES 39*: 203–7.

1984. "Radiocarbon chronology of predynastic Nagada settlements, Upper Egypt." *Current Anthropology 25*: 681–3.

Hayes, William C., 1939. "A fragment of a prehistoric Egyptian victory monument." *BMMA 34*: 48–9.

1945–6. "An archaic Egyptian statue." *BMMA*, n.s. *4*: 113–16.

1953. *The scepter of Egypt, I.* New York: Metropolitan Museum of Art.

Hegel, G. W. F., 1977. *Phenomenology of spirit.* Edited by J. N. Findlay, translated by A. V. Miller. Oxford: Oxford University Press.

Helck, Wolfgang, 1962. *Die Beziehungen Aegyptens zu Vorderasien im 3. und 2. Jahrtausend v. Chr.* Wiesbaden, Harrassowitz.

1975. *Wirtschaftsgeschichte des alten Aegypten im 3. und 2. Jahrtausend v. Chr.* Leiden: Brill.

Hellström, Pontus, 1970. *The rock drawings.* Scandinavian Joint Expedition to Sudanese Nubia 1. Odense: Scandinavian University Books.

Hermann, Alfred, 1936. "Zur Anonymität der ägyptischen Kunst." *MDAIK 6*: 150–7.

Hoffman, Michael, 1979. *Egypt before the pharaohs.* New York: Knopf.

Hornung, Erik, 1973. "Bedeutung und Wirklichkeit des Bildes im alten Aegypten." *Akademische Vorträge gehalten an der Universität Basel 8*: 35–46.

1978. *Le don du Nil.* Basel: Kunsthalle.

1982. *Conceptions of god in ancient Egypt.* Translated by J. R. Baines. Ithaca, N.Y.: Cornell University Press.

Iversen, Erik, 1955. *Canon and proportions in Egyptian art.* 1st ed. London: Sidgwick and Jackson.

1960. "A canonical master-drawing in the British Museum." *JEA 46*: 71–9.

1968. "Diodorus' account of the Egyptian canon." *JEA 54*: 215–18.

1971a. "The canonical tradition." In *The legacy of Egypt*, edited by J. R. Harris, 55–82. 2d ed. Oxford: Oxford University Press.

1971b. "The hieroglyphic tradition." In *The legacy of Egypt*, edited by J. R. Harris, 170–96. 2d ed. Oxford: Oxford University Press.

1975. *Canon and proportions in Egyptian art.* 2d ed. with Y. Shibata. Warminster: Aris and Phillips.

1976. "The proportions of the face in Egyptian art." *SAK 4*: 135–48.

James, Jean M., 1980. "Signs in ancient Egypt: another look at the relation of figure to hieroglyph." *Visible Language 14*: 52–61.

James, T. G. H., 1955. *The mastaba of Khentika called Ikhekhi.* London: Egypt Exploration Society.

Jameson, Frederic, 1981. *The political unconscious.* Ithaca, N.Y.: Cornell University Press.

Janssen, J., 1978. "The early state in Egypt." In *The early state*, edited by Henri Claessen, 213–34. The Hague: Mouton.

Jéquier, G., 1938. *Le monument funéraire de Pépi II, II-III.* 2 vols. Cairo: IFAO.

Jones, Grant D., and Robert R. Kautz, 1981. *The transition to statehood in the New World.* Cambridge: Cambridge University Press.

Junker, Hermann, 1938. *Giza, XII.* Vienna: Hölder-Pichler.

    1956. "Der Maler 'Irj." *Wien Anzeiger 93:* 59–79.

    1957. "Zu dem Idealbild des menschlichen Körpers in der Kunst des alten Reiches." *Wien Anzeiger 94:* 171–81.

    1959. *Die gesellschaftliche Stellung der Künstler im alten Reich.* Oesterreiche Akademie der Wissenschaften, philosophische-historische Klasse, Sitzungsberichte 193. Vienna: Akademie Verlag.

Kaiser, Werner, 1956. "Stand und Problem der ägyptischen Vorgeschichtsforschung." *ZAS 81:* 87–109.

    1957. "Zur inneren Chronologie der Naqadakultur." *Archaeologia Geographica 6:* 69–77.

    1964. "Einige Bemerkungen zur ägyptischen Frühzeit, III: Die Reichseinigung," *ZAS 91:* 86–125.

Kaiser, Werner, and Günther Dreyer, 1982. "Umm el-Qaab: Nachuntersuchungen im frühzeitlichen königsfriedhof." *MDAIK 38:* 211–69.

Kanawati, Naguib, 1977. *The Egyptian administration in the Old Kingdom.* Warminster: Aris and Phillips.

    1981. "The living and the dead in Old Kingdom tomb scenes." *SAK 9:* 213–25.

Kantor, Helene J., 1942. "Early Mesopotamian relations with Egypt." *JNES 1:* 174–213.

    1944. "The final phase of predynastic culture: Gerzean or Semainean(?)." *JNES 3:* 110–36.

    1947. "The Aegean and the Orient in the second millennium B.C." *AJA 51:* 1–103.

    1952. "Further evidence for early Mesopotamian relations with Egypt." *JNES 11:* 239–50.

    1965. "The relative chronology of Egypt and its foreign correlations before the late Bronze Age." In *Chronologies in Old World archaeology,* edited by R. W. Ehrich, 1–46. Chicago: University of Chicago Press.

    1974. "Aegypten." In *Frühe Stufen der Kunst,* edited by J. Filip and M. Mellink, 67–72. Propyläen Kunstgeschichte 13. Berlin: Propyläen Verlag.

Kaplony, Peter, 1958. "Zu den beiden Harpenenzeichen der Narmerpalette." *ZAS 83:* 76–8.

    1963. *Die Inschriften der ägyptischen Frühzeit.* 2 vols. Wiesbaden: Harrassowitz.

    1966a. *Kleine Beiträge zu den Inschriften der ägyptischen Frühzeit.* Wiesbaden: Harrassowitz.

    1966b. "Die Handwerker als Kulturträger Aegyptens." *Asiatische Studien 20:* 101–25.

Kees, Hermann, 1926. *Totenglauben und Jenseitsvorstellungen der alten Aegypter.* Leipzig: J.C. Hinrichs.

Keimer, Ludwig, 1941. *Sur un certain nombre d'ostraca figurés, de plaquettes sculptées, etc.* Cairo: IFAO.

    1948. Review of Vandier-d'Abbadie, 1936–59. *Bibl. Or. 5:* 18–25.

    1957. Review of Brunner-Traut, 1956. *Bibl. Or. 14:* 148–51.

Kelley, Allyn L., 1974. "The evidence for Mesopotamian influence in predynastic Egypt." *Newsletter of the Society for the Study of Egyptian Antiquities 4,* no. 2: 2–13.

REFERENCES   Kemp, Barry J., 1963. "Excavations at Hierakonpolis fort, 1905." *JEA 49*: 24–8.

    1967. "The Egyptian First Dynasty royal cemetery." *Antiquity 41*: 22–32.

    1968. "The Osiris temple at Abydos." *MDAIK 23*: 138–55.

    1973. "Photographs of the Decorated Tomb at Hierakonpolis." *JEA 59*: 36–43.

    1982. "Automatic analysis of predynastic cemeteries: a new method for an old problem." *JEA 68*: 5–15.

    1983. "Old Kingdom, Middle Kingdom, and Second Intermediate Period, c. 2686–1552 B.C." In B. G. Trigger et al., *Ancient Egypt: A Social History*, 71–182, 352–6, 371–99. Cambridge: Cambridge University Press.

    1987. "The Amarna workmen's village in retrospect." *JEA 73*: 21–50.

Kennedy, John, 1976. "Attention, brightness, and the constructive eye." In *Vision and artifact*, edited by M. Henle, 33–47. Berlin: Springer.

Keuls, Eva C., 1978. *Plato and Greek painting*. Leiden: Brill.

el-Khouli, Ali, 1978. *Egyptian stone vessels, predynastic period to Dynasty III: typology and analysis*. 3 vols. Mainz-am-Rhein: von Zabern.

Kielland, Else C., 1946. *The human figure*. Oslo: Aschehoug.

    1955. *Geometry in Egyptian art*. London: Tiranti.

Klasens, A., 1965. "A stela of the Second Dynasty in the Leiden Museum of Antiquities." *Oudheidkundige Mededelingen uit het Rijksmuseum van Oudheden te Leiden 46*: 1–9.

Klebs, Luise, 1914. "Die Tiefendimension in der Zeichnung des alten Reiches." *ZAS 52*: 19–34.

    1915. *Die Reliefs des alten Reiches*. Heidelberg: Winter.

    1922. *Die Reliefs und Malereien des mittleren Reiches*. Heidelberg: Winter.

    1934. *Die Reliefs und Malereien des neuen Reiches*. Heidelberg: Winter.

Kozloff, Arielle P., 1979. "A study of the painters of the tomb of Menna, No. 60." In *Acts of the First International Congress of Egyptology*, 395–402. Berlin: Akademie Verlag.

Krahmer, Gerhard, 1931. *Figur und Raum in der ägyptischen und griechischen Kunst*. Halle: Niemeyer.

Kripke, Saul, 1980. *Naming and necessity*. Cambridge, Mass.: Harvard University Press.

Kuentz, Charles, 1928. *La bataille de Qadesh: les textes et les bas-reliefs.* MIFAO 55. Cairo: IFAO.

Labrousse, A.; J.-Ph. Lauer; and J. Leclant, 1977. *Le temple haut au complèxe funéraire de roi Ounas*. IFAO Bibl. d'Et. 73. Cairo: IFAO.

Landström, Bjorn, 1970. *Ships of the pharaohs*. New York: Doubleday.

Lange, Julius, 1899. *Darstellung des Menschen in der älteren griechischen Kunst*. Strassburg: Heitz.

Lange, Kurt, and Max Hirmer, 1967. *Egypt*. 4th ed. London: Thames and Hudson. (Plates identical to German ed. 1967.)

Lange, Kurt, and Heinrich Schäfer, 1908. *Grab- und Denksteine des mittleren Reiches, II*. CCG 36. Cairo and Berlin: Reichsdruckerei.

Lansing, Ambrose, 1935. "Report of the Egyptian expedition." *BMMA Egyptian Expedition*. New York: Ayer Co.

Lauer, J.-Ph., 1962. *Le pyramide à degrés*. IFAO Bibl. d'Et. 39. Cairo: IFAO.

Lauer, J.-Ph., and J. Leclant, 1973. *Le temple haut du complèxe funéraire du roi Teti*. IFAO Bibl. d'Et. 51. Cairo: IFAO.

258

Leclant, J., 1980. "La 'famille libyenne' au temple haut de Pépi Ier." In *IFAO Livre du centénaire, 1880–1980*. 49–54. Cairo: IFAO.

Lee, R. W., 1940. " 'Ut pictura poesis': the humanistic theory of painting." *Art Bulletin 22*: 197–296.

Legran, L., 1971. "A propos des statuette d'hommes à l'époque archaïque et à l'ancien empire." *CdE 46*: 11–22.

Lepsius, Karl Richard, 1884. *Die Längenmasse der Alten*. Berlin: Wittertz.

    n.d. *Denkmaeler aus Aegypten und Aethiopien*. 6 Abtheilungen. Berlin: Nicolaische Buchhandlung.

Levinson, Jerrold, 1979. "Defining art historically." *BJA 29*: 232–50.

Lichtheim, Miriam, 1973. *Ancient Egyptian literature, I: the Old Kingdom*. Berkeley: University of California Press.

Liepsner, Thomas F., 1980. "Modelle." In *Lex*. IV, 168–80.

Lloyd, Alan B., 1983. "The Late Period, 664–323 B.C." In B. G. Trigger et al., *Ancient Egypt: a social history*, 279–348, 359–64, 412–27. Cambridge: Cambridge University Press.

Lorenzen, E., 1977. "Canon and 'thumbs' in Egyptian art." *JAOS 97*: 531–9.

    1980. "The canonical figure 19 and an Egyptian drawing board in the British Museum." *SAK 8*: 181–99.

Lucas, A., and J. R. Harris, 1962. *Ancient Egyptian materials and industries*. 4th ed. London: E. Arnold.

MacIver, Randall, and A. C. Mace, 1902. *El Amrah and Abydos*. London: Egypt Exploration Fund.

Mackay, E., 1917. "Proportion squares on tomb walls in the Theban necropolis." *JEA 4*: 74–85.

Manuelian, Peter, 1983. "Prolegomena zur Untersuchung saitischer 'Kopien.' " *SAK 10*: 221–45.

Marr, David, 1982. *Vision*. New York: W. H. Freeman.

Matz, Friedrich, 1922. "Zur Komposition ägyptischer Wandbilder." *JDAI 37*: 39–53.

    1923–4. "Das Motiv des Gefallenen." *JDAI 38–9*: 1–27.

    1930. Review of V. Müller, 1929. *Gnomon 6*: 245–62.

    1934. Review of Krahmer, 1931. *Deutsche Literaturzeitung 55*: 1901–14.

    1944–5. "Die Stilphasen der hellenistischen Malerei." *JDAI, Archäologischer Anzeiger 60*: 89–112.

    1950. *Geschichte der griechischen Kunst, I: Die geometrische und die fr   harchaische Form*. 2 vols. Frankfurt-am-Main: Klostermann.

    1964. "Strukturforschung und Archäologie." *Studium Generale 17*: 203–19.

Meillassoux, Claude, 1972. "The mode of production of the hunting band." In *French perspectives in African studies*, edited by P. Alexandre, 187–203. Oxford: Oxford University Press.

    1978. "The 'economy' in agricultural self-sustaining societies." In *Relations of production*, edited by D. Seddon, translated by Helen Lackner, 127–58. London: Cass.

Mekhitarian, Arpag, 1954. *Egyptian painting*. Geneva: Skira.

    1956. "Personnalité de peintres thébains." *CdE 31*: 238–48.

    1957. Review of Brunner-Traut, 1956. *CdE 32*: 59–63.

Meyer, K.-H., 1974. "Kanon, Komposition, und 'Metrik' der Narmer-Palette." *SAK 1*: 247–65.

    1975a. "Zur Konstruktion ägyptischer Flachbilder." *SAK 3*: 187–200.

1975b. "Flachbild." In *Lex*. II, 244–56.

Michalowski, K., 1969. *The Art of Ancient Egypt*. London: Thames and Hudson.

Mitchell, William P., 1973: "The hydraulic hypothesis: a reappraisal." *Current Anthropology 14*: 532–5.

Moessel, E., 1926. *Die Proportion in Antike und Mittelalter*. Vol. 1. Munich: Beck.

Mogenson, Maria, 1930. *La collection égyptien de la Glypothèque Ny Carlsberg*. Copenhagen: Ny Carlsberg Glyptothek.

Mohr, Herta T., 1943. *The mastaba of Hetep-her-akhti*. Leiden: Brill.

Mond, Robert, and Oliver H. Myers, 1937. *Cemeteries of Armant, I*. 2 vols. London: Egypt Exploration Fund.

Montet, Pierre, 1925. *Les scènes de la vie privée dans les tombeaux de l'ancien empire*. Strassburg: Istra.

    1928–9. *Byblos et l'Egypte*. 2 vols. Paris: Geuthner.

Morenz, Siegfried, 1973. *Egyptian religion*. Translated by Ann E. Keep. Ithaca, N.Y.: Cornell University Press.

Müller, Hellmuth, 1937. "Darstellungen von Gebärde auf Denkmälern des alten Reiches." *MDAIK 7*: 57–118.

Müller, H.-W., 1959. *ZAS 84*: 68–70.

    1970. *Aegyptische Kunst*. Munich: Umschau Verlag.

    1973. "Der Kanon in der ägyptischen Kunst." In *Der 'vermessene' Mensch: Anthropometrie in Kunst und Wissenschaft*, edited by S. Braunfels, 9–31. Munich: Moos.

Müller, Maja, 1980. "Musterbuch." In *Lex*. IV, 244–5.

Müller, Valentin, 1928. "Die Raumdarstellung der altorientalischen Kunst." *AfO 5*: 199–206.

    1929. *Frühe Plastik in Griechenland und Vorderasien*. Augsburg: Filser.

    1938. "The origin of the early dynastic style." *JAOS 58*: 140–7.

Munro, Peter, 1971. "Untersuchungen zur altägyptischen Bildmetrik." *Städel Jahrbuch 3*: 7–42.

Murray, M. A., 1920. "The first mace-head of Hierakonpolis." *Ancient Egypt*, 15–17.

    1956. "Burial customs and beliefs in the hereafter in predynastic Egypt." *JEA 52*: 86–96.

Myers, Oliver H., 1958. "Abka re-excavated." *Kush 6*: 131–41.

    1960. "Abka again." *Kush 8*: 174–81.

Mysliwiec, Karol, 1972a. "Towards a definition of the 'sculptors' model' in Egyptian art." *Etudes et travaux 6*: 71–5.

    1972b. "A propos des signes hieroglyphiques 'hr' et 'tp.' " *ZAS 92*: 85–99.

Naville, E., 1898. *Deir el-Bahari, III*. London: Egypt Exploration Fund.

Needler, Winifred, 1980. "Two important predynastic graves from Henri de Morgan's excavations." *Bullétin de l'Association international pour l'étude de la préhistoire égyptienne 1*: 1–15.

    1984. *Predynastic and early dynastic Egyptian art in the Brooklyn Museum*. Brooklyn: Brooklyn Museum.

Nelson, H. H., 1929. *Medinet Habu, 1924–1928, I*. Chicago: University of Chicago Press.

Newberry, P. E., 1908. "The petty-kingdom of the harpoon and Egypt's earliest port." *Liverpool Annals of Archaeology and Anthropology 1*: 17–22.

1913. "Some cults of prehistoric Egypt." *Liverpool Annals of Archaeology and Anthropology* 5: 132–6.

Nims, C. F., 1973. "The transition from the traditional to the new style of wall relief under Amenhotep IV." *JNES 32*: 181–7.

O'Connor, David, 1983. "New Kingdom and Third Intermediate Period, 1552–664 B.C." In B. G. Trigger et al., *Ancient Egypt: A Social History*, 183–278, 357–9, 400–11. Cambridge: Cambridge University Press.

Otto, Eberhard, 1972. "Abstraktionsvermögung." In *Lex.* I, 18–23.

Page, Anthea, 1976. *Egyptian sculpture archaic to Saite in the Petrie Collection*. Warminster: Aris and Phillips.

1983. *Ancient Egyptian figured ostraca in the Petrie Collection*. Warminster: Aris and Phillips.

Panofsky, Erwin, 1939. *Studies in iconology*. Oxford: Oxford University Press.

1955. *Meaning in the visual arts*. New York: Doubleday.

1956. *Tomb sculpture*. New York: Abrams.

1960. *Renaissance and renascences in Western art*. Copenhagen: Russak.

Peck, C. P., 1958. "Some decorated tombs of the First Intermediate Period at Naga ed-Der." Ph.D. diss., Brown University.

Peck, W. H., 1977. "A newly discovered example of decorated predynastic pottery in the Detroit Institute of Arts." *Bulletin of the Detroit Institute of Arts 55*: 216–18.

Peck, W. H., and J. G. Ross, 1978. *Egyptian drawings*. New York: Dutton.

Peebles, Christopher, and Susan Kus, 1977. "Some archaeological correlates of ranked societies." *American Antiquity 42*: 421–48.

Peet, T. E., 1913. *The cemeteries of Abydos, I*. London: Egypt Exploration Fund.

Peterson, Bengt E. J., 1973. *Zeichnungen aus einer Totenstadt: Bildostraka aus Thebenwest*. Stockholm: Medelhavsmuseet.

Petrie, W. M. F., 1892. *Medum*. London: Egypt Exploration Fund.

1896. *Koptos*. London: Egypt Exploration Fund.

1898. *Deshasheh*. London: Egypt Exploration Fund.

1900–1. *Royal tombs of the First Dynasty*. 2 vols. London: Egypt Exploration Fund.

1901. *Diospolis Parva*. London: Egypt Exploration Fund.

1902–3. *Abydos*. 2 vols. London: Egypt Exploration Fund.

1906. *Researches in Sinai*. London: J. Murray.

1909. *Memphis, 1908*. London: Egypt Exploration Fund.

1914. *Tarkhan, II*. London: Egypt Exploration Fund.

1920. *Prehistoric Egypt*. London: Egyptian Research Account.

1921. *Prehistoric Egypt Corpus*. London: Egyptian Research Account.

1926. "Egyptian working drawings." *Ancient Egypt*, 24–6.

1927. *Tombs of the courtiers*. London: Egyptian Research Account.

1953. *Ceremonial slate palettes* and *Corpus of protodynastic pottery*, Edited by H. F. Petrie and M. A. Murray. London: Egyptian Research Account.

Petrie, W. M. F., and J. E. Quibell, 1896. *Naqada and Ballas*. London: Egypt Exploration Fund.

Pevsner, Nikolaus, 1940. *Academies of art*. Cambridge: Cambridge University Press.

Pieper, Max, 1929. "Die grosse Inschrift des Königs Neferhotep in Abydos." *Mitteilungen der Vorderasiatisch-aegyptischen Gesellschaft 32*: 8–14.

REFERENCES   Porter, Bertha; Rosalind L. B. Moss; and J. Malek, n.d. *Topographical bibliography of ancient Egyptian hieroglyphic texts, reliefs, and paintings.* Oxford, 1927–51, 2d ed., Oxford, 1960–.

    1960. *Topographical bibliography of ancient Egyptian hieroglyphic texts, reliefs, and paintings.* 2d ed., *Theban tombs.* Oxford: Oxford University Press.

    1972. *Topographical bibliography of ancient Egyptian hieroglyphic texts, reliefs, and paintings.* 2d ed., *Theban temples.* Oxford: Oxford University Press.

    1974. *Topographical bibliography of ancient Egyptian hieroglyphic texts, reliefs, and paintings.* 2d ed., *Memphis.* Oxford: Oxford University Press.

Quibell, J. E., 1902–4. *Archaic objects.* 2 vols. CCG 23–4. Cairo: IFAO.

    1913. *Excavations at Saqqara, 1911–12: The tomb of Hesy.* Cairo: IFAO.

    1923. *Excavations at Saqqara, 1912–14: Archaic mastabas.* Cairo: IFAO.

Quibell, J. E., and F. W. Green, 1900–1. *Hierakonpolis.* 2 vols. London: Egypt Exploration Fund.

Radwan, A., 1973. "Gedanken zum 'Würfelhocker.' " *GM 8*: 27–31.

Ranke, Hermann, 1925. *Alter und Herkunft der Löwenjagd Palette.* Heidelberg: Winter.

Raphael, Max, 1947. *Prehistoric pottery and civilization in Egypt.* Princeton: Princeton University Press.

Reisner, G. A., 1927. "The tomb of Meresankh." *BMFA 25*: 64–79.

    1930. *Mycerinus.* Cambridge, Mass.: Harvard University Press.

Reuterswürd, Patrik, 1958. *Studien zur Polychromie der Plastik, I.* Stockholm: Almqvist and Wiksell.

Riegl, Alois, 1927. *Spatrömische Kunstindustrie.* 1901. Reprint. Vienna: Oesterreichische Staatsdruckerei.

Robins, Gay, 1983a. "Amarna grids, 1." *GM 64*: 67–72.

    1983b. "Anomalous proportions in the tomb of Haremhab (KV 57)." *GM 65*: 91–6.

    1983c. "The canon of proportions in the tomb of Ramesses I (KV 16)." *GM 68*: 85–90.

    1983d. "Natural and canonical proportions in ancient Egyptians." *GM 61*: 17–25.

    1984. "Analysis of facial proportions in Egyptian art." *GM 79*: 31–42.

    1985. "Application of the canon of proportions and grid system to figures shown in special postures." In *Abstracts of papers at the Fourth International Congress of Egyptology*, 185–7. Munich: ICE.

Roeder, G., 1912. "Namenunterschriften von Künstlern unter Tempelreliefs in Abu Simbel." *ZAS 50*: 76–8.

    1947. "Waren die Künstler des Pharaonenreichs auch Persönlichkeiten?" *FuF 21–3*: 198–204.

    1956. Review of Kielland, 1955. *Orientalistischen Literaturzeitung 51*: 509–11.

    1957. Review of Brunner-Traut, 1956. *Deutsche Literaturzeitung 78*: 912–15.

Rostem, O. R., 1948. "Remarkable drawings with examples in true perspective." *ASAE 48*: 167–77.

Russmann, Edna R., 1980. "The anatomy of an artistic convention: representation of the near foot in two dimensions through the New Kingdom." *Bulletin of the Egyptological Seminar 2*: 57–81.

Saad, Zaki Y., 1951. *Royal excavations at Helwan, 1945–1947.* Cairo: IFAO.

1957. *Ceiling stelae in Second Dynasty tombs from the excavations at Helwan.* ASAE Supplement 21. Cairo: Imprimerie Nationale.

Sahlins, Marshall, 1983. "Other times, other customs: the anthropology of history." *American Anthropologist 85*: 517–44.

Saleh, Janine Monnet, 1987. "Remarques sur les representations de la peinture d'Hierakonpolis (Tombe No. 100)." *JEA 73*: 51–8.

Saleh, M. M., 1977. *Three Old Kingdom tombs at Thebes.* Mainz-am-Rhein: von Zabern.

Sauneron, Serge, 1957. *Les prêtres de l'ancienne Egypte.* Paris: Editions du Seuil.

Säve-Söderbergh, T., 1953. *On Egyptian representations of hippopotamus hunting as a religious motive.* Horae Soederblominae 3. Uppsala: Gleerup.

Sayce, A. H., and E. Somers Clarke, 1906. "Report on certain excavations made at El-Kab during the years 1901, 1902, 1903, 1904." *ASAE 6*: 239–72.

Scamuzzi, E., 1965. *Egyptian art in the Egyptian Museum of Turin.* New York: Abrams.

Schäfer, Heinrich, 1911. "Scheinbild oder Wirklichkeitsbild?: Ein Grundfrage für die Geschichte der ägyptischen Zeichenkunst." *ZÄS 48*: 134–42.

1916. *Aegyptische Zeichnungen auf Scherben. Jahrbuch der preussischen Kunstsammlung 38,* Hefte 1–2. Berlin: Preussische Kunstsammlung.

1926. "Die angebliche Entstehung der ägyptischen Wandbilder aus Wandbehang." *Deutsche Literaturzeitung 47*: 1879–84.

1936a. *Das altägyptische Bildnis.* Leipziger Aegyptologische Studien 5. Hamburg: Augustin.

1936b. *Atlas zur altägyptischen Kulturgeschichte, III,* edited by Walter Wreszinski, 1–3. Leipzig: J. C. Hinrichs.

1938. "Ungewöhnliche ägyptische Augenbilder und die sonstige Naturwiedergabe." *ZÄS 74*: 27–41.

1957. "Das Niederschlagen der Feinde." *Wiener Zeitschrift für die Kunde des Morgenlandes 54*: 168–76.

1974. *Principles of Egyptian art.* 1919. 4th ed. Edited by Emma Brunner-Traut, translated by J. R. Baines. Oxford: Oxford University Press.

Scharff, Alexander, 1937. "Egyptian portrait sculpture." *Antiquity 11*: 174–82.

1939. "Typus und Persönlichkeit in der ägyptischen Kunst." *Archiv für Kunstgeschichte 29*: 1–24.

1941. "On the statuary of the Old Kingdom." *JEA 26*: 41–50.

Schott, Erika, 1979. "Künstler." In *Lex.* III, 833–6.

Schott, Siegfried, 1950. *Hieroglyphen: Untersuchungen zum Ursprung der Schrift.* Akademie der Wissenschaften, Geistes- und Sozialwissenschaftliche Klasse 24. Wiesbaden: Akademie der Wissenschaften.

Scranton, Robert L., 1964. *Aesthetic aspects of ancient art.* Chicago: University of Chicago Press.

Seidel, Matthias, and Dietrich Wildung, 1975. "Rundplastik der Frühzeit und des alten Reiches." In Vandersleyen, 1975b, 212–29.

Senk, Herbert, 1933. "Vom perspektivischen Gehalt in der ägyptischen Flachbildnerei." *ZÄS 69*: 90–94; 74: 125–32.

1950. "Bemerkungen zur kontrapostischen Form in der ägyptischen Flachbildnerei." *ASAE 50*: 281–320.

1956. Review of Kielland, 1955. *Bibl. Or. 13*: 213–16.

REFERENCES

1958a. Review of Brunner-Traut, 1956. *Orientalistischen Literaturzeitung* 53: 35–41.

1958b. "Zur kunstgeschichtliche Bedeutung altägyptischer Scherben-zeichnungen (Bildostraka)." *Fuf 32*: 50–6.

1958c. "Kunstgeschichtliche Bemerkungen zu Emma Brunner-Traut, *Bildostraka, 28, 29, 30.*" In *Akten des 24. Internationalen Orientalistenkongresses,* 53–4. Wiesbaden: Harrassowitz.

1959. "Eine 'sondergeometrische' Stilphase in der ägyptischen Ersten Zwischenzeit." *FuF 33*: 236–41, 272–7.

1965. "Zum aspektivischen Formcharakter der ägyptischen Kunst." *FuF 39*: 301–3.

Service, Elman, 1975. *The origins of the state and civilization.* New York: Norton.

Sethe, Kurt, 1929. *Amun und die acht Urgötter von Heliopolis.* Leipzig: de Gruyter.

Shoukry, A., 1951. *Die Privatgrabstatue im alten Reich.* ASAE Supplement 15. Cairo: Imprimerie Nationale.

Simpson, W. K., 1955. Review of Groenewegen-Frankfort, 1951. *AJA 59*: 325–7.

1956. "A statuette of King Nyneter." *JEA 42*: 45–9.

1972. "Two Egyptian bas reliefs of the late Old Kingdom." *North Carolina Museum of Art Bulletin 11*, no. 3: 4–13.

Simpson, W. K., ed., 1973a. *The literature of ancient Egypt.* New ed. New Haven: Yale University Press.

Simpson, W. K., 1973b. "Organisation des Bauwesen." In *Lex.* I, 668–72.

1973c. "Ptolemaic-Roman cartonnage footcases with prisoners bound and tied." *ZAS 100*: 50–4.

1977. *The face of Egypt: permanence and change in Egyptian art.* Katonah, N.Y.: Katonah Gallery.

Smith, H. S., and H. M. Stewart, 1984. "The Gurob shrine papyrus." *JEA 70*: 54–64.

Smith, W. S., 1949. *A history of Egyptian sculpture and painting in the Old Kingdom.* 2d ed. Cambridge, Mass.: Harvard University Press.

1952. "An Eighteenth Dynasty toilet box." *BMFA 50*: 74–9.

1958. "Egyptian painter's sketch on a flake of limestone." *BMFA 56*: 102.

1963. "The stela of Wepemnofret." *Archaeology 16*: 2–13.

1965. *Interconnections in the ancient Near East.* New Haven: Yale University Press.

1967. "An archaic Egyptian wooden face." *BMFA 65*: 79–83.

1971. "The Old Kingdom in Egypt and the beginning of the First Intermediate Period." *CAH* I, pt. 2, 145–207.

1981. *The art of ancient Egypt.* 2d ed., revised with additions by W. K. Simpson. The Pelican History of Art. Harmondsworth: Penguin.

Spencer, A. J., 1979. *Brick architecture in ancient Egypt.* Warminster: Aris and Phillips.

1980. *Early dynastic objects.* Catalogue of Egyptian antiquities in the British Museum 5. London: British Museum Publications.

Spencer, Patricia, 1984. *The Egyptian temple: a lexicographical study.* London: Kegan Paul.

Sperber, Dan, 1975. *Rethinking symbolism.* Cambridge: Cambridge University Press.

1985. "Towards an epidemiology of representations." *Man 20*: 73–89.

Spiegel, Joachim, 1936. *Die Idee von Totengericht in der ägyptischen Religion.* Glückstadt and Hamburg: J. J. Augustin.

1940. "Typus und Gestalt in der ägyptischen Kunst." *MDAIK 9*: 156–72.

1957. "Zur Kunstentwicklung der zweiten Hälfte des alten Reiches." *MDAIK 15*: 225–61.

Speigelberg, W., 1902. "Eine Künstlerinschrift des neuen Reiches." *Recueil de travaux 24*: 185–7.

1918. "Der Maler Heje." *ZAS 54*: 77–9.

Steindorff, Georg, 1897. "Eine neue Art ägyptischer Kunst." In *Aegyptiaca: Festschrift Ebers*, 122–41. Leipzig: W. Engelmann. (Reprint of an earlier article.)

1910. "Der *Ka* und die Grabstatuen." *ZAS 48*: 152–9.

1920. *ZAS 56*: 96–8.

Steinmann, Frank, 1980–4. "Untersuchungen zu den in der handwerklich-künstlerischen Produktion beschäftigen Personen und Berufsgruppen des neuen Reiches." *ZAS 107*: 135–57; *109*: 66–76, 149–56; *111*: 30–40.

Stiles, Daniel, 1979. "Paleolithic culture and culture change: experiment in theory and method." *Current Anthropology 20*: 1–21.

Suys, E., 1935. "Refléxions sur la loi de frontalité." *Annuaire de l'Institut de philologie et d'histoire orientale 3*: 545–62.

Tefnin, Roland, 1979a. "Image et histoire: refléxions sur l'usage documentaire de l'image égyptienne." *CdE 54*: 218–44.

1979b. *La statuaire d'Hatshepsout.* Monumenta Aegyptiaca 4. Brussels: Fondation égyptologique Reine Elisabeth.

1981. "Image, écriture, récit: à propos des representations de la bataille de Qadesh." *GM 47*: 55–76.

1983. "Discours et iconicité dans l'art égyptien." *Annales d'histoire de l'art et d'archéologie 5*: 5–17.

Terrace, E. L. B., 1961. "A fragmentary triad of King Mycerinus." *BMFA 59*: 41–9.

Terrace, E. L. B., and Henry G. Fischer, 1970. *Treasures from the Cairo Museum.* London: Thames and Hudson.

Trigger, Bruce G., 1969. *Beyond history: the methods of prehistory.* New York: Holt, Rinehart, and Winston.

1983. "The rise of Egyptian civilization." In B. G. Trigger et al., *Ancient Egypt: a social history*, 1–70, 349–52, 365–71. Cambridge: Cambridge University Press.

Ucko, Peter J., 1968. *Anthropomorphic figurines of predynastic Egypt and neolithic Crete.* Royal Anthropological Institute Occasional Papers 24. London: Royal Anthropological Institute.

Vandersleyen, Claude, 1974. Review of Groenewegen-Frankfort, 1951. *CdE 49*: 90–2.

1975a. "Objectivité des portraits égyptiens." *BSFE 73*: 5–27.

Vandersleyen, Claude, ed., 1975b. *Das alte Aegypten.* Propyläen Kunstgeschichte 15. Berlin: Propyläen Verlag.

Vandersleyen, Claude, 1978. Review of Iversen, 1975. *CdE 53*: 84–90.

1982. "Porträt." In *Lex.* IV, 1074–80.

Vandier, Jacques, 1952–69. *Manuel d'archéologie égyptienne I-V.* Many vols. Paris: Picard.

1952. *Manuel d'archéologie égyptienne.* Vol. 1, *Les époques de formations.* 2 vols. Paris: Picard.

REFERENCES

1958. *Manuel d'archéologie égyptienne*. Vol. 3, *Les grandes époques: la statuaire*. Paris: Picard.

1964. *Manuel d'archéologie égyptienne*. Vol. 4, *Bas reliefs et peintures: scènes de la vie quotidienne*. 2 vols. Paris: Picard.

Vandier-d'Abbadie, Jeanne, 1936–59. *Catalogue des ostraca figurés de Deir el-Medineh*. 4 vols. Cairo: IFAO. See also Gasse, 1986.

1941. "Deux nouveaux ostraca figurés." *ASAE 40*: 467–88.

1946a. *Catalogue des ostraca figurés de Deir el-Medineh*. Vol. 3. Cairo: IFAO.

1946b. "A propos des bustes des laraires." *RdE 5*: 33–5.

1957. "Deux ostraca figurés." *BIFAO 56*: 21–34.

1960. "Deux sujets originaux sur ostraca figurés." *RdE 12*: 83–8.

Varille, Alexandre, 1947. *A propos des pyramides de Snefrou*. Cairo: IFAO.

von Bissing, F. W., 1898. "Les origines de l'Egypte." *L'Anthropologie 9*: 241–59.

1929. "Der Meister des Grabes des Merreruka-Meri in Saqqara." *ZÄS 65*: 116–19.

1930. "Palette mit dem Namen der Königen Tije im Museum in Kairo." *AfO 6*: 1–2.

1947. "Aegyptische Baumeister als künstlerische Persönlichkeiten." *FuF 21–23*: 134–6.

von Kaschnitz Weinberg, Guido, 1933. "Bemerkungen zur Struktur der ägyptischen Plastik." 1933. Reprinted in *Kleine Schriften zu Struktur*, edited by Helga von Heintze, 15–37. Berlin: Gebr. Mann.

1946–7. "Aegyptische und griechische Plastik: Versuch einer Strukturvergleichung." 1946–7. Reprinted in *Kleine Schriften zu Struktur*, edited by Helga von Heintze, 146–55. Berlin: Gebr. Mann.

1965a. "Ueber die Rationalisierung der 'mythischen Form' in der klassichen Kunst." In *Kleine Schriften zu Struktur*, edited by Helga von Heintze, 203–13. Berlin: Gebr. Mann.

1965b. *Mittelmeerische Kunst*. Berlin: Gebr. Mann.

von Recklinghausen, H., 1928. "Rechtsprofil und Linksprofil in der Zeichenkunst der alten Aegypter." *ZÄS 63*: 14–36.

Wainwright, G. A., 1963. "The origin of storm-gods in Egypt and the origin of Amūn." *JEA 49*: 13–23.

Ward, W. A., 1963. "Egypt and the east Mediterranean from predynastic times to the end of the Middle Kingdom." *Journal of the Economic and Social History of the Orient 6*: 1–57.

1977. "Neferhotep and his friends." *JEA 63*: 63–6.

Ware, Edith W., 1927. "Egyptian artists' signatures." *AJSL 43*: 185–207.

Weber, Max, 1976. *The agrarian sociology of ancient civilizations*. Translated by R. I. Frank. Atlantic Highlands, N.J.: Humanities Press.

1978. *Economy and society*. Edited by Günther Roth and Claus Wittich. 2 vols. Berkeley: University of California Press.

Weeks, Kent, 1979. "Art, word, and the Egyptian world view." In *Egyptology and the social sciences*, 59–81. Cairo: American University in Cairo Press.

Weill, R., 1950. "Une nouvelle stèle de la première dynastie (de Helouan?)." *RdE 7*: 180–2.

Werbrouck, Marcelle, 1932. "Ostraca à figures." *BMAA 4*: 138–40.

1934. "Ostraca à figures." *BMAA 6*: 138–40.

Westendorf, Wolfhart, 1966. *Altägyptische Darstellungen des Sonnenlaufes auf der abschüssigen Himmelsbahn*. MAS 10. Munich: B. Hessling.

266

White, John, 1957. *The birth and rebirth of pictorial space*. London: Faber and Faber.

Wildung, Dietrich, 1975. "Erschlagen der Feinde." In *Lex.* II, 14–17.
1977. "Imhotep." In *Lex.* III, 145–8.

Willats, John, 1977. "How children learn to draw realistic pictures." *Quarterly Journal of Experimental Psychology 29*: 367–82.

Williams, Bruce, 1986. *Excavations between Abu Simbel and the Sudan frontier.* Pt. 1, *The A-Group royal cemetery at Qustul: Cemetery L.* Oriental Institute Nubian Expedition 3. Chicago: University of Chicago Press.
1988. "Narmer and the colossi of Min." Paper delivered at the Annual Meeting of the American Research Center in Egypt, Chicago, April 1988.

Williams, Bruce, and Thomas J. Logan, 1987. "The Metropolitan Museum knife handle and aspects of pharaonic imagery before Narmer." *JNES 46*: 245–84.

Williams, C. R., 1921. "An Egyptian sketch on limestone." *Quarterly Bulletin of the New York Historical Society 4*: 91–9.
1929–30. "Wall decorations of the main temple of the sun at el 'Amarneh." *Metropolitan Museum Studies 2*: 135–51.
1932. *The decoration of the tomb of Per-nēb: the technique and the color conventions.* New York: Metropolitan Museum of Art.

Wilson, John A., 1946. "Egypt." In *The intellectual adventure of ancient man*, edited by H. and H. A. Frankfort, 31–122. Chicago: University of Chicago Press.
1947. "The artist of the Egyptian Old Kingdom" (review of Smith, 1949). *JNES 6*: 231–49.

Winkler, Hans A., 1947. "The origin and distribution of Arab camel-brands." *JAOS Supplement 15*: 25–35.

Wittfogel, Karl, 1957. *Oriental despotism*. New Haven: Yale University Press.

Wittgenstein, Ludwig, 1921. *Tractatus logico-philosophicus*. London: Routledge and Kegan Paul.

Wolf, W., 1935. *Individuum und Gemeinschaft in der ägyptischen Kultur.* Leipziger Aegyptologische Studien 1. Glückstadt: Augustin.
1951. *Die Stellung der ägyptischen Kunst zur Antiken und Abendländischen und das Problem des Künstlers in der ägyptischen Kunst.* Hildesheim: Gebr. Gerstenberg.
1957. *Die Kunst Aegyptens: Gestalt und Geschichte.* Stuttgart: Kohlhammer.
1957–8. Review of Kielland, 1955. *AfO 18*: 433–4.

Wollheim, Richard, 1980. *Art and its objects*. 2d ed. Cambridge: Cambridge University Press.

Wood, Wendy, 1978. "A reconstruction of the reliefs of Hesy-re." *JARCE 15*: 9–24.
1987. "The archaic stone tombs at Helwan." *JEA 73*: 59–70.

Worringer, Wilhelm, 1928. *Egyptian art*. Translated by B. Rackham. London: Putnam.

Wreszinski, Walter, 1923. *Atlas sur altägyptischen Kulturgeschichte, I.* Leipzig: J.C. Hinrichs.

el-Yakhy, Farid, 1981. "Remarks on the armless figures represented on Gerzean boats." *JSSEA 11*: 77–83.

Yeivin, S., 1960. "Early contacts between Palestine and Egypt." *IEJ 10*: 193–203.

INDEX